101
GREAT MARQUES

101
GREAT MARQUES

ANDREW WHYTE

PEERAGE BOOKS

First published in Great Britain in 1985 by
Octopus Books Limited

This edition published in 1988 by
Peerage Books
Michelin House
81 Fulham Road
London SW3 6RB

ISBN 1 85052 085 2

Printed by Mandarin Offset in Hong Kong

Special photography by Ian Dawson

The publishers would like to thank The Patrick Collection
of Birmingham for kindly providing cars for photography.
In particular they would like to thank J. Alexander Patrick,
Mr and Mrs Ian Robinson and John Ward for their help
and co-operation.

The publishers would like to thank the manufacturers for permission
to reproduce their badges. Reproduction of Rolls-Royce and Bentley
trademarks and copyright material is made with the kind permission
of their owners. The three-pointed star logo is a registered
trademark and is the property of Daimler-Benz AG of Stuttgart,
Federal Republic of Germany. The BMW logo is the copyright of
BMW AG of Munich, Federal Republic of Germany.

PAGE 1 *1938 SS Jaguar 100, provided
by The Patrick Collection.*

PAGES 2-3 *1973 Ferrari 365 GTB4
Daytona from The Patrick Collection.*

THIS PAGE *1936 Auburn Model 852
Cabriolet from the Auburn-Cord-
Duesenberg Museum.*

CONTENTS

INTRODUCTION

BY ANDREW WHYTE

What makes a motor car great?

In the 101 years since the car's birth, literally thousands of marques have been born through whim, fantasy, or ambition – probably about five thousand if one is considering only the serious attempts.

To choose 101 Great Marques representing what has been achieved over the past, fleeting century is to do an injustice to many great names. Greatness has been short-lived for many companies or the individuals who inspired them. In some cases it is difficult to see why an inspired product should emerge from, apparently, a sea of mediocrity. In other cases – and there are many in this book – a great manufacturer can change course, to lose his credibility and his customers overnight.

Above all, economics, politics and luck have affected the car maker and his customer from the very beginning; and there were three events, the effects of which could be seen time and time again during the research for this book. There were the First and Second World Wars and, more lethal commercially, the Wall Street Crash. It might be argued that any company that could survive, let alone return to profit, following the New York stock market collapse of October 1929 should qualify for greatness.

Internal combustion

The motor car of today is thoroughly international. In many respects, this has always been so. Nevertheless, there is a national core to almost every great product; and the individual characteristics of individual cars and their makers still show through, to add to the fascination of almost any vehicle – no matter how clinically conceived.

Ubiquitous as the car has become, with factories in every corner of the globe, the great makers are concentrated where they have always been: on the European and North American continents. Then there is Japan, which is, of course, the shining modern example of greatness in sheer manufacturing skills.

Europe is the natural starting point for this preliminary investigation of the Great Marques.

It is, perhaps, unfair to have omitted steam traction from the book, but it is in effect a separate subject. There have been some magnificent steam cars, the American Doble and Stanley of the 1920s getting further than any. The last Doble could raise a head of steam remarkably briskly and, like the early de Dion, Serpollet and other European steam vehicles of 20 to 30 years earlier, the Doble would out-accelerate, and climb hills much more readily, than most of its petrol-engined contemporaries. For many years, Stanley was the world's fastest car.

The electric vehicle is almost as old as the motor car itself but, like the 'steamer', it has not achieved the same level of convenience as a means of personal transport.

Of all the great 19th-century inventors, Carl Benz stands out as the father of the motor car. His compact three-wheeler was a practical and original machine. It was made in 1885, and the patent was dated January 1886. Although Germany, like Britain, was relatively slow to follow up the invention of the car, it nevertheless fathered the device that has transformed our way of life for more than a century ever since.

Germany

The first choice for any story of Great Marques must be the Benz, despite the general feeling that it soon rested upon its laurels. The company did produce some magnificent racing and touring cars before the link with Mercedes, but its biggest contribution to the combine was probably in diesel engine development. Mercedes was the marque name used by the German Daimler company; it had strong ties with the birth of the motor car, too, for Gottlieb Daimler had been experimenting with the internal combustion engine for a considerable time before agreeing to use it in roadgoing vehicles.

The formation of Daimler-Benz as a company in 1926, and subsequent use of the name Mercedes-Benz for its product, gave this marque a prime position among the Greats. Nor has the position altered, for the Mercedes-Benz is one of the most respected names in the whole automotive world. (The British Daimler car was never connected directly with the German make, and was something of a misnomer.)

One car that Daimler-Benz helped into the world was the Volkswagen, the creation of Ferdinand Porsche, a towering figure of modern automobile history.

Some early German firms 'borrowed' from France – what country did not do so? The first car makers of Eisenach began in 1898 with Decauvilles; soon afterwards Adler was turning out de Dion-powered Renault-like machines, before Edmund Rumpler came and changed the cars of this near-great firm. The early Benz was, however, the inspiration for the ancestors of today's fine Audis and Opels. And what of the magnificent

The mighty Mercedes-Benz 7.1-litre supercharged SSK of 1928 was a product of the merger of Benz and Daimler, and thus a direct descendant of the very first cars. The earliest BMWs, such as this 1931 DA 4 (or fourth German version, inset left), were based on the British Austin Seven, 100 examples of which had been imported in 1927. The announcement of the KdF-Wagen – Adolf Hitler's name for the Volkswagen – was, in effect, at the factory foundation stone laying ceremony of May 1938 (inset right); well over 20 million Beetles have been built since then.

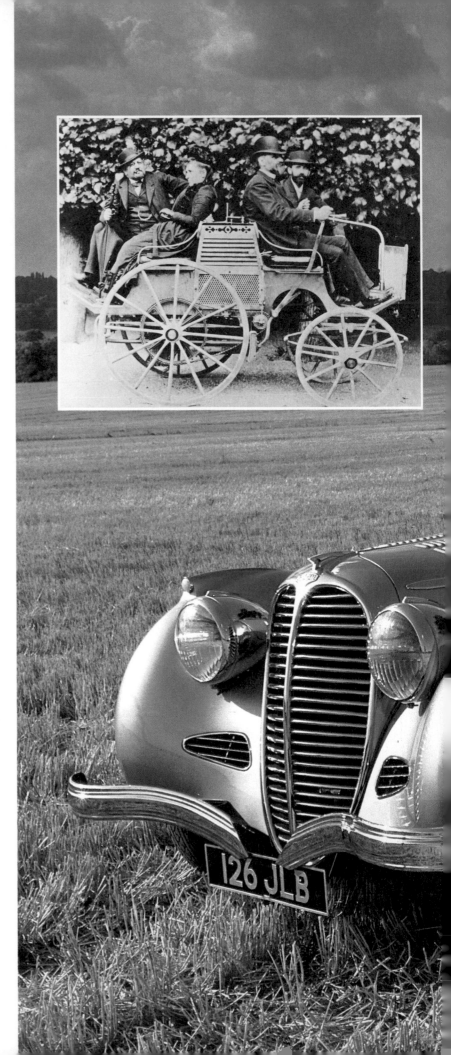

youngster of the German motor industry, BMW? Actually, the first cars to carry those famous initials in the late 1920s were Austin Sevens built under licence.

The division of Germany after the Second World War meant the loss of some very important factories, including BMW's, but West Germany has returned to the forefront of design.

France

Daimler and Benz sold patent rights to the French, who became the world's first commercial producers.

France was the most difficult country when it came to choosing marques of representative greatness for this book. Two examples, which were rejected only at the short list stage, had touched greatness before settling for the postwar cult of the two-seater miniature economy car. From 1904 the marine engineers Delaunay-Belleville of St Denis had set out to find perfection by much the same means as Rolls-Royce: by building in refinement without regard to expense, providing pure luxury without ostentation. One model was named after the Tsar of Russia, a regular customer. But the Delaunay-Belleville did not modernize, and lost its premier place to Hispano-Suiza – more French than Spanish or Swiss in character – from 1919, although it did stay in car manufacture in a desultory way. From 1946, Robert de Rovin built 260 cc and 425 cc baby cars in the factory where once Delaunay-Belleville limousines of 20 and 30 times that engine size had been lovingly assembled. (The Lorraine-Dietrichs that won at Le Mans in 1925 and 1926 were designed by Marius Barbarou, formerly of Benz *and* Delaunay-Belleville.)

The other four-wheeled baby of famous French ancestry was Spain's Autonacional Biscuter, designed by the ageing but imaginative Gabriel Voisin. He had been renowned for aircraft design, and much of this was reflected in the exotic and sometimes aerodynamic cars he created between the wars.

Other spectacular cars of the early 1920s with aerial connections included the Farman, the Fonck, and the Gnome et Rhone, but there was room on the market for only one Hispano-Suiza!

At the other end of the scale, the inventive French were strong on scaled-down cars, of which the de Dion-Bouton (one of our 101 Great Marques) was the original and most famous. Whatever happened, for example, to the French Simplicia of 1909, which apparently had the first backbone chassis? Earlier, Decauville had probably been the first in the market with independent front suspension: a feature of the lightweights produced by Maurice Sizaire and Louis Naudin, so successful in voiturette racing.

After the Second World War, the French luxury car market virtually disappeared, although several great marques did try to find it again. The coachbuilder in the case of this late-1940s Delahaye 135 was, in fact, Pennock of Holland. Mme Levassor is the most important person in this photograph of a c. 1890 prototype Panhard (inset left), for she held Daimler's engine patent rights in France. Production Panhards had front-mounted engine, setting the pattern for the world. France has always been in the forefront of design – no one more so than Citroen with the 1955 DS19 (inset right).

France was where racing began, and some weird monsters appeared in the first few years of the 20th century, like the opposed-piston Gobrons and the V8 Aders – the first of their kind – which took part in the ill-starred Paris-Madrid race of 1903. So casualty-stricken was the event that it was halted at Bordeaux; it would be the last of the heroic (or mad?) inter-city races. It was won by yet another of France's many mighty machines, the Mors, designed by Ingénieur Brasier. Brasier had, by then, joined Georges Richard and was to create the most successful Gordon Bennett Cup racer of them all. For that reason the Brasier has been chosen, along with Renault, to represent the great racers of old.

If one was asked to choose a marque which represents consistent French individuality through the years, Citroën must be the first choice, for it was also the first truly mass-produced continental car.

Italy

Like France, although it started later and on a smaller scale, Italy has had its share of great white hopes.

Perhaps the most advanced of these was the San Giusto, a light rear-engined car with all-independent suspension and a backbone chassis: all this in 1922, well ahead of its time. So why did it fail?

FIAT tends to overshadow all else in Italy, and controls Ferrari and Lancia today. At an early date FIAT took over the Ceirano brothers' business, but the Ceiranos were indepen-dent souls and went their own way again. There were also Ceirano family connections with the SCAT, the SPA and the Itala: the last-named made fame by winning 'The Great Race' of 1907, from Peking to Paris. For this book, however, the Isotta Fraschini has been selected as Italy's whitest of elephants from a dead era, alongside the six marques that must be considered the most typical of Italy's wonderful, stylish and sporting heritage.

Of all great marques, Ferrari is one of the most universally adored. There are several reasons for this extraordinary devotion. Firstly, there have been few unlovely or unlovable Ferraris, from the chunky sports-racers of 1947 to today's sleek and sophisticated monsters. Secondly, Ferrari has an unequalled record of success overall in Grand Prix, sports, and GT racing at international level. Thirdly, and above all, the man who started it all, Enzo Ferrari, was still going strong as the marque's founder and father figure in 1985! He is respected throughout the whole motoring business, and for many people his cars are the world's ultimate. They typify Italy's exciting approach to styling, engineering and manufacture – as well as its ability to come up with dramatic new designs apparently at the drop of a hat.

Enzo Ferrari once ran the Alfa Romeo racing team, Italy's pride in the 1930s. Alfa Romeo then occupied a position in the industry not unlike that of Ferrari today. It manufactured racing and sports cars, and was as famous for them as for the exotic Gran Turismo models which it produced in small quantities.

The Alfa Romeo sporting image is still there but, since 1950, the accent has been on volume production of high-performance cars of reasonable price rather than exclusivity. Modern technical cooperation with Japan has helped keep the Alfa Romeo name among the most admired in Italy, and there are still models of great character.

Lancia, too, remains firmly in the forefront of advanced design. Like Alfa Romeo, the company has been out of Grand Prix racing for many years. On the other hand, in the 1980s Lancia was deeply committed to prototype racing and international rallying, the latter having become an immensely popular branch of the sport since special stages (or timed sections) were shown regularly on film or television. This meant that by 1985 Lancia was joining the 'rat race' of four-wheel-drive specials which was changing the face of rallies and rally-type events, by then as costly a business as any in the motor sporting field. However, non-motoring multi-national companies (notably Martini in Lancia's case) were responsible for the financing of such endeavours.

Italy's other two great marques, Lamborghini and Maserati, have managed to survive many a crisis to continue as further examples of Italy's highly individual motor industry.

With its modern front-wheel-drive Strada (above), FIAT maintains its dominance of the Italian mass market, which it has achieved throughout the 20th century. Italian glamour and high performance are typified by Zagato's sweeping lines for this 1930 Alfa Romeo 1750 Gran Sport (left) – a Vittorio Jano masterpiece and now in the company's museum in Arese. Running Alfa Romeo's racing team in the 1930s led Enzo Ferrari into car manufacture himself. The Ferrari marque today remains one of the most revered in the world, and its special flair is summed up very well in this sleek and purposeful 1982 BB 512i (below).

Great Britain

The British were late starters in the motor industry, but soon made up for this with a sparkling variety of cars. Britain's first production cars – of 1897 – took their name from Germany (Daimler) and their design from France (Panhard); but the

Coventry Daimler became a car of true character very quickly. By contrast, the first Lanchester car of 1895 was as original in its design as the first Benz of ten years before. The Rolls-Royce is a youngster by comparison.

These, and many other great British marques, are included here but, even so, the cars whose creator took them to third place at Le Mans and outright victory in the Monte Carlo Rally (Allard) have had to be omitted: likewise the Beverley Barnes, the Crossley, the GN, the GWK, the H.E., the Sheffield Simplex, the Squire, the Swift and the Vanwall Grand Prix car, all of which had something special about them.

The British car industry has produced a hotchpotch of types, mostly built in the Midland area, which developed quickly as factories mushroomed, only to find life harder in times of recession. Recoveries like that of Jaguar may be miraculous, but need not be isolated cases. Fewer than half the marques chosen are still being made, however; and of these, only a handful remain independent.

Jaguar (which had been combined with Daimler in 1960) is Britain's shining star of the 1980s. Indeed, in 1984 it produced an all-time record number of cars – over 33,000 in all – mostly XJ saloons of the type originated by Sir William Lyons in 1968. Although he retired some time later after 50 years at the head of the firm he had founded, Sir William was (at 83) still Jaguar's very influential President until his death in February 1985. By then, of course, the company had thrown off the unwelcome mantle of British Leyland which it had worn for so long, and had been brought back to a position of strength by John Egan – a modern hero of industry – and his team.

The biggest British producers of the 1930s, Austin and Morris, were also British Leyland's mass-producers of the 1970s. As the company changed its form, the Austin stayed and the Morris vanished. Austin-Rover, as the 1980s group is called, dropped the Triumph range but reinstated M.G.; and there are many more 'BL ancestors' to be found in this book – long gone, but not forgotten.

If BL gave Britain its biggest motoring shake-up, the next most disturbed conglomerate must be Peugeot-Talbot, formerly Chrysler, formerly Rootes, and before that Hillman, Humber, Sunbeam and Talbot. With these four great marques is allied the French Darracq, which is at the heart of their complex relationship.

As in other countries, both General Motors and Ford have a strong foothold, and GM in particular has made great strides with its modern Vauxhalls. Britain still boasts many idiosyncratic sports models, of which the Morgan is the classic; and of course the Rolls-Royce, one of the greatest of all great marques, continues to occupy the premier position in the world for sheer unashamed luxury.

The British convertible, as interpreted by Triumph for the 1970s: this V8-engined Stag, which may become a classic one day, is in The Patrick Collection. The breadth of Britain's creativity is seen clearly in the cheeky supercharged 1927 Austin Seven Super Sports (upper inset) and the superbly proportioned Park Ward-bodied 1933 Rolls-Royce Phantom II Continental touring saloon (lower inset) provided by John A. Young.

Scandinavia

Denmark, Norway and Sweden originated several cars at the very beginning of motoring. The roads were so narrow that a Norwegian, H.C. Bjerring, designed one with half the usual track width and tandem seating, with the driver aft: the idea was that if the passenger were a lawbreaker the person in charge could watch his every move.

Only Sweden has developed a modern motor industry, and Saab and Volvo are undoubtedly Great Marques, in view of the manner of their progress.

Benelux and the Iberian countries

The Minerva is the best known of the 60 or so Belgian marques but others – notably the Excelsior, the Germain, the Imperia and the Métallurgique – were very worthy ones. Today, Belgium assembles many cars of the international groups.

The Spijker (or Spyker) stood out among the few Dutch cars of the early 20th century. Later came the DAF, with its infinitely variable belt drive, but it was taken over by Volvo who developed the marque the Swedish way.

While the SEAT company has developed a range separate from that of its originator, FIAT, most Spanish cars are assembled by the internationals. The Hispano-Suiza originated in Spain, but somehow it is generally thought of as French: although in fact the Barcelona factory carried on making cars the longer of the two. The Hispano-Suiza probably comes into anyone's top ten among the all-time great marques. Not so the Pegaso, which was produced in the old factory in Barcelona in the 1950s. It was a splendid Italian-type grand touring car; but it was only economic to make trucks by then and production soon ceased. The Pegaso, although a fascinating car, does not quite make the top 101.

Central Europe

Switzerland and Austria produced interesting cars in the early years. Austria, in particular, has a background of brilliant engineers: especially if we consider the days of the Austro-Hungarian empire. The names of Ledwinka, of Porsche and Rumpler will be found frequently in the pages of this book. All three men learned their craft in Vienna. There were some grand cars from that territory, too: Austro-Daimler, Gräf und Stift, Steyr, Laurin-Klement (later Skoda), Praga, Jawa, Walter and many more. Engineers such as Břetislav Novotný and Karl Rabe added their ideas to those of Ledwinka, the acknowledged master. The modern air-cooled rear-engined Porsche and Tatra models (described in this book) are living tributes to the principles established long before conformity took over.

North America

From the beginning, the people of the New World made use of everything within their power to develop their land.

The motor car was not, therefore, a plaything. It was a workhorse and had to be functional, capable of cheap manufacture and reliable service. On the whole, the American car

---

HIGHLIGHTS OF 101 YEARS OF THE MOTOR CAR

1885	First purpose-built internal combustion-powered road vehicles produced by Carl Benz and Wilhelm Maybach in Germany.
1891	Commercial car production begins in France, Panhard and then Peugeot using Daimler-patent engines, Peugeot claiming first sale. John William Lambert of Ohio produces America's first petrol-engined car.
1896	British motor industry gets under way with lifting of anti-motoring restrictions.
1901	First modern motor car, the Mercedes, introduced by German Daimler company (another Maybach design).
1904	The meeting of Rolls with Royce.
1906	The first Grand Prix is won by Renault.
1907	Japan makes its first production car.
1908	Henry Ford launches Model T.
1911	First Indianapolis 500; first Monte Carlo Rally.
1913	British Talbot car covers 160 km (100 miles) in one hour.
1914-18	The First World War.
1922	Ford makes over one million cars in the year.
1923	First Le Mans 24-Hour race (winning car: Chenard-Walcker).
1927	End of Model T Ford production, with over 16 million made.
1929	New York stock market failure.
1933	Adolf Hitler becomes Chancellor of the German Third Reich.
1939-45	The Second World War.
1955	Volkswagen 'Beetle' becomes first European car to pass million-a-year mark.
1963	Launch of new Wankel rotary piston engine by NSU.
1971	Japan becomes world's second-largest car producer.
1973	Fuel crisis (OPEC oil embargo).
1980	Japan becomes world's largest car producer.
1985	Centenary of the internal combustion-engined motor car.

The Model T Ford (above right), seen here at Piquette Street works in Detroit in its early days, was built with relatively few changes for nearly two decades. The remarkable production total of over 16 million cars has been exceeded by only one other model in automobile history – the VW Beetle. By contrast, the 1929 Cord L-29 with Miller-patent front-wheel drive (right) was a classic victim of the Depression.

makers have taught the world – especially in production matters. Henry Ford was the undoubted giant of motoring, so it is easily forgotten that his amazing Model T was preceded by that ultra-practical buggy, the Merry Oldsmobile. Those two cars are essential to any representative account of great cars.

If 'practicality' was the American watchword, it did not prevent a host of exciting, and sometimes distinctly odd, machines from establishing themselves. Among those vehicles whose greatness can only receive a passing mention in a book of this size were the Apperson, the Chadwick (the first

supercharged car), the Christie (first transverse engine with front drive), the Kissel, the Locomobile, the Marmon, the Pope-Toledo, the Wills-Sainte Claire, or the Winton. More recent groups such as Kaiser-Frazer and Hudson-Nash have also had to be left out.

Ford's constant rival has been General Motors, of which the Oldsmobile was one of the earliest member marques. General Motors is still a world leader, with the Chevrolet, Buick, Pontiac and Cadillac as well as the Oldsmobile; but nowadays, there is considerable collaboration with Japan, too.

While it is true that America taught the world about car production, the New World has fathered many a splendid failure. Three of the United States' greatest marques were Auburn, Cord and Duesenberg, brought together by the sharp businessman Errett Cord. These brilliant designs were styling dreams, engineering wonders, and the toast of the Hollywood set in the early 1930s; and each of these marques has been brought back to life in modern times, utilizing modern materials and components – a true measure of their appeal.

Another famous name can be recalled in the distinctive Avanti 11, which is still made in small numbers at South Bend, Indiana, where it began life as a Studebaker. Studebaker had merged with Packard (to many, the 'Rolls-Royce' of America) but neither survived the 1960s. The Avanti is living proof that American styling *can* be timeless, and that the United States is as capable as any nation of producing an attractive specialist car commercially. Since 1965, output has increased fairly steadily from one to four or six cars a week and there have been regular improvements. Its predecessors – the revered Packard and

Studebaker – are covered in this book, for they are among the great classics.

There have been so many great American specialists, but for this edition there was a particular one that could not be left out, the Pierce-Arrow. The magnificent beast, originated by George Pierce of Buffalo, retained a special confidence and swagger for close on 40 years and became a household word; yet, like so many other luxury cars, it finally succumbed – though well after the stock market crash.

Perhaps as famous but not quite as long-lived as the Pierce-Arrow was the Stutz, a truly sporting American marque with European influence in it. It has been revived not only as a modern marque but also musically. The Bearcat was always the most famous of the Stutzes!

Of the very early car makers, the Duryea name is the most highly honoured, and it has a place here – even though none was made after the First World War.

Japan

Japan is the country whose almost incredible growth from a late start can be attributed partly to the effect of war and, of course, to earthquake . . .

If Japan seems to have been short-changed in this selection of Great Marques, all that can be said is that her day will come. Had this book been based only on qualities of productivity and growth, all her manufacturers would have been represented here.

One GP winner, Honda, is an outstanding omission: unless the reader cares to turn to the Rover page! The Japanese motor industry is not old and perhaps this has been to its advantage. It is difficult to realize that Honda did not start

producing four-wheelers until 1962! The first Subaru was made in 1958; the first Suzuki car in 1961; in the early 1970s the Japanese pioneered the use of four-wheel drive for everyday small family cars. No excuse is made, however, for selecting Mazda from among the Japanese specialists – because of its successful pursuit of the Wankel rotary-piston engine. Naturally, Nissan (still more familiar as Datsun?) and Toyota have been selected, too, for they are the firms that have led their industry to the head of the world's manufacturing league table.

The rest of the world

What North America started, Japan has continued. These are the nations that have taught the non-industrial ones the ways of motor manufacture – and the results of manufacture alone bear no relation to the selecting of Great Marques.

There are many – perhaps five hundred? – makes worthy of short-listing.

What I have tried to do in this book, where there have been veritable queues of contestants, is to nominate classic representatives of certain types. Examples are the Arrol-Johnston (for Scotland), the Clyno (for the no-hopers), the Brasier (for the great French racers), the Miller (for the American racing scene) and so on. While perhaps half of the marques that have been chosen were absolutely essential to the intentions of the title, an element of personal bias may also be detected.

The people of the motor industry are as fascinating as the cars they make. What a pity there is no place for *101 Great Tycoons* as a book in itself . . . or is there?

The 1980 Cadillac Seville shows that individuality has been retained for the modern flagships of General Motors – still the world's biggest motor manufacturer.

101
GREAT MARQUES

The main section of the book, which follows, describes the history of 101 famous marques from AC to Wolseley. Each entry contains information on the company, the principal cars, the people behind the marque, the major engineering achievements, and the celebrated sporting successes. Several of the entries also include a brief chronology outlining the significant events in the company's history.

AC Great Britain

Although its name may sound rather ordinary, the AC typifies the ability of certain great, specialist marques to survive much longer than business economics would normally permit. Change of ownership meant that, from the mid-1980s, AC cars were still being hand-built: no longer in Thames Ditton, Surrey, but by AC Scotland plc at Hillington, near Glasgow.

John Weller was the man responsible for bringing the AC car the recognition it deserved, for it was his overhead-camshaft six-cylinder 2-litre engine of 1919, that gave the marque its sporting reputation.

Weller and a wealthy trader, John Portwine, pooled their technical and commercial resources. The company was named Autocars and Accessories Ltd and the first single-cylinder Autocarrier, a three-wheeled commercial delivery vehicle, appeared in 1904. Such was its success that Autocarriers Ltd was formed to produce the AC tricar or Sociable (the first vehicle to be named AC) from 1907. A four-wheeled AC followed shortly before the First World War, by which time

manufacture had moved from West Norwood to Thames Ditton, Surrey.

Weller's six-cylinder power unit ultimately replaced the proprietary fours hitherto used and helped AC expand its markets during the 1920s. S.F. Edge (*see* Napier) was a board member then, and saw to it that the company went racing and record breaking. However, it was in rallying that the AC found true fame; in 1926 it became the first British make to win the winter trek to Monte Carlo outright. In 1929, Edge resigned and the company went into voluntary liquidation, although the service department was kept operating. By 1931 the new owners, the Hurlock brothers, had drawn up a plan to revive the AC with a series of attractive sixes.

Distinctive styling could not disguise the lack of chassis development in the postwar 2-litre saloon, which lasted only until the mid-1950s. Economy cars, invalid carriages and other products helped keep AC afloat while a new route into the sports car market was sought. It was found in an all-independently sprung tubular chassis created for racing by John Tojeiro. With their delightful Ferrari-esque lines, the AC Ace open model and Aceca coupé gave new life to Thames Ditton. Still John Weller's old engine was being offered, suitably modernized and tuned. (Eventually, Bristol and Ford engines were to supplement and replace it.)

In 1961 discussions between the American Carroll Shelby and AC led to the Ford V8-powered Cobra – soon a marque in its own right. The shape is a truly classic one, and much copied in the so-called replica market. (Between 1966 and 1973, 'British' ACs had Frua luxury coachwork from Italy.)

The next design to be bought by AC was a mid-engined one, the Bohanna Stables, a two-seater spaceframed GT car dating from 1972, when it had an Austin Maxi engine. In AC form it had a 3-litre Ford V6

RIGHT *First all-British winners of the Monte Carlo Rally, in 1926, were the Hon. Victor Bruce and this 2-litre AC tourer. 'The World's Finest Light Six' was the AC company's justifiable claim for John Weller's great engine, which was built for a period of some 40 years.*

BELOW *The AC Ace had beautiful lines, which took on an aggressive look as the V8 Cobra was developed. In the 1960s Jack Sears, seen here at the Goodwood chicane, was Britain's most effective and entertaining Cobra driver.*

Vittorio Jano's first great Alfa Romeo sports car was introduced in 1925 and went on general sale in 1927. This is the ultimate version of it, the 1929 6C 1500 Super Sport. It had an excellent power-to-weight ratio, and led to many more superb Jano designs.

power unit, and was called the ME3000. Few were built during an excessively long gestation period. One consequence of all this, in the winter of 1983–4, was a new plan to develop the AC in Scotland. So in the mid-1980s the AC marque was still alive; Thames Ditton, its spiritual home, continued to house the service and spares organization.

ALFA ROMEO Italy

The evocative words Alfa Romeo have a special ring to them in any language, especially Italian.

The first products of ALFA, the Società Anonima Lombarda Fabbrica Automobili ('Lombardy Motor Works'), were made in 1910. For several years before that, the Milan factory had assembled lightweight Darracqs. Giuseppe Merosi, a noted FIAT and Bianchi engineer, designed the original ALFA as a truly Italian high-performance car. Nicola Romeo, who took charge of the company in 1915, added his name to the marque. It was, however, another former FIAT man, Vittorio

Jano, who turned a promising (but abandoned) Merosi design into the famous all-conquering supercharged Alfa Romeo 2-litre twin-overhead-camshaft eight-cylinder engine, which helped the Tipo P2 Grand Prix car dominate racing in 1924–5. He also created a fine series of six-cylinder sports cars.

Jano continued to produce brilliant and successful designs for Alfa Romeo which, nevertheless, was affected by the Depression, like every other manufacturer. So high was Alfa Romeo's repute, however, that the company was rescued in 1933 and from then on it was state-owned.

Racing continued, being run by Enzo Ferrari (*see* Ferrari). A heroic drive in a 3.8-litre P3 by Tazio Nuvolari in the 1935 German Grand Prix gave Alfa Romeo one of its very few victories over Auto Union and Mercedes-Benz. Alfa Romeo came up with a more powerful racing car with a 4.1-litre 12-cylinder unit, and Nuvolari and Carlo Pintacuda did beat the German team drivers occasionally in 1936–7.

In 1938 Scuderia Ferrari, the independent Alfa Romeo team, was taken over by the works when Alfa

ABOVE *1951 was the last season for Alfa Romeo's highly developed Alfetta which had originated in Modena, in the Scuderia Ferrari workshops, in 1937. Juan Manuel Fangio (here en route to the fastest lap in the German Grand Prix) had to work hard for his first world title. The supercharged Alfa Romeo 159 was usually faster than the new 4.5-litre Ferrari, but it used much more fuel and could lose through pitstops – as Fangio did on this occasion at the Nürburgring.*

Corse was formed. Soon Ferrari left; he had been organizing racing for Alfa Romeo for long enough. Now he would go it alone (*see* Ferrari); his achievements continue to make motoring history. Jano had left Alfa Romeo by 1938, and the last prewar racing cars were largely the work of Gioacchino Colombo. Most significant was the Alfetta, or Tipo 158, a 1.5-litre supercharged straight-8 voiturette that developed 190 bhp at 6500 rpm. It fitted the postwar Grand Prix formula ideally and, as the Tipo 159, could produce over 400 bhp at 9300 rpm by the end of its useful development life. Its last two racing seasons were also the first two for the new World Drivers' Championship. Those first champions – Giuseppe Farina in 1950, and Juan Manuel Fangio in 1951 – drove Alfa Romeos.

Although there were some further successes later,

1951 was to be the last year of what could be termed dominance by Alfa Romeo in Grand Prix or sports car racing. It was with its production cars that the marque would continue to achieve great things in racing and rallying.

Throughout the 1930s, Alfa Romeos had been costly and exotic. The postwar 1900 saloon was mundane to look at, but it performed well and brought Alfa Romeo to the everyday sporting motorist. Much more of an inspiration was the 1954 Giulietta: neat, elegant, and very very fast for a 1300. The coach-builders Bertone gave the regular model its classic lines, designer Orazio Satta its technical features. The Giulietta made Alfa Romeo (with Jaguar) the only early postwar volume producer of double-camshaft engines; and it led to the Giulia saloon and many subsequent attractive rear-wheel-drive Alfa Romeos.

ABOVE *Most exotic of modern Alfa Romeos, the front-engined Montreal V8 GT model was built from 1970 to 1975. This example was provided by The Patrick Collection.*

LEFT *This mid-1980s Alfa Romeo was called the Alfetta. The old nickname had been revived in 1972 for a new saloon range, which held a special appeal for the sporting motorist.*

HIGHLIGHTS

1906: SA Italiana Darracq moves into Portello works, Milan.

1910: SA Lombarda Fabbrica Automobili (ALFA) begins producing Italian-designed cars, following departure of Darracq personnel.

1915: Nicola Romeo takes charge of Portello works; all cars now named Alfa Romeo.

1926: Vittorio Jano takes over from Giuseppe Merosi as technical chief.

1927: First of 11 Alfa Romeo victories in Mille Miglia road race.

1931: First of four successive Le Mans 24-Hour race wins.

1932: Alfa Romeo now the top make in Grand Prix racing.

1933: Nationalization of company.

1946: Return to Grand Prix domination.

1950: Giuseppe Farina is first World GP Champion.

1951: Juan Manuel Fangio succeeds Farina as World Champion.

1954: Giulietta starts new trend in Alfa Romeo design.

1971: Alfa Romeo's ninth and last victory in Targa Florio road race. Alfasud introduced at new Naples plant.

1984: Alfa Romeos score maximum points in European Touring Car Championship for third year running.

1985: The Alfa Romeo company celebrates its 75th anniversary.

The GTV6 scored maximum marks in the first three European touring car race championships, in 1982, '83 and '84, following the adoption of Group A regulations: not that there was much opposition for them in their class.

In many respects the ideal compact front-wheel-drive car, the Alfasud ('Alfa South', so called because it was made in a new factory near Naples, in southern Italy) represented a new departure in 1971. It had a flat-4 engine and disc brakes all round. At the other end of the scale, in the early 1970s, the Bertone-styled Montreal coupé kept Alfa Romeo firmly in the exotic *gran turismo* class. Its V8 engine was based on a competition unit, for Alfa Romeo had achieved some success with its Tipo 33 sports racing car, which had its engine behind the driver.

In Grand Prix racing, Niki Lauda scored a victory in the 1978 Swedish Grand Prix with the controversial Brabham 'fan' car, which drew air from underneath to promote downforce, and had an Alfa Romeo engine. Alfa Romeo's own return to Grand Prix racing soon afterwards had produced some good performances but no outright victories by 1985.

The wide range of more recent sporting saloons and coupés – including the Alfa 90, the first production car to have an adjustable aerodynamic spoiler – successfully maintains the Alfa Romeo's individuality and international appeal. They are worthy successors to those 'muscle' cars that – with monotonous regularity in the 1930s – ran away with the Mille Miglia, Targa Florio, and with the Le Mans 24-Hours. For, when Germany took over Grand Prix racing in that period, Alfa Romeo had still dominated sports car racing.

ALVIS Great Britain

Some of this company's recent military vehicles have had Jaguar engines, but that is where the connection between Alvis and the modern car ends. Sold in the early 1980s to United Scientific by the failing BL conglomerate, Alvis still occupies its famous Holyhead Road, Coventry, factory; but there has been no new Alvis car since 1967. Yet, in its day, the Alvis was considered one of the finest cars of its class.

The name Alvis was coined by Geoffrey de Freville, linguist, businessman, and engineer. He managed a car import business before setting up his own Aluminium Alloy Pistons Ltd in Wandsworth, London, in 1914. His pistons were stamped with the word 'Alvis' in a triangle. Among his customers was Siddeley-Deasy of Coventry (see Armstrong Siddeley). A Welsh marine engineer, Thomas George John, worked at Siddeley-Deasy before starting up in car manufacture, utilizing a Freville-designed 1.5-litre four-cylinder engine. He also acquired the right to use the Alvis name and insignia which (after modifications because of a complaint from Avro) developed into the distinctive and legendary Red Triangle.

Production began in 1920, and in 1922 John was joined (from Daimler) by George Thomas Smith-Clarke, a creative designer and inventor who had

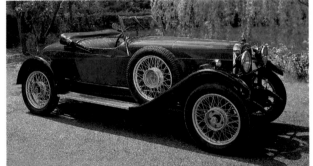

RIGHT *The first commercially successful Alvis was the 12/50, which established a sporting character for the marque. This one dates from 1927 and, like its contemporaries, carries the symbolic hare mascot on its radiator cap.*

already built several vehicles of his own. He became chief engineer and general manager and, with the 12/50 model, helped Alvis through receivership and back into liquidity. Victory by Major C. M. Harvey in the 1923 Brooklands 200-Mile race did much to promote the new marque.

Although Smith-Clarke and his team worked hard on innovations such as front-wheel drive, all-synchromesh gears, supercharging and independent suspension, it was on orthodoxy and style that later Alvis cars would sell. Some of the most attractive coachwork of the 1930s came on Alvis chassis. The company's body engineer Roland Fox had trained not only at the London works of Vanden Plas (run by his father), but also at the famous Continental coachbuilding house of Gangloff.

Agreements with the French company Gnome et Rhône and with the Hungarian cross-country pioneer Nicholas Straussler brought Alvis into the fields of aero engines and military vehicles respectively – and nearly to financial ruin in 1937. New designs and plenty of war contracts restored the company.

From 1946, the year of T. G. John's death, former de Havilland director John Joseph Parkes became Alvis's chief executive.

Smith-Clarke retired at the end of 1950. Alec Issigonis, the creator of the Morris Minor, was in 1952 appointed to inject new life into Alvis design. His T175 (four-cylinder) and T350 (V8) would have had rubber suspension, a two-speed rear axle and other novel features – but finance was withdrawn. The only (T350) prototype of what could have been a Jaguar rival was eventually scrapped. Meanwhile Issigonis had gone back to what was now BMC, to design the Mini. Before he was killed, Parkes's son Michael, a successful engineer and racing driver, had hoped to revive the Issigonis eight-cylinder engine for a competition car. Another proposal that might have kept Alvis going as a car maker was joining forces with Aston Martin-Lagonda.

RIGHT *Bought for The Patrick Collection in 1984, this Charlesworth-bodied Alvis Speed 25 dates from 1939. It was photographed at Bordesley Hall in Worcestershire where its former owner, Joseph Patrick, once lived.*

In fact, no other serious long-term development took place. A twin-carburettor version of the 3-litre six-cylinder engine did make the attractive Grey Lady a genuine 160 km/h (100 mph) saloon; but the car's classic lines were too dated for some customers.

Graber had been putting special coachwork on Alvis chassis for Swiss customers from the late 1940s, and in 1955 the rights were acquired to manufacture similar bodies in Britain: first by Willowbrook of Loughborough and then, in a more organized fashion, by Park Ward of London.

In 1965, at the invitation of John Parkes, the Rover company bought Alvis. The mid-engined Rover BS prototype car was made at Alvis soon afterwards, and there was even a new Alvis coupé: the GTS. (Nicknamed Gladys, it became the property of the man who styled it, Rover's David Bache.)

There was little time for the Alvis and Rover people to work as partners. Rover and Triumph came together in 1967; British Leyland was born in 1968. The last Alvis car – a traditional 3-litre (boosted by triple carburettors) with, by now, very expensive Mulliner Park Ward coachwork – was completed in September 1967.

AMÉDÉE BOLLÉE France

The Bollée family of Le Mans were pioneers of road transport well before the days of the internal combustion engine. Ernest-Sylvain Bollée set up the company in 1842, and was joined by his son Amédée (*père*). The Bollée bell foundry began to turn out large, roadgoing steam buses in the early 1870s.

Amédée Bollée had three sons, two of whom became manufacturers in their own right. Léon Bollée's original voiturette (1895: the first use of that term) preceded a chequered history that included the acquisition of his works by Morris in 1925. The Léon Bollée marque name disappeared in 1933.

The eldest son, Amédée (*fils*), made his first vehicle, a steam coach, in 1885: the year of Benz's first car and Daimler's first motorcycle. Amédée Bollée's first true motor car was completed in 1896, after much trial and error. Like his brother Léon, Amédée sold manufacturing rights to others: both showed great originality of thought in matters of power and weight.

Probably the younger Amédée's greatest claim to fame was his introduction of serious streamlining for motor racing, an activity in which France and French manufacturers were the true pioneers. The first-ever race to cross national boundaries was the Paris–Amsterdam–Paris of 7–13 July 1898, in which four of these 8 hp two-cylinder air-cooled Amédée Bollée *torpédos* made their impressive début, driven by Bollée himself, Etienne Giraud, Loysel and Vinet.

Havoc had been caused beforehand by the *préfecture ingénieur*, a Monsieur Bochet, turning down nearly all the vehicles after keeping everyone waiting while he

had a two-hour dinner. When he threatened to use the 23rd Hussars to blast unauthorized racers off the roads, the simple expedient of moving the start to Villiers, in the next *département* (Seine-et-Oise), was taken. Amédée Bollée, anxious to prove his new cars, ran the gauntlet of the furious Bochet and his troops with a horse and cart to collect the fuel and take it to the new starting point.

At Amsterdam, Giraud's Bollée led from Léonce Girardot's Panhard. Unfortunately, Giraud's car skidded and rolled over on the return run. This, and other problems, dropped it to third place at the finish (repositioned just short of Bochet territory), and Loysel's car came in fifth. The other two cars were not classified as finishers; Bollée is known to have lost a lot of time after a crash. All the same it was a fine début for this extraordinary machine, which went on to win the Bordeaux–Biarritz race six weeks later.

Those Amédée Bollées were, probably, the fastest of the petrol-driven cars for straight-line speed. (The wind-cheating Jeantaud and Jamais-Contente record cars of 1898–9 were electric powered.)

An even bigger Amédée Bollée (20 hp, four-cylinder) raced in the 1899 Tour de France, showing speed but less reliability. One example did finish fifth behind the inevitable Panhards in this 2165 km (1350-mile) seven-stage marathon. After that, and up to the First World War, Amédée Bollée made small quantities of luxury touring cars and the marque lived on only until 1922.

ARMSTRONG SIDDELEY Great Britain

RIGHT *Armstrong Siddeley was ready to announce its stylish postwar models, the Hurricane and Lancaster, as early as May 1945, when few manufacturers had managed even to get their 1930s designs back on the road. This range was later expanded with the arrival of the Typhoon, the Whitley and an up-market pick-up truck. The lines of the Whitley (seen here) were to inspire those of the last great Armstrong Siddeley, the 1953 Sapphire.*

John Davenport Siddeley, later Lord Kenilworth, was a draughtsman in Thomas Humber's bicycle works before moving into the developing motor tyre business. This led him, via sales of Peugeots and other imports, to motor manufacture.

Wolseley made many components for Siddeley whose next move, in 1905, was to take the post of general manager of the Wolseley motor works when Herbert Austin left in 1905. Siddeley, in turn, fell out with his masters and moved to H. H. P. Deasy's new motor works in Coventry in 1909. From 1912, these Deasy cars, characterized by their bulkhead-mounted radiators, were called Siddeley-Deasy.

Meanwhile, in Newcastle upon Tyne, Sir W. G. Armstrong, Whitworth & Co. had been manufacturing the advanced Wilson-Pilcher car, before creating an Armstrong-Whitworth design. This company's cars already had a reputation for solid British engineering and craftsmanship when, in 1919, a merging of interests produced the Armstrong Siddeley.

For many years the distinctive radiator grille surmounted by a Sphinx represented all that was best from Coventry, Britain's car-making capital.

From 1929, the Wilson preselect epicyclic gearbox was an optional extra, and later it became standard. The 'gear-change' pedal (replacing the normal clutch pedal) caused the engagement of gears previously selected by hand on a quadrant. Thus both hands were free for the actual change. The most exciting model of the 1930s was the 5-litre Siddeley Special, for which a 145 km/h (90 mph) top speed has been quoted. Generally, however, the Armstrong Siddeley retained an aura of high quality with average performance, even with the attractive postwar range.

It was not until 1953, when the excellent six-cylinder Sapphire was launched, that Armstrong Siddeley began to look as if it had a world-beater. A twin-carburettor engine put it firmly in the Jaguar class in 1954, when Tommy Sopwith drove his Sapphire-powered Sphinx sports car effectively in British club races.

Unfortunately the compact 234 and 236 saloons of 1956 had none of the Sapphire's class, and Hawker Siddeley (newly merged with Bristol Aircraft) stopped making cars in 1960.

ARROL-JOHNSTON Great Britain

ABOVE RIGHT *The Arrol-Johnstons of 1906 to 1912, like this 24/30 model, had distinctive dashboard radiators.*

Scotland has been able to boast several great marques of its own, including the 'Three As': the Albion; the Argyll (perhaps most famous for the architectural excesses of its factory at the south end of Loch Lomond); and, the most historic of them all, the Arrol-Johnston. Sir William Arrol and Partners are best known for their bridges and other great civil engineering works. However, the same Arrol, with

George Johnston, put Scotland on the motoring map in 1897 with their rugged opposed-piston, twin-cylinder dogcart.

Design did not advance with the times – at least not until the arrival of John Napier as engineer-in-chief. In 1905 he used an Arrol-Johnston, still a flat-twin, to win the original Tourist Trophy race on the Isle of Man, to the chagrin of Charles Rolls, S. F. Edge and other strong publicists.

The company was re-formed in 1906 as the New Arrol-Johnston Car Co. Ltd of Paisley, and made orthodox production models and experimental electric cars. Another company reorganization in 1913 took Arrol-Johnston to Dumfries where a luxury model, the overhead-camshaft Victory, was introduced immediately after the First World War. It was not a success, and a revised version of the cheaper, prewar 15.9 hp side-valve car was reintroduced.

A merger with Aster in 1927, to make Arrol-Aster cars with sleeve-valve engines, brought the company to its knees for the last time in 1931, not long after the Wall Street crash.

ASTON MARTIN Great Britain

Big, bespoke, and very expensive indeed, today's Aston Martin has the longest pedigree of all the traditional sports cars, with the exception of the unique Morgan. This essentially British luxury car enjoys Royal patronage: notably that of the Prince of Wales.

The name of the marque comes from the Buckinghamshire village of Aston Clinton, scene of a once-famous speed hill climb in which Lionel Martin took part with a tuned and lightened Singer just before the First World War.

Aston Martins have always been produced individually. The original, which ran in late 1914, had an Italian Isotta Fraschini chassis powered by a Coventry Simplex (forerunner of the Coventry Climax) engine. The engineer who built it with Martin, Robert Bamford, left the partnership when the marque was barely established.

Racing successes began in 1921, when *Motor* published the first test report of a roadgoing Aston-Martin (the name tended to carry a hyphen then). That car lapped Brooklands at nearly 106 km (66 mph) 'in full touring trim', with two people aboard. Its performance was considered outstanding for a 1½-litre;

RIGHT Purposeful 1949–50 Aston Martin DB2, styled by Frank Feeley and powered by the W. O. Bentley team's 2.6-litre six-cylinder Lagonda engine. This ex-works prototype was provided by the Nigel Dawes Collection.

BELOW Ultimate expression of the A. C. Bertelli period, this 1935 Mark II model had a dry-sump 1.5-litre overhead-camshaft engine. This car, owned by D. J. E. Proffitt, was provided by the Nigel Dawes Collection.

53 km/h (33 mph) was averaged on the 430 km (268-mile) journey from Holyhead in Anglesey to London. In May 1921, *Motor*'s report summed the Aston Martin up as 'a high-efficiency, high-class large car in miniature'. The price was expected to be about £700. By October, when *Autocar* carried out a Continental road test of the very same car, the nominal price was a stunning £850: and there was the clear implication that in buying 'the car that is built for its owner's pleasure' (to quote a subsequent slogan), the customer was now having to pay substantially towards the development costs. The accidental death of a major sponsor, Count Louis Zborowski, in 1924, was most likely the main reason for Lionel Martin's declaration of insolvency the following year.

From 1926, after moving from Kensington, Aston Martin began its second, 'Bertelli' period at Feltham, Middlesex. Augustus and Enrico Bertelli had been taken from Italy to Wales in their early childhood. Augustus was a fine engineer and he took the marque in hand, turning it into a great one by modernizing the chassis and fitting his own design of four-cylinder overhead-camshaft engine. Another financier pulled out of the business, however, and in 1931 the Frazer Nash company held the purse strings. In 1932, control of the company passed to Sir Arthur Sutherland and his son Gordon. Bertelli stayed on, designing a new 2-litre engine. Next door, his brother Enrico ran his own coachbuilding works and produced some lovely low-slung bodies for Aston Martin (see below).

There were successes in racing – as reflected in such model names as International and Ulster – but high prices and low sales meant a constant battle for survival. Gordon Sutherland wanted to modernize and 'soften' the Aston Martin to give it wider appeal. Augustus Bertelli disagreed with this policy and left in 1936; his protégé Claude Hill took charge of engineering. In 1947 Sutherland put Aston Martin on the market as a going concern and it was bought by David Brown.

FAR RIGHT *The Aston Martin DBS was styled in Sir David Brown's days by William Towns, and it still has a timeless look. This 1978 V8-engined car was provided by The Patrick Collection.*

Claude Hill had produced a pushrod overhead-valve four-cylinder engine for postwar use; but David Brown bought Lagonda soon afterwards, and insisted on Aston Martin's new production model being powered by the double-overhead-camshaft unit that W. O. Bentley had designed for Lagonda. And like Bertelli before him, Hill marched out.

To its credit, Aston Martin's reputation, if not its finances, went from strength to strength. The DB2 of 1949–50 was a beautifully smooth coupé, styled by Lagonda designer Frank Feeley with or without apology to – but certainly improving upon – Carrozzeria Touring's early Ferraris. It starred in classic events like the TT, the Mille Miglia, the Alpine Trial, and of course the Le Mans 24-Hour race. Had it been a two-plus-two, then Aston Martin might have been heralded as the maker of the first Grand Touring car (in fact Lancia had this distinction). Aston Martin's DB2 did, however, acquire the sophistication of two small seats and a hatchback in 1953, but at the same time lost its near-perfection of form.

The 1951 DB3 was an Eberan-Eberhorst design for sports car racing. Like Sir William Lyons of Jaguar,

ABOVE *Roy Salvadori takes one of the works DBR1s through the chicane at Goodwood during the 1959 Tourist Trophy: the race that clinched the World Sports Car Championship for Aston Martin.*

RIGHT *Lex Davison (Essex Racing Stable Aston Martin DB4GT Zagato) overtook Jack Sears (Coombs Jaguar E-Type) on the last lap to win the 1961 Aintree International GT race in spectacular style. New cooperation between Aston Martin and Zagato was being prepared in 1985.*

David Brown had a burning ambition to win at Le Mans. The DB3 was succeeded by the DB3S (1953) and the DBR1 (1956), but it was not until 1959 – after a decade of struggle, including three second places – that the Aston Martin racing team under John Wyer

gained that special victory as part of a brilliant season which, quite unexpectedly, brought the World Sports Car Championship Trophy to Britain for the first time.

The road cars continued with the DB4, DB5 and DB6, which had a new twin-cam engine designed by a Polish engineer, Tadek Marek, and bodywork on the Carrozzeria Touring Superleggera principle (aluminium panels over tube frame). Beautiful they all were, but without the pugnacious purity of the very rare DB4GT Zagato, 19 of which were built in the early 1960s: magnificent, classic beasts from any point of view.

A proposed link with Alvis came to nothing and, in 1972, Sir David Brown sold out: his main company was unable to justify the losses any longer. Racing successes have been elusive, but a succession of enthusiastic proprietors has kept the firm going and the present V8-engined Aston Martins, based upon the William Towns-styled DBS first seen in 1967, can be numbered among the worthiest claimants to the description 'Supercar'.

AUBURN USA

The small town of Auburn near Fort Wayne, Indiana, gave its name to a car in 1903, when two coachbuilders, Frank and Morris Eckart, first marketed their single-cylinder runabout. The firm grew to make proprietary-engined two-, four-, and six-cylinder cars labelled Auburn and (from 1911 to 1914) Zimmerman.

Small quantities of rather over-ornamented models, including a confection called the Beauty Six, were made in uneconomic numbers until 1924, when the most important event in Auburn history occurred: E. L. Cord bought the company.

In 1919, at the age of 25, Errett Lobban Cord had started selling the Moon, which was a St Louis-built copy of the Rolls-Royce. Like the Auburn, the Moon had a four-bearing Continental engine. Cord rose to the position of general manager before being head-hunted to sell off several hundred of Auburn's slow-retailing cars. Within only two years Cord became the chief

shareholder (and president) of the Auburn company.

Style, quality and value made the Auburn famous across North America. Cord's sales successes with Auburn enabled him to buy the Midwestern Ansted, Checker, and Duesenberg companies (see Duesenberg), then in 1929 he created a marque of his own (see Cord). Other acquisitions included the Lycoming engine company in Pennsylvania.

Such were Cord's abilities that Auburn was able to weather the Wall Street crash better than most, and made well over 30,000 cars in 1931: but that was to be an all-time record.

In 1932, at $975, Auburn was offering the cheapest-ever 12-cylinder car; but sales were plummeting by now. Harold Ames, August Duesenberg and Gordon Buehrig produced the boldly styled Auburns for 1935 – by which time E. L. Cord had fled the country, under suspicion of financial irregularities. It was after Cord's return to the United States, while his financial affairs were undergoing scrutiny, that the proposed 1937 range was shelved.

ABOVE *Flamboyant speedster – this c. 1930 boat-tailed Auburn 8-98A is from the Auburn-Cord-Duesenberg Museum.*

For 30 years the Auburn name lay dormant. Then the owner of a new Auburn-Cord-Duesenberg company, Glenn Pray, began making copies of the more impressive Auburns at Tulsa, Oklahoma, using modern V8 engines and transmissions beneath the classical clothing.

AUDI Germany

The word quattro has become part of the international vocabulary of motoring since Audi NSU Auto Union AG of Ingolstadt announced its advanced four-wheel-drive high-performance road car of that name in 1980. For years the Audi marque had failed to project its individual personality, which is unusual for a make of such engineering integrity. The complexity of the Audi's background is probably the main reason for this.

Cars called Horch were made from the turn of the century until about 1940. It was only when 40-year-old former Benz engineer August Horch fell out with his colleagues, and left to set up a new car-making company with new partners, that he found he could not take his own name with him. So it was that his first new car of 1909 bore an Audi badge. (This new name was the translation of Horch, which means 'Hark!' or 'Listen!' in German, into its Latin equivalent.)

The early Audis were sporting enough for Horch and others to win major prizes in the Austrian Alpine Trials of 1911 and 1912. An interesting parallel with modern times was the introduction of a short-wheelbase version (the Alpensieger), which maintained the rally success in 1913 and 1914.

Despite a financial crisis in 1925, Audi cars kept their individuality until 1928 when J. S. Rasmussen (*see* DKW) took a controlling interest. He had bought up the tooling and existing materials (including stocks of 3.8- and 4.4-litre six- and eight-cylinder power units) of the Rickenbacker Motor Company, Detroit. Edward Vernon Rickenbacker ('Captain Eddie') had been a fine racing driver with Duesenberg, Maxwell and others; and he was a First World War hero, too, having shot down a record 26 German aircraft. After the war he had gathered a good team around him and made top quality cars; but under-pricing and a shortage of dealers had led to receivership and a sale of all assets in 1927. The six-cylinder Audi Dresden and the eight-cylinder Audi Zwickau *could* have been called Rasmussen Rickenbackers. Rasmussen also ordered the assembly of a few 1.1-litre four-cylinder DKW-based Peugeot-engined cars using the name of Audi.

In 1932, the company lost its personal identity still further when it was combined with Horch, Wanderer and DKW in the Auto Union group. Audi became a middle-of-the-range model and, ironically, production was transferred to the nearby works of A. Horch in 1934. The Audi Front or Type UW was a compact and often attractive 'up-market DKW' while its successor,

RIGHT *Front-wheel-drive 1935 Audi UW225, built at the Horch works in Zwickau, bears Auto Union insignia beneath the traditional Audi bonnet badge. Coachwork on this example is by Heinrich Gläser of Dresden.*

ABOVE *The Audi Quattro led the world trend towards four-wheel-drive competition cars, and dominated the rally scene between 1982 and 1984, by which time several other manufacturers were following suit. This action shot was taken during the 1984 Portugal Rally, which Hannu Mikkola won for the Audi team.*

the 3.3-litre rear-wheel-drive 920, verged on the exclusive. Production ended in April 1940. After the Second World War, the Zwickau factory came within the Russian zone. Today its product is East Germany's maid of all work, the tiny Trabant.

Meanwhile Auto Union gradually came back to life in West Germany. The Audi name remained dormant until 1965 when a new 'big DKW' – in effect the DKW's replacement – set the marque firmly on a front-drive course once again. It had a four-stroke 1.7-litre overhead-camshaft four-cylinder engine and disc brakes at the front. By now Audi's parent company was VW and production of these two marques

increased rapidly at the Ingolstadt works, which had been put into operation for DKW in 1959.

Even more outstanding technically, the Audi range developed along somewhat mundane lines from a styling point of view, often closely akin to Volkswagen. A 1973 Audi 80 styling exercise by Giorgetto Giugiaro's Ital Design and the Karmann company hinted at the new concept which, as the five-cylinder fuel-injection turbocharged Quattro, was to be the motoring sensation of 1980, and a natural rallying competitor. As early as 1982 the Quattro won the World Rally Championship, and by 1985 four-wheel drive was being offered across the Audi range.

RIGHT *Mid-1980s Audi 200 Turbo, typical of the Ingolstadt firm's aerodynamic and sophisticated road cars.*

AUSTIN Great Britain

ABOVE *The Austin Seven was introduced in 1922, and was soon influencing car manufacture abroad. This 1928 Chummy tourer epitomizes Austin's catch phrase – Motoring for the Million.*

Herbert Austin's first big adventure came when, as a teenager, he sailed to Australia in 1884 to enter the world of agricultural engineering. After nearly ten years, he returned and designed the first Wolseley car (*see* Wolseley).

Austin and the board of Vickers (Wolseley's owners) fell out and parted, and the now successful engineer started looking for premises of his own. In November 1905, near the Lickey Hills, just to the southwest of Birmingham, he came across the disused White & Pike metal works. In January 1906 it became the Austin Motor Company's rapidly expanding Longbridge factory.

Design of the first Austin car was already well under way and by April 1906, when the official opening of Longbridge as a motor works took place, it was already running. By 1917 Longbridge had established itself as Britain's biggest motor factory, due in part to large-scale war contracts, including a very large order from Tsarist Russia, and in September of that year Herbert Austin was knighted for his services. Just afterwards came the Russian Revolution, and some cancellations!

The Austin car had already acquired its 'dependable' reputation when a postwar one-model policy was announced: there would be a 20 hp car combining American production technology with traditional craftsmanship. The formula was not destined to succeed and only Sir Herbert Austin's skill, confidence and strength of character enabled the company to escape both from the receiver and from the possibility of a merger with General Motors.

Two cheaper cars, the Twelve and the Seven, introduced in 1921 and 1922 respectively, saved the company. The Twelve was good and solid, and formed the basis for the most familiar version of the London taxicab. The Seven was to become one of the world's best-loved cars, bringing motoring to many of the people of Britain as the Ford Model T had done in America. Both models received wide acclaim and were made in many parts of the world. The simple Austin Seven found its way to the United States and Rosengart made a French version; but the most famous overseas Austin Seven was the German Dixi, or BMW-Dixi (*see* BMW). The success of the car is shown by the annual production figures at Longbridge, which leapt from just under 10,000 in 1924 to over 26,000 in 1929, a figure bettered only once (and by a small margin) in 1935. Throughout the 1930s,

RIGHT *The Austin Seven came of age with the delightful £120 Ruby of 1934. The later 'Big Seven' lacked charm, however, and was to hasten the Seven's departure in 1939. This 1937 Ruby is from The Patrick Collection.*

BELOW *Longbridge revisited in the 1980s by a 1952 Austin A90 Atlantic from the nearby Patrick Collection. (In 1953 the A90's engine and gearbox were adapted for Austin's sports car, the Healey 100.)*

however, the Austin and Morris concerns waged war as Britain's top producers. (Ford began to feature in this commercial conflict once the new factory at Dagenham was in full swing.) For Austin, 1937 was another great year, with over 89,000 cars produced including some 23,000 Sevens. In that year, a less successful 'Big Seven' joined the Austin range, and the idea suddenly began to look outdated.

HIGHLIGHTS

1906: Austin works open at Longbridge, Birmingham.

1922: Austin Seven announced.

1927: The Seven built in Germany as Dixi.

1928: The Seven built in France as Rosengart.

1930: The Seven built in United States as American Austin (later called Bantam; led to prototype of Jeep.)

1933: The Seven adapted by Datsun, made in Yokohama.

1936: Introduction of new bestseller, Austin Ten Cambridge.

1941: Death of Lord Austin.

1952: Austin merges with Nuffield Group to form British Motor Corporation.

1959: Introduction of new 'Austin Seven' (also as Morris Mini-Minor), designed by Alec Issigonis.

1966: British Motor Holdings formed by merger of BMC and Jaguar.

1968: British Leyland formed by merger of BMH with Leyland Motors.

1975: BL nationalized.

1982: Decentralization of BL leads to formation of Austin-Rover Group Ltd.

In updating the Seven, however, Austin avoided the battle that was developing between Ford and Morris for the 'eight horsepower' market. In 1938 demand for the Austin Seven tailed off rapidly and a new Eight was brought out for 1939; but in fact the Ten (or Cambridge) was Austin's top-selling car from 1936 to 1939.

Lord Austin, who had been made a peer in 1936, died in 1941, and Leonard Lord, who had left Morris after a quarrel, became the top man at Longbridge from 1938. This was the second disagreement (Sir) Leonard Lord, later Lord Lambury, had had with Morris (Lord Nuffield).

Leonard Lord, however, evened the score when, having quickly and successfully launched a range of postwar Austins – the A40, A70, A90, A125 and A135 – he became senior executive following the 1952 merger with Morris which resulted in the formation of the British Motor Corporation. Lord Nuffield was 74 by then, Lord Lambury nearly 20 years younger and, it seemed, very belligerent and not much concerned with popularity.

RIGHT *The 1959 Austin Seven (and Morris Mini-Minor) represented as big an advance in motoring concepts as the original Seven nearly 40 years earlier. Under British Leyland rule 'Mini' would be used as a marque name.*

BELOW *The Mini layout – front-wheel drive and engine mounted crosswise – was to be adopted for all new designs bearing the name Austin. The Maestro (seen here) followed the Metro in the new generation of Austins for the 1980s.*

The memory of the Austin Seven lingered on but the postwar version, the A30/A35, was to be dropped after little more than a decade. It was just too austere and too small to compete with the Morris Minor, which had a lifespan twice as long as its Austin counterpart. The overlapping 'baby Austin' replacement was the simple yet cleverly conceived Austin A40 Farina series, a design that could have led to the modern hatchback, but did not. One probable reason for this was the launch of the next 'Austin Seven': the car we know today as the Mini. Alec Issigonis, the man who had created the 1948 Morris Minor, was behind this sensational small car of 1959.

The Mini was not the first vehicle in the world to have its engine placed crosswise; but it was the first car – cheap and available – with this feature that could also accommodate four people in reasonable comfort within an overall length of 3 m (10 ft). Ford's new small car of 1959, the 105E Anglia, was nearly 4 m (13 ft) long.

Front-wheel drive and transverse engines became the trend from then on, the last rear-driven Austin model being the anachronistic 3-litre saloon of 1967–71. In 1966, BMC and the Jaguar Group merged to form British Motor Holdings. Soon afterwards it was seen that, despite the apparent success of the Mini and the larger 1100, the British Motor Corporation was incurring heavy losses. British Leyland was formed in 1968, with Sir Donald Stokes in command. At first the prospect seemed good, but the corporation failed and was nationalized in the mid-1970s.

The Austin name has lived on through the rise and fall of that controversial organization while Morris, Triumph, Riley and Wolseley have gone (although Morris was kept on as a commercial vehicle marque). The Metros, Maestros and Montegos of the mid-1980s were infinitely more sophisticated than their predecessors, and the new company name, Austin Rover, seemed to indicate a clear return to the understanding that a strong marque identity is desirable. The Austin name is, certainly, one of Britain's worthiest.

BENTLEY Great Britain

DFP (Doriot, Flandrin et Parant) of Courbevoie had found invaluable importers of their cars to Britain in the brothers H. M. and W. O. Bentley, who did useful development work, took part in competitions and in general worked hard to promote the obscure French marque. Then came the First World War and the DFP was never quite the same again, for it had lost the Bentleys' services.

Walter Owen Bentley was a designer of rotary aero engines. When peace came in 1918, he designed his first car, which appeared as a prototype at the London motor show the following year.

The Bentley factory was in Cricklewood, London,

and a near neighbour was the British Vanden Plas coachbuilding company. The first sales of the marque were made in 1921, and Bentleys took 2nd, 4th and 5th places in the 1922 Isle of Man Tourist Trophy race: Bentley himself came 4th in what was to be his last race as a driver. On the other hand, a Bentley legend was about to unfold.

It began in 1923 when a privately owned Bentley was the only non-French car to take part in the first-ever Le Mans 24-Hour race. Its owner was a Canadian soldier of fortune named John Duff, who was to be Bentley's London agent for a brief period, and his co-driver was Bentley's chief tester Francis Clement. This was a very satisfactory début for Bentley because they came fourth. In 1924, again the only overseas entrants, they returned to win outright. Bentleys subsequently became a force at Le Mans, winning four times in succession between 1927 and 1930. These were great victories for Britain – as were the many other races won and records broken, notably the 1929 500-mile and 1930 Double Twelve races at Brooklands, and in 1926 the world's 12-hour record at over 160 km/h (100 mph) at Montlhéry in France. The Bentley soon came to be regarded as the most splendid expression of the British sports car. The business side was, however, very shaky. Bentley, the technician and creator of the great sports cars, could not keep the company going unaided, and so playboy driver Woolf Barnato – three times a winner for Bentley at Le Mans – invested a large amount of money in the firm.

Nevertheless, the writing was already on the wall when, at the height of the Depression, W. O. Bentley's greatest masterpiece, the 8-litre, took its stately bow, replacing the famous Speed Six. It was strong and it was fast, but it was prohibitively expensive, too, and out of the reach of most.

ABOVE *The last Tourist Trophy race for cars to be held on the Isle of Man took place in what the winning Sunbeam driver, Jean Chassagne, described as 'a nightmare in a sea of mud'. Frank Clement (Bentley) is seen here working hard for his second place. The works Bentleys of Clement, Bentley and Hawkes took the team prize. The year was 1922.*

RIGHT *A mid-1930s 3.7-litre Bentley, with the grace and beauty typical of the Rolls-built 'silent sports cars', which were so different from their predecessors. The coachwork in this case is by Park Ward.*

Perhaps the most covetable of all 'W. O.' Bentleys, the 1929 4.4-litre supercharged model developed 175 bhp. This fine example, provided by the Nigel Dawes Collection, was once a factory demonstration car.

HIGHLIGHTS

1919: First Bentley 3-litre displayed at London show.

1924: First Le Mans 24-Hour race victory.

1926: Six-cylinder 6.6-litre model introduced.

1927: Four-cylinder 4.4-litre model announced.

1929: Speed Six model brought out.

1930: Speed Six wins Le Mans for second successive year, bringing Bentley total to five.

1931: 8-litre model coincides with company's collapse.

1933: First 'Rolls' Bentley.

1952: Bentley Continental introduced.

1966: Discontinuation of Continental chassis.

1980: Rolls-Royce and Bentley future reshaped through acquisition by Vickers engineering group (whose forebears once owned Wolseley).

The end of the company's independence marked the arrival of the 'Silent Sports Car' to replace its thunderous machines; for the Bentley name, unlike that of so many failed companies, seemed desirable to more than one potential buyer. Napier had stopped making cars in the early 1920s. In 1931, however, with Bentley in liquidation, it was considering a return (*see* Napier); but Rolls-Royce managed to outbid it. Still keen, the Napier directors hoped they might yet obtain the services of Bentley himself; but Rolls-Royce saw to it that 'W. O.' would not be free to join another car company right away. At this point Napier gave up. W. O. Bentley later did a fine job for Lagonda and other concerns, although they were not allowed to put his name on the product. Without 'W. O.' himself to

influence it, the new company – Bentley Motors (1931) Ltd – kept quiet for a while, and the first Rolls-Bentleys appeared at the 1933 motor show.

Built at the Derby plant, the 3.7- and later 4.3-litre pushrod overhead-valve Bentleys of the 1930s were based on the 'small' Rolls-Royce 20/25. The performance potential was still there, however, and one man in particular proved it. E. R. Hall was a regular competitor in the Tourist Trophy race, by then transferred from the Isle of Man to Ulster. Three times he raced his modified Derby Bentley in that classic road race (1934 to 1936), and three times he came home the runner-up, just failing to beat the handicappers but creating an all-time race record for the tricky Ards course at an average speed of over 128 km/h (80 mph).

History has endowed the first Bentley decade with a special aura; but there is little doubt that the second manifestation of the marque was a better car altogether. Thanks largely to the understanding of development chief W. A. Robotham, who had spent his working life with Rolls-Royce, the new cars were not simply 'badge-engineered', not just Rolls-Royces with Bentley embellishments. Another thing that set Bentley apart from Rolls-Royce was the delightful and varied coachwork, from open tourer to sleek sedanca. In particular, Gurney Nutting and Vanden Plas of Great Britain, who had clothed many a vintage Bentley, seemed to have a special rapport with the marque in its new guise.

The French, too, knew a thing or two about style. The low-drag body designed by Louis Paulin and executed in 1938 on a Bentley chassis by the French coachbuilder Van Vooren was a classic. Walter Sleator, who represented Rolls-Royce's interests in France, was the key man in developing this car, and its successors, in the Rolls-Royce–Van Vooren relationship. In 1939, George Eyston covered 184.48 km (114.63 miles) in one hour at Brooklands race track, proving the overdrive-equipped Van Vooren Bentley to be one of the grandest tourers the world has seen. After the war, this 4¼-litre streamliner completed the 24-Hour race at Le Mans three times, finishing as high as sixth in 1949, driven by its owner H. S. F. Hay and Fleet Street journalist T. H. Wisdom.

The Second World War interrupted the progress of a Mark V Bentley and the postwar 'Silent Sports Car', the Mark VI – built at Crewe, rather than Derby – represented a new departure with its standardized bodywork. Chassis could, of course, be bought separately, to be fitted with special bodies; but the Standard Steel Bentley, a very good-looking car, spelled the beginning of the end for the last of the great bespoke coachbuilders. (However, some names, like Vanden Plas, which was taken over by Austin, do still exist.) In 1951 H. J. Mulliner, soon to combine with Park Ward, created the beautiful two-door Bentley Continental, a thoroughly civilized successor to the 1939 Van Vooren fastback, and not just a one-off. The six-cylinder engine, with overhead inlet and side exhaust valves, went up in size from 4.3 to 4.6, and ultimately to 4.9 litres, before giving way to an even bigger overhead-valve V8.

Since the Continental, Bentleys in general have become more and more like Rolls-Royces, yet every so often a more distinctive version is announced. The Mulsanne model of the 1980s, named after the long straight at Le Mans, was an intentional reminder of this fine marque's great beginnings.

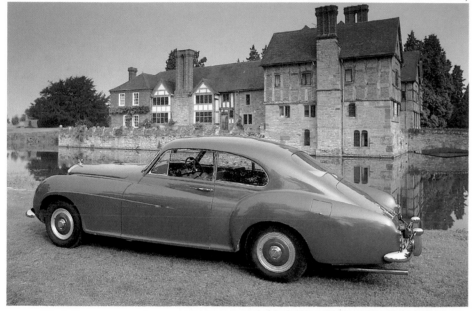

ABOVE *The 'silent sports car' theme was maintained in postwar years by the glorious Continental. This 1954 H. J. Mulliner-bodied model was photographed by courtesy of the Nigel Dawes Collection.*

RIGHT *The Bentley of the 1980s was still a Rolls-Royce in all but name, but no less prized because of that. A mechanical distinction was retained through this turbocharged version of the 6.7-litre V8 Mulsanne saloon. An even more sporting Bentley was forecast for the 1990s.*

BENZ Germany

Few people disagree that the motor car was born in Mannheim in 1885, when 40-year-old Carl Friedrich Benz placed his 1.7-litre single-cylinder internal-combustion engine horizontally on a purpose-built roadgoing chassis.

From the age of two, Benz had been brought up by his widowed mother who was determined that her son should have the technical education he wanted. He gained experience at several engineering works, before setting up his own Rheinische Gasmotorenfabrik.

The 1885 Benz was built as a three-wheeler for the sake of simplicity. The sophisticated steering of two front wheels would come a little later in the development of the motor car. Mechanical valve operation and water cooling were distinctive features of the vehicle.

RIGHT *Although the world''s first car – the three-wheeled Benz – had been made in 1885, regular production of four-wheelers did not begin until 1893 with the Victoria, seen here with Carl and Clara Benz on board.*

RIGHT *Most influential of the later 'independent' Benz cars was this 1923 Grand Prix car in which Hans Nibel made use of patents established by Edmund Rumpler. With its double-overhead camshaft six-cylinder engine mounted behind the driver (in this case Willy Walb) and independent rear suspension, it anticipated the layout of the Auto Union and the Cooper and their successors in Formula 1 racing.*

In 1888, Benz's wife took their children on a successful drive from Mannheim to Pforzheim and back: an important event in the progress towards personal transport.

At about this time, Emile Roger of Paris began promoting Benz's cars, as well as the stationary engines he was already selling for him. Improvements were made and low-volume production began in 1890. The arrival of business partners to let the founding genius pursue his art has been a common occurrence in motoring history, and it happened to Benz in that year. In 1891 came the first four-wheeled Benz and, from 1895 to 1899, annual production (mainly of the Benz Velo) went up from 100 to over 600 vehicles.

After the turn of the century, sales began to slide and in 1906 Benz joined his sons Eugen and Richard who made motor cars (C. Benz Söhne) in small numbers until 1926 at Ladenburg in the Neckar valley. Carl Benz lived until 1929.

Marius Barbarou and Hans Nibel were, successively, the men who brought the products of the Mannheim Benz company up to date and involved the marque in motor racing: something that had been of no interest at all to Benz himself, although his French agent and assembler, Roger, had been all for it from the beginning. David Bruce-Brown of the United States and the fiery Frenchman Victor Hémery were the top Benz drivers of their day. In 1910 Bruce-Brown won the American Grand Prize at Savannah, Georgia, an event in which Benz cars were the runners-up on four occasions. Hémery was first in the St Petersburg to Moscow race of 1908, and very nearly won that year's French Grand Prix, too. Shortly before the finish a stone broke his goggles and glass got into his eye, but he managed to go on and finish second to Christian Lautenschlager in the rival Mercedes.

The 21.5-litre Blitzen ('Lightning') Benz probably

German and Austrian engineering, Italian style, and a British (FF) four-wheel-drive transmission system give this 1982 Bitter coupé (from The Patrick Collection) a special individuality. Erich Bitter's particular talents have enabled him to establish his own great marque.

was the most powerful car of the pre-First World War era. Robert Burman of the United States exceeded 225 km/h (140 mph) with one at Daytona Beach, Florida, as early as 1911, but the French rule makers would not count it as a world record.

The Benz company wanted to return to competition during Germany's years of recovery after the war, and to do so acquired the rights to adapt Edmund Rumpler's remarkable 'teardrop car' (*Tropfenwagen*) of 1921 (with rear engine and swing-axle suspension) for motor racing. The very advanced Benz racers produced by this adaptation came fourth and fifth in the 1923 Italian Grand Prix, but never appeared in a major race again.

Benz began close commercial and technical co-operation with Mercedes (as the Daimler company had become known) at about this time, contributing swing-axle rear suspension, the compression-ignition (or diesel) and other features to the marque that would become Mercedes-Benz from 1926, the year in which Benz and Daimler finally merged.

BITTER Germany

In return for a high initial price, Erich Bitter of Schwelm, near Düsseldorf, offers style without ostentation and high performance with dependability.

A former cyclist and competition driver, Bitter went into business in the late 1950s. His firm, Rallye-Bitter, grew quickly and took on agencies for specialist Italian cars. He discovered, through experience and customer dissatisfaction, that individuality alone cannot

turn unusual designs into great cars. A hand-built car ought to match the very best 'machine-made' ones. In 1971, Erich Bitter set about proving that it could be done. He went to the big names: to Opel for the mechanical components, and to Karl Baur, a long-established Stuttgart coachbuilder, for the bodywork.

The Bitter CD was introduced in 1973. A smooth and well-proportioned fastback coupé, it had all the technical features of the top-of-the-range Opel Diplomat, including its 5.4-litre Chevrolet V8 engine. During the first few years, output averaged one or two cars a week. By the mid-1980s, plans to widen the range and increase production substantially had reached an advanced stage, and preparations on a big scale were being undertaken by Steyr-Daimler-Puch in Graz, Austria. From 1979 the CD was replaced, gradually, by the 3-litre six-cylinder SC coupé and cabriolet models, based on the Opel Senator.

In 1984 a new prototype sports car, with Manta 400 power unit, was being assessed as world markets appeared to be opening up for the Bitter. Of more practical appeal, a new model for 1985 was the long-wheelbase Bitter SC four-door saloon: really an extended version of the coupé, sharing its quiet good looks and its luxurious appointments. The new saloon's 3.9-litre engine gave it sports car performance, too.

An export drive to the United States was started in 1984; and the first regular sales in Britain began in 1985, with prices in the £30,000 to £35,000 bracket. The optional British FF (Ferguson Formula) four-wheel drive and anti-lock braking system added even more to the cost of acquiring this relative newcomer to the ranks of the world's great marques.

BMW Germany

The modern achievements of the Bayerische Motoren Werke, in view of its virtual collapse in 1959, are little short of miraculous. A high-flying image is quite appropriate, too, for BMW's origins lie in the early days of aviation. The Bayerische Flugzeugwerke ('Bavarian Aircraft Factory') was formed in 1916 as a merger between Karl Rapp and Gustav Otto: both were engine makers in Munich. BMW was established soon afterwards, also in the Bavarian city.

After the First World War BMW made motorcycle engines designed by Max Friz. (These were developed by Martin Stolle, soon to be a noted car designer.) In 1921 and 1922 the company made motorcycles for Helios, using BMW flat-twin engines. BMW considered these machines to be poorly designed and in consequence it turned to producing complete motorcycles from 1923. Designed by Friz, these machines had a flat-twin 500 cc power unit mounted transversely, with transmission by shaft rather than chain drive. These have remained features in the BMW over the years, right up to the revered examples of today. In the

intervening period there would be many racing successes and speed records by riders of the calibre of Ernst Henne, Ludwig Kraus, and 1939 TT winner Georg Meier.

In the meantime, BMW had looked at car manufacture several times. Remarkably little appears to be known about a small 1922 Tatra chassis (the Tatra 11 prototype would suit the date), which BMW fitted with its regular 500 cc flat-twin M2B15 motorcycle engine and converted to a crude form of front-wheel drive.

In the mid-1920s, three prototypes of a more sophisticated form of car were commissioned by BMW engineering director Franz-Josef Popp. Planned by the imaginative Professor Wunibald Kamm, the SHW, made by the Schwäbische Hüttenwerke of Böblingen, had front-wheel drive, independent suspension and a chassis-less alloy body constructed in the Zeppelin works. A ZF preselective gearbox was another feature of this car, the specification of which would not look out of place today. BMW, in the midst of recapitalization after the effects of the First World War, dropped its support for the project and chose a much simpler design of small car with which to broaden its product range. Professor Kamm, however, was to influence

RIGHT *Derived from the life-saving* Neue Klasse *saloons of the early 1960s, the 02 coupés gave BMW a further sales boost from 1966. This 2002, provided by Derek Waller, dates from 1972.*

LEFT *Still looking more like an Austin Seven than anything else, the 1932–4 BMW 3/20 AM represented the Bavarian marque's first step towards individuality.*

BELOW *In September 1937, Paul Heinemann and Dr Noll (seen here on the starting line) arrived from Germany to dominate the sports car category at the Shelsley Walsh hill climb in England with their BMW 328s. Note the non-standard rear bodywork of Noll's car.*

BMW's aerodynamic design again in the 1930s.

In 1928, the Munich company was able to acquire a subsidiary company, the Dixi-Werke of Eisenach. Cars had been made in Eisenach ever since 1898, when Heinrich Ehrhardt had arranged the building of French Decauville Voiturelles under licence, using the name Wartburg (after the castle that is Eisenach's main landmark). Later products were called Dixi (Latin for 'I have spoken'), and it was the newest of these that appealed to BMW's directors.

Dixi production had never been great; the cars were good, solid, and not very exciting. In 1927 Jakob Schapiro, a leading light in the Gotha railway wagon works (which had owned the Eisenach motor works since 1921), concluded a crucial deal with Sir Herbert Austin, resulting in the importation of 100 units followed by volume production of the famous Austin Seven at Eisenach. It was this simple British design that became the first BMW car soon after the purchase of Dixi-Werke from the Gotha company.

In July 1929 the name of the German Austin Seven

The modern BMW has established itself at the forefront of every racing category for which it has been eligible. This particular example is seen in 1975–6 American IMSA racing guise. In roadgoing form, this CSL coupé was sleek and beautiful: features that are sometimes sacrificed for optimum performance.

admired by many British automotive engineers.

The Second World War brought BMW's first flush of commercial success to a sudden end. In 1945 the company found itself without a car factory. The problem was not so much war damage as the fact that the town was in East Germany, under Russian control. In 1945, the factory began a decade of BMW (later called EMW, for Eisenacher Motoren Werke) production, using the prewar BMW designs. In due course, the Eisenach factory was used for making DKW-type cars, with three-cylinder two-stroke engines but these reverted to the Wartburg marque name in 1956.

The Munich company, not far away across the border, retained the BMW name, of course, but had to start car production from scratch. Fiedler had gone to Britain (*see* Bristol and Frazer Nash), and West Germany's occupation by the Western Allies meant a slow recovery for industry.

HIGHLIGHTS

1916: Formation of Bayerische Flugzeugwerke, Munich.

1922: BMW formed, as result of diversification. Experimental Tatra-based car tested.

1924: Sponsorship of three advanced Kamm-designed front-wheel-drive SHW prototypes, later shelved.

1928: Acquisition of Dixi-Werke (formerly Fahrzeugfabrik Eisenach, founded 1898) and manufacture of Austin Seven under licence, renamed BMW.

1933: First six-cylinder BMW cars.

1936: Legendary BMW 328 wins its first race, at the Nürburgring.

1945: Eisenach car factory now in Russian-occupied E. Germany.

1952: BMW car production restored at Munich.

1960: BMW company reorganized.

1961: *Neue Klasse* saloons set the scene for today's success story.

1966: BMW expanded from touring to single-seater racing, leading to success in Formula 2.

1975: Domination of European Touring Car Championship racing, through to 1983.

1983: Turbocharged BMW engine powers Formula 1 Brabham driven by World Champion Nelson Piquet.

was changed from Dixi to BMW; the type name, 3/15 DA, remained the same. There were already subtle changes, however, and during its three years of production the German version (DA stood for *Deutsche Ausführung*) was modernized in several ways. Over 25,000 3/15 DAs had been made by the time Max Friz cut short the agreement with Austin.

From 1932 to 1934, the BMW 3/20 AM (*Auto München*) range bridged the gap to the first of the classic BMWs: the '300' series, with its famous two-lozenge grille, inspired by the cowl of a BMW-Dixi 3/15 with sports bodywork by the Ihle brothers, coachbuilders of Bruchsal, near Karlsruhe.

In 1933, former Horch designer Fritz Fiedler and Rudolf Schleicher, who had worked with Friz in the early motorcycle days, joined BMW. Within three years their 326 became Europe's trend-setter in the compact six-cylinder category. It was followed by the legendary 328, an ultramodern two-seater which won its first race at the Nürburgring in June 1936, driven by Ernst Henne. Many race and rally victories were to follow, even well into the 1950s. The 2-litre 327 and 327/8, and the 3.5-litre 335 of the immediate prewar period, put BMW in the forefront of world car design. Imported into Britain as Frazer Nash-BMWs, these Eisenach products were – like those of Citroën – much

Encouraged by Georg Meier, BMW was able to find the means to get back into motorcycle production during the late 1940s. (Meier was also involved in the creation of the short-lived Veritas sports and competition cars based on the BMW 328.) Other big firms like Mercedes-Benz did not have quite the same problem as BMW, who had never produced cars in Munich before.

Soon, however, Fiedler went back to Germany, and a number of other senior engineers returned – including Baron Alexander von Falkenhausen, a fine driver who had spent several years making competition cars named AFM (for *A*lexander *F*alkenhausen *M*ünchen).

From 1952, when production of the first of a new range of BMW 501/502 luxury saloon cars began, there was an element of uncertainty of direction at Munich. The magnificent V8 503 coupé and 507 roadster were much admired but were made and sold only in small quantities. At the other end of the scale, a fine little car, rather like a Fiat Topolino, was designed by the Fiedler team, only to be sidelined in favour of the Isetta 'bubble car' which was acquired and modified. There was no middle-range BMW, no true family car, let alone an interesting one like the 326.

The company narrowly avoided affiliation with Mercedes-Benz during a crisis in 1959, and the future still looked bleak until a group led by industrialist Herbert Quandt took matters in hand. While Austrian distributor Wolfgang Denzel organized the updating of the small car (the 700, with Michelotti styling), BMW prepared to present its new image at the 1961 Frankfurt motor show. There the big 500 series of saloons and coupés was replaced by a beautiful new Bertone-styled coupé, the 3200 CS. Although it retained the V8 engine of its predecessors, its concept foretold the shape of today's BMW coupés. However, it was the 1500 saloon, the other BMW débutant at Frankfurt in 1961, that set the seal on

BMW's survival as a great car manufacturer.

This new model, the first of the *Neue Klasse* of BMWs, did have several initial problems but these were overcome with determination, and from 1963 sales and profits rose with agility. Such was its success that by 1967 BMW was able to buy another car maker, Hans Glas GmbH of Dingolfing, some 100 km (60 miles) from Munich.

The four-cylinder BMW engine, developed by Alex von Falkenhausen and his colleagues, became highly successful in racing. It is even recognizable in the modern turbocharged power unit of the Formula 1 Brabham which brought Brazilian Nelson Piquet the title of World Grand Prix Champion of 1983.

BMW has dominated many forms of motor racing in the period since its recovery in the early 1960s. This fact, plus superb styling and engineering, has made every new series of BMW road cars of special interest to the car-conscious customer. Every so often this appeal is further boosted by something really special, like the spectacular mid-engined M1, sold in tantalizingly small numbers in the early 1980s. For many people, however, each one of those sleek, slightly aggressive four- and six-cylinder front-engined rear-wheel-drive saloons and coupés from BMW of Munich is something out of the ordinary. Despite the large numbers in which they are now made, they still have great character.

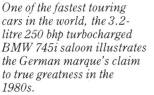

One of the fastest touring cars in the world, the 3.2-litre 250 bhp turbocharged BMW 745i saloon illustrates the German marque's claim to true greatness in the 1980s.

BRASIER France

ABOVE *Léon Théry drove like this for over seven hours to win the last Gordon Bennett race, in July 1905. This atmospheric photograph shows the 11.3-litre Brasier hurtling under one of the temporary bridges near Volvic on the tortuous 137 km (85-mile) Auvergne circuit, which had to be covered four times.*

In many respects France was the true birthplace of motoring and of motor racing, and the country produced many great marques for both purposes. Not all can be represented in this book: Delaunay-Belleville, de Dietrich, Gobron-Brillié, Mors, Serpollet and very many more made history in particular ways. The Brasier is chosen because it typifies the ability of engineers to create great racing machines in a very short time, only to see them vanish just as quickly into relative obscurity.

After designing cars for Emile Mors, *ingénieur* Henri Brasier moved in 1902 to work for Georges Richard, who had been making light cars at Ivry-Port since 1897. The cars they made together were called Richard-Brasiers. Very soon, however, Richard moved out to form a new company, Unic.

What made Henri Brasier famous was the performance of his cars in the 1904 and 1905 Gordon Bennett races. The cars were vast, but their large cylinder displacements – 9.9 litres for 1904 and 11.3 litres for 1905 – were not unusual for those days when the only real regulation was the one that dictated a maximum weight limit of 1000 kg (2200 lb).

The Gordon Bennett races, for national teams of three cars, were held in the country of the previous winning make; and some national teams were selected beforehand by eliminating trials in their own country.

In 1904, 29 cars from ten different manufacturers took part in the French trials, based on Mazagran, near the Belgian border, and Léon Théry (Brasier) was the winner. In the race proper, run in the Taunus area, Germany, he won from 1903 winner Camille Jenatzy (Mercedes), which meant that the 1905 race would be in France. Once again, the remarkable Théry won the trials and the race, both this time in the Auvergne, from a very strong team from Italy. Yet there seemed to be no inclination to generate new business through these successes.

The Brasier was quite well placed in the 1906 and 1907 Grands Prix; but there were no dramatically new designs. The firm went downhill steadily in the 1920s, not helped by a merger and an attempt to join the popular car market with the Chaigneau-Brasier TD-4. It was followed by a return to the luxury market with the DG-8, which coincided with the Wall Street crash in 1929. As with so many other companies, the event led to the speedy disappearance of a great marque.

BRISTOL Great Britain

RIGHT *The 1947 Bristol 400 had many BMW features (even the shape of the radiator grille) due largely to the cooperation of BMW engineer Fritz Fiedler, who went on to Frazer Nash before returning to Germany. It was, however, a precision-built car and very 'British' on the inside.*

BELOW *Modern Bristols are as exclusive as ever. Zagato of Italy inspired this modified 412, the 5.9-litre turbocharged Beaufighter. This 1982 example was provided by The Patrick Collection.*

Whenever motor car and aircraft engineering meet, there is something special about the outcome. As a manufacturer of military aircraft with a car maker on its board of directors, the Bristol Aeroplane Company was in an interesting situation as the Second World War came to a close in 1945. The man in question was H. J. Aldington, importer of BMWs before the war, and also the head of AFN Ltd (*see* Frazer Nash).

Bristol wanted to make cars and it was Aldington who arranged for the release of BMW engineer Fritz Fiedler and a large quantity of technical documentation to be brought from Germany to the factory at Filton, Bristol. It was no surprise, therefore, that the first Bristol car, the 1947 Type 400, bore a strong technical and visual resemblance to the BMW 327/28. (At first, it was called the Frazer Nash-Bristol, but the marques were soon separated.)

The 2-litre cross-pushrod overhead-valve engine was capable of excellent performance and was fitted to the second series of Bristols, the 401/402/403, with aerodynamic coachwork, based upon a shape created by Carrozzeria Touring of Milan. This utilized, and improved upon, its famous *Superleggera* construction system of aluminium panelling over small-diameter steel tubing. Aircraft engineering standards were again applied and full use was made of the wind tunnel and the long runway at Filton.

A short-wheelbase coupé, the 404, was added to the range from 1953 to 1955; an interesting variation was the Bertone-bodied Arnolt-Bristol open two-seater for the North American market. A stretched version – the 405, on the original wheelbase – was

Bristol's only four-door model. The 406 (1958 to 1961) was the last type to use the six-cylinder engine, and for this model it was enlarged to 2.2 litres. Throughout the 1950s the 2-litre version of this unit had been developed beyond all expectation. Bristol cars were raced and rallied successfully, and other firms, including AC, Cooper, Lister and Lotus, used this fine, reliable power unit for their special sports and racing models.

Since the early 1960s, Bristols have featured Chrysler V8 engines, but the change of character has not altered the marque's position as an exclusive, understated, high-performance luxury car built by craftsmen for the kind of owner who is fastidious but not flashy.

BRM Great Britain

More than a decade of disappointment, and even despair, preceded that moment of glory when the great Graham Hill became World Champion for the first time, bringing BRM the Grand Prix manufacturers' title.

The original V16 BRM had been a product of national pride. In the 1930s Raymond Mays and Peter Berthon had created Britain's most successful racing car in the voiturette or 'Formula 2' category (see ERA), but had also seen the absolute domination of 'Formula 1' by Germany's state-sponsored Auto Union and Mercedes-Benz teams. British industry responded to Mays's plea for support of a project intended to put Britain at the top when Grand Prix racing returned after the Second World War.

As early as 1939 Mays and Berthon had created a 'paper' company called Automobile Developments Ltd which, as the project got under way, became British Racing Motors – BRM. As contributions came in, the British Motor Racing Research Trust was formed in 1947, and December 1949 brought the first press demonstrations of the Type 15 BRM: a beautifully purposeful machine in its original guise.

Graham Hill clinches the 1962 World Grand Prix Championship in South Africa, where Jim Clark's leading Lotus lost a small bolt and, as a result, most of its engine oil – and thereby the title. Hill's 1.5-litre V8 BRM won him his crown on reliability as well as speed. It was BRM's finest hour, and this historic car can now be seen in The Patrick Collection.

The first postwar Grand Prix formula was for 1.5-litre supercharged cars or for 4.5-litre unblown machines. Berthon took the former course, choosing a high-revving 16-cylinder 1.5-litre with two camshafts for each bank of cylinders which had an included angle of 135 degrees. With two-stage supercharging, a maximum power output of 485 bhp at 12,000 rpm was quoted.

Unfortunately, after weeks of engine trouble (related largely to difficulties in the machining and locating of the cylinder liners), the transmission broke on the start line of the BRM's first race – the 1950 International Trophy at Silverstone. That débâcle set the scene for a whole series of non-starts and failures to finish. The fifth and seventh places of Reg Parnell and Peter Walker in the 1951 British Grand Prix were

attributed to sheer determination, in view of the near-unbearable cockpit temperatures. Parnell had won two short races in the wet, at Goodwood in September 1950; he and José Froilan Gonzalez won three more sprints between them in 1952.

In that year the Trust sold out to Rubery Owen, a strong ally of the BRM project from its inception. Unfortunately, 1952 and 1953 were interim years in Grand Prix racing and there were few big races in which the BRM could find suitable opposition.

Juan Manuel Fangio's win in Heat 1 of the 1953 Albi Grand Prix was probably the car's most impressive performance, and in fact what prevented an overall victory was that all three BRMs threw tyre treads at high speed. The only other victories were in short races in Britain by Ken Wharton, Ron Flockhart and Peter Collins, mostly with the shorter, lighter Mk II model. The sound of all 16 cylinders firing in unison was unforgettable, but a total of 19 race victories between 1950 and 1955 could not offset the failure of the first BRM to meet its objectives, and unkind critics called it 'Britain's Racing Mistake'.

In 1954 ORMA (the Owen Racing Motor Association) issued a souvenir book containing fine cutaway drawings of the amazing engine. In his foreword, Sir Alfred Owen wrote of the cost and the hazards he had discovered in motor racing: 'There is plenty of criticism to face, and one's patience is tried to the utmost, but one's greatest reward is to see our country's prestige enhanced in the field of engineering.'

The new Grand Prix formula of 1954 led to the manufacture of a new BRM, the 2.5-litre four-cylinder Type 25. It proved to be rather a luckless car and several top drivers, including Jean Behra, Tony Brooks, Mike Hawthorn and Stirling Moss, had spectacular accidents – fortunately with little injury to themselves. It was the Swede, Joakim Bonnier, who gave an overjoyed BRM pit crew its first-ever major Grand Prix victory at Zandvoort in Holland in 1959, by which time the trend away from front-engined racing cars was well advanced.

It took BRM a while to catch up with Ferrari, Cooper and Lotus as the formula changed to 1.5 litres unsupercharged for 1961, but the compact new BRM V8 took Graham Hill to victory four times in 1962, and BRM secured the championship, thanks to a great extent to the work of the technical chief, Tony Rudd. BRM continued to win regularly, and Hill was runner-up in the championship for the next three years. But then a newcomer to the BRM team scored his first win in 1965, and was placed third in the World Championship; his name was Jackie Stewart.

The 3-litre formula came in for 1966 but Stewart managed to win the Monaco GP with the obsolete model powered by a 2-litre engine. A 3-litre H16 engine (based on two V8s) was replaced by a more effective V12 and BRM kept competitive; but only temporarily. The last two Grand Prix wins for BRM were spectacular ones. Peter Gethin took the 1971

Italian Grand Prix by just one hundreth of a second at over 242 km/h (150 mph): a record in itself. Jean-Pierre Beltoise won the following spring's Monaco GP in the pouring rain at little more than 102 km/h (63 mph), but this was nonetheless a brave drive.

Sir Alfred Owen's brother-in-law, Louis Stanley, tried to keep BRM in touch – but found he could not, and the marque became a memory, probably due more to trying to run too big a team than to anything else.

BUGATTI France

The Type 35 Bugatti was both a Grand Prix machine and a sports car (this one dates from 1926). In either form it represented all that was best in Ettore Bugatti's conception of the motor car as an art form. Provided by H. G. Conway.

The automotive art of Ettore Bugatti (1881–1947) and his son Gianoberto, or Jean (1909–39), is rightly revered throughout the motoring world, for it blends visual and mechanical integrity uniquely.

Even if the car's *pur-sang* image was rather deliberately cultivated by its horse-loving creator, the Bugatti car was nevertheless a genuine thoroughbred technically and aesthetically. The son of an Italian furniture maker, Ettore Arco Isidoro Bugatti inherited certain creative gifts and put them into practice as an apprentice with the Milanese engineering company of Prinetti & Stucchi. Even as a teenager he designed two cars, one of which gained an award at an exhibition in Milan in 1901. Among those present was the Baron de Dietrich, whose plants in Lunéville (Lorraine) and Niederbronn (Alsace) assembled Amédée Bollées.

The baron was looking for new designs and arranged for the young Bugatti to create them for him at Niederbronn, then in German territory; but Bugatti was more interested in racing than in developing cars for the road. In 1904, he and the baron parted company and soon afterwards the Alsace works stopped producing cars. (Those from Lunéville then became Lorraine-Dietrichs.)

For a brief period, Bugatti designed cars for Emil Mathis, Strasbourg agent for de Dietrich, who may have hoped to find the customers who had been lost to Niederbronn. Few cars were made under this arrangement, however, and Mathis fell out with Bugatti for much the same reasons as de Dietrich had done.

Bugatti then became designer for the Gasmotorenfabrik Deutz of Cologne, where such great men as Nikolaus August Otto, Gottlieb Daimler and Wilhelm Maybach (*see* Mercedes-Benz) had worked. In 1907 Deutz decided to enter car manufacture – which is why Bugatti was appointed. Once again, in 1909, the agreement ended. The difference this time was that Bugatti used his Deutz design as the basis for the first car to bear his own name. (Deutz pulled out of car making in 1911 and, in 1938, combined with Magirus of Ulm.)

At the end of 1909, Bugatti obtained sponsorship and moved back to Alsace. With a small team he began making cars in an abandoned dye works at Molsheim,

was persuaded to try aerodynamics of a sort for his straight-8 Type 30 and 32 racing cars; but they were neither stable nor particularly quick and were beaten by the FIATs and the Sunbeams.

The more orthodox Type 35 – arguably the greatest 'production' racing car of all time – followed in 1924. Its cast-alloy wheels and other ultra-light components, its beautifully functional body and its jewel-like, meticulously balanced engine brought Bugatti's special art out into the open. By 1926 the Type 35 was Europe's top racing car and it remained competitive until the early 1930s.

Bugatti's next racing car, the 1931 Type 51, marked a switch to a twin-camshaft power unit, incorporating the experience gained from examination of two Miller racing cars (see Miller) bought at the instigation of Jean Bugatti. It was successful from 1931 to 1933 when a more nearly perfect Grand Prix model, the Type 59, appcarcd. René Dreyfus and Jean-Pierre Wimille won the 1934 Belgian and Algerian Grands Prix respectively. From 1935, however, the Germans ruled big-time racing, and most of the Type 59's later victories were in sports car races.

Probably Ettore Bugatti's most famous road car, the Type 41 was also one of the great white elephants of motor manufacturing. Only six of these Royale monsters were built, between 1929 and 1933 in the depths of the Depression. The engine was a 12.8-litre straight-8, the wheels were 610 mm (24 in) in diameter and the wheelbase, at 4.3 m (over 14 ft), was considerably longer than that of the biggest Rolls-Royce. Its proportions were superb; its sales potential virtually nil.

The wide variety of models in the Bugatti range did

Late version of an early racing Bugatti, this Type 13 dates from 1925, but the design was a prewar one. The model became known as the Brescia after its impressive win there in 1921. The car was provided by D. R. Marsh.

near Strasbourg. Automobiles Ettore Bugatti began trading on 1 January 1910.

From the outset, the accent was on advanced engineering and light weight and, even before the war, the marque was gaining fame. An 'outside contract', Bugatti's design of the 1911 Bébé for Robert Peugeot, also broke new ground in small-car technology. It looked like a 'big car in miniature', and had a unique drive-line involving two concentric propeller shafts.

Bugatti spent most of the First World War in Paris designing aero engines. Molsheim had become French by the time he returned there afterwards. A whole series of brilliant touring and competition cars began to flow from the drawing boards of the Molsheim technicians, always quickly turning into metal. For a brief period, in the early 1920s, Bugatti

RIGHT *Works Ventoux coupé body on the Type 57 chassis typifies Jean Bugatti's period as day-to-day boss at Molsheim. This 1939 car was provided by G. Perfect.*

BELOW *This awesome 12.8-litre Bugatti Royale prototype was Ettore Bugatti's personal car, and was rebuilt several times. With other historic Molsheim gems, it joined the Schlumpf Collection quietly in the 1960s. This is now the Musée National de l'Automobile, Mulhouse.*

not help the company's financial situation. Fortunately Ettore Bugatti was not too obsessive over his flights of fancy. During the 1930s he worked on railcars (in which the Royale engines were used) and other projects. Usually he was based in Paris, entrusting the running of Molsheim to his son.

Jean Bugatti used the 3.3-litre straight-8 engine as the basis for his own policy of theme-and-variations, rather than a multiplicity of models. His types 57, 57C, 57S and 57SC represented rationalization without loss of individuality. The leading coachbuilders could work wonders with that low-slung chassis, and this made the Type 57 the best of all the non-independently sprung sports cars.

The Bugatti works itself undertook the manufacture of some of the most memorable Type 57 bodies, including the Atalante and Atlantic coupés. The latter had externally riveted panels, turned outwards along the wing tops and on the centre of the roof: a styling *tour de force*.

Just as distinctive in its own way was the four-door Galibier saloon, a 57C (supercharged) version of which covered over 182 km (113 miles) in an hour on the banked circuit of Linas-Montlhéry in the summer of 1939. (It was driven by Bugatti's Paris depot manager, former Grand Prix ace Robert Benoist, whose work with the Resistance in the Second World War was to take him to Buchenwald concentration camp and execution.)

Ironically, if the war had started a few days earlier, the Bugatti story might have continued into the modern era. As it was, Jean Bugatti was killed avoiding a cyclist while testing a car near Molsheim in August 1939.

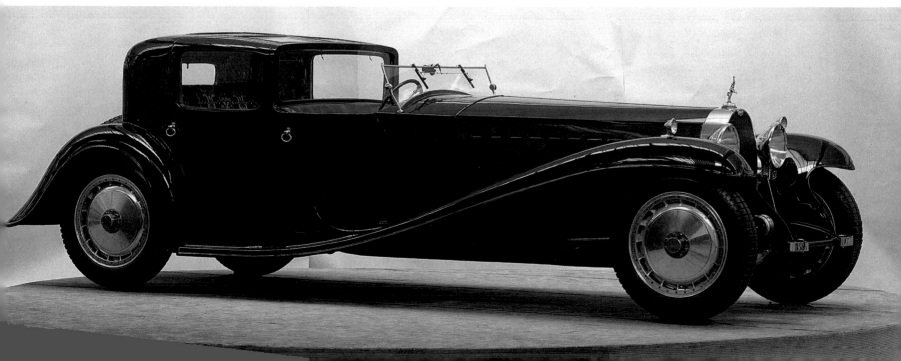

After the German occupation, Ettore Bugatti repossessed Molsheim and announced plans for a postwar programme. He lived only until 1947, after which all inspiration evaporated. A younger son, Roland, led an attempt to modernize the Type 57, but few cars were made. Then he brought in Gioacchino Colombo, the famous Italian designer, to make a modern GP car; but the inexperienced Roland Bugatti dabbled with the design, and the project failed. In its one race, the 1956 French GP, that car proved virtually undrivable.

Posterity is serving the Bugatti marque well. Not only is there untold treasure in the Musée National de l'Automobile (formerly the Schlumpf Collection) in Mulhouse, quite near the Bugatti's spiritual home, but around the world museums and private collections preserve a large proportion of the relatively few Bugattis made. This fact alone proves that, in all the decades of motoring history, the Bugatti car has been regarded as a true work of art.

of overhead valves, the venture failed; under Durant, production was started up again in 1904 at Flint, Michigan.

The year 1908 saw the first official manifestation of General Motors, which went through a chequered early life. Stability came only after 1920, when the Du Pont company bought the shares (and the liabilities) of Durant, who continued to gamble in the motor industry, but on a much smaller scale. General Motors, which includes several great marques (Cadillac, Chevrolet, Oldsmobile, Pontiac, Opel and Vauxhall), went on to become the world's biggest manufacturer of motor vehicles.

The Buick was developed as a marque noted for innovation. It specified four-wheel brakes early on, and maintained David Buick's original engine design policy: 'Valve in Head – Ahead in Value' ran one piece of Buick publicity.

Big and burly, the straight-8 Buicks of the 1930s and 1940s were good-looking and popular with top professional people. They were among the more familiar of several North American cars to be seen at that time in Britain, perhaps since the then Prince of Wales had shown a penchant for them. However, garishness followed: Buick was responsible for 1949's dubious title of the Year of the Porthole. Beneath the glitter, the styling and the engineering were good and solid. V8 engines were brought in for 1953.

Buick models still cover the whole GM range – valued members of an industry that has survived by moving with the times.

BUICK USA/Canada

The Buick was the original cornerstone of General Motors; William Durant, the architect of that organization, acquired the marque as early as 1904.

David Dunbar Buick was a Scottish plumber-of-fortune who, on visualizing the future of the car, turned to making engines in 1902. The first Buick cars were made in Detroit in 1903. Despite the advanced feature

1906 Buick 22 hp Model F tourer, one of the key models in the formation of General Motors, and an antecedent of the Ford Model T.

CADILLAC USA

Star of the General Motors conglomerate, this marque was named in honour of Antoine de la Mothe Cadillac, the French commander of the fortified village built in 1701 on the narrow passage (*d'étroit*) between Lakes Huron and Erie. That fort was to become Detroit where, over two centuries later, Henry Leland created the Cadillac car.

Born in Vermont in 1843, Henry Martyn Leland was trained in the disciplines of New England's small arms industry, in which he worked for many years. He moved to Detroit and, in 1890, set up a precision engineering works. When the motor industry began, his company, Leland and Faulconer, was well qualified to make engines. Leland supplied R. E. Olds with power units for the curved-dash runabout. Another customer was the Detroit Automobile Company, whose engineering chief was Henry Ford. Ford objected to the company's policy of making individual cars to order and charging the earth for them so, in March 1902, he left to continue his own experiments. Leland took over and the first Cadillac was completed that September.

March 1903 saw the start of Cadillac production on a genuine basis. That is to say, Leland insisted on accuracy of manufacture. In 1908 the policy was tested in Britain, under RAC observation. Three single-cylinder Cadillacs were dismantled and their parts intermixed; when they were reassembled each car started up right away and ran smoothly. For this achievement Cadillac was awarded the Dewar Trophy. Soon, Leland coined the phrase: 'Standard of the World'. Much of the success of this exercise was attributed to the first industrial use of Johansson gauges to check Leland's machine tools.

In addition to the single-cylinder, Leland introduced a four-cylinder model in 1906. In 1913 a second Dewar Trophy, for the motor industry achievement of the year, went to Cadillac, this time for the Dayton Engineering Laboratories (Delco) application of electric self-starter and lights. Charles Kettering was the brilliant inventor in conjunction with the Lelands, father and son, who had standardized these revolutionary features on their cars in 1912.

Wilfred Leland, Henry's son, was a similarly gifted engineer and businessman. Through his negotiations, a good price was paid for Cadillac when it had become part of General Motors in 1909; and when GM founder William Durant ran into difficulties in 1910, it was the younger Leland's powers of persuasion that prevented the sacrifice of Cadillac. Durant managed to regain control of GM in 1916 and the Lelands left in 1917, ostensibly to retire. Their story continues under the Lincoln heading.

One of the many Leland legacies at Cadillac was the first-ever production V8 engine, introduced in 1915. It was not the first of its kind, but it was the first to be sold in quantity. Moreover, it became the smoothest-running V8 when the brilliant Charles Kettering altered the crankshaft in 1923.

Membership of the consolidated GM corporation kept Cadillac's head above water in January 1930 when a V16 engine was introduced, to be followed by a V12 in September. These power units stamped the name Cadillac with a special authority in the world of motoring – but the marque was not allowed to rest on its laurels. The problem in the 1940s, that a Cadillac

BELOW *Actress Jean Harlow adds the Hollywood touch to this handsome 1934 Cadillac V12 Fleetwood town car.*

RIGHT *A befinned 5.4-litre V8 Cadillac Series 60 of this type finished, remarkably, tenth at Le Mans in 1950.*

ABOVE *In 1976 it was thought that this Cadillac Eldorado would be the last of the great American convertibles. By the mid-1980s, however, several open-top cars were beginning to reappear on the US market.*

RIGHT *Mid-1980s Eldorado retains Cadillac charisma – and the front-wheel-drive system which originated in Oldsmobile's Toronado.*

limousine. That, in turn, was inspired by one of Britain's oldest coachbuilders, Hooper, who had established a precedent back in the late 1940s by ignoring the rear wheel arch in its razor-edge work.

That distinctive Cadillac Seville was the first car to combine front-wheel drive, disc brakes all-round, and a V8 diesel engine as standard.

Responding to the age of economy, Cadillac also had its version of the 'European-sized' front-wheel-drive J-car for the 1980s. (i.e. equivalent to Britain's Vauxhall Cavalier). The Cadillac may not be quite the American dream it represented in the 1930s but, in most people's minds, it is America's answer to the Rolls-Royce.

might be mistaken for a cheaper model, was overcome when GM styling chief Harley Earl introduced the tailfin. Shortly afterwards, in 1949, Cadillac was among the first companies to produce a high-performance, modern 'oversquare' V8 engine.

The Anglo-American enthusiast Tom Cole (of the E. K. Cole radio-making dynasty) was the first person to have a Cadillac engine fitted to an Allard chassis. He shared the wheel of one of these impressive British sports cars with its maker, Sydney Allard, at Le Mans in 1950, where they came third. Tenth and eleventh in that event came two Cadillac cars prepared for Briggs Cunningham by Bill Frick (*see* Cunningham), but this was an isolated competition foray for the Cadillac car in road racing.

Cadillac has always kept certain model names in use for very special cars. One of these is the Eldorado. The 1967 version of this car ushered in the large front-wheel-drive Cadillac, a follow-on from the Oldsmobile Toronado. This particular car was also a big step forward in dignifying the style and finally getting rid of the unattractive fins.

The Cadillac individuality still exists. The latest Seville (another old Cadillac model name) is probably the most distinctive. Introduced in 1980, its rear styling is clearly related to Sir William Lyons's treatment of the 1968 Jaguar-powered Daimler

HIGHLIGHTS

1903: Henry Leland produces first Cadillac car in Detroit.

1909: Cadillac joins General Motors.

1915: First Cadillac V8 engine.

1927: Harley Earl joins company to create slightly cheaper marque, named LaSalle (after another explorer of a former age).

1929: This year's models have first synchromesh gearboxes.

1930: V16 engine closely followed by V12.

1940: Cadillac range broadened so production of LaSalle ends.

1949: New 'oversquare' overhead-valve V8 engine introduced.

1950: Cadillac-engined Allard finishes third at Le Mans, followed by Cadillac cars in tenth and eleventh places; more Allard successes later, mainly in United States.

1952: Cadillac-engined Allard wins RAC Rally, but GM still not interested in competition.

1967: New Eldorado starts trend to front-wheel drive.

1980: New Seville keeps Cadillac individuality, but compact Cadillacs now also available.

CHEVROLET USA

Chevrolet was the last of the big names to come into General Motors. William Durant wanted to regain his position in the car industry after losing control of his brainchild, General Motors, in 1910. The main companies of GM at that time were Buick, Cadillac, Oldsmobile and Oakland (later Pontiac) – but there were over half a dozen more, now defunct.

Durant was not happy sitting on the sidelines and began tackling new enterprises. In 1909, he had set up a successful Buick stock-car racing team, with Louis Chevrolet as the top driver. Later, Durant approached him with a view to producing a new car to match the popularity of the Model T Ford, one that would have Chevrolet's name on it.

The Swiss-born Chevrolet collaborated with Durant for a time; but he was in fact a racing man through and through, and a disagreement with Durant was enough to make him tear up their contract and depart. Louis Chevrolet set up his own company, Frontenac, and cars designed by him won the Indianapolis 500-Mile race in 1920 and 1921. Later he went into the tuning business, mainly converting dirt-track Ford Model T

engines to overhead valves. The cars were called Fronty-Fords, not Chevrolets.

Meanwhile, using his possession of the name Chevrolet Motor Company, which incorporated his other acquisitions, Durant exchanged Chevrolet shares for General Motors ones, and from 1915 a complex game of combining his old and his new empires was played. Durant could not maintain his position so long this time. Rid of him once more, General Motors went from strength to strength after 1920, with the Chevrolet as its cheapest line.

Many of the innovations within the new corporation were passed on to its youngest marque, and the Chevrolet soon began to challenge the Ford Model T: its big opportunity came when the Ford plant shut down for the changeover to the Model A. From then on, Chevrolet and Ford were to vie for leadership as the mass market blossomed.

Louis Chevrolet would have been proud to see his name attached to such postwar winners as the Corvette, often worthy of the title of sports car, which was launched in 1953 to counter imports like the Jaguar XK120. The compact rear-engined Corvair was another new departure in 1960, but it died by the end of the decade (if not at the hand of safety campaigner

BELOW *Two ages of the Chevrolet Corvette. The main photo shows a 1967 Stingray, provided by Russell Schacter. Above this is a Corvette of 1985, which is still made of glass fibre. It continues to represent American individuality at its best*

Ralph Nader, then by GM themselves). The later Corvair was well-behaved and sporting, and won the SCCA manufacturers' rally championship and the D Production national racing title in 1967; but by that time the Ford Mustang was far ahead in the 'ponycar' field (the name coined for this new breed of compact coupés). Chevrolet responded with the Camaro.

Through the 1970s and 1980s came a variety of medium and small-scale Chevrolets for manufacture in GM plants at home and abroad. The pattern of motoring was altering and the Chevrolet was keeping pace with the changes. The sporting Corvette, although modernized, remained a fine-looking if crude-handling V8-powered 'muscle car' as it entered its fourth decade of production, still America's 'sports car'.

CHRYSLER USA

As the third of America's big manufacturers, the Chrysler Corporation has frequently been overshadowed by GM and Ford; and it has often had to struggle hard to survive. Walter Percy Chrysler was with Buick for a decade, and was works director when he left in 1921 to become a motor magnate. He acquired two failing but reputable Detroit makes, the

Maxwell and the Chalmers, and by 1924 the first Chrysler car was on the market. Two new Chrysler marques were launched in 1928: the DeSoto and the Plymouth, intended to rival GM's Oldsmobile and Chevrolet respectively. These were supplemented by acquisition of the Dodge company. (The Dodge brothers had been engine suppliers to Ford before starting their own car-making enterprise in 1914.)

Chryslers were among the few American cars to be seen racing in Europe, and they did well in the classic Belgian and French 24-Hour races at Spa and Le Mans in 1928.

The classic Chrysler was the 1931 Custom Imperial straight-8, a masterpiece of smoothness and style. The smoothness was helped by the use of rubber buffers between the engine and the chassis. The style came from making the ultra-long wheelbase chassis available to top coachbuilders (who were already getting practice at designing long, low bodywork with the recently introduced Cord L-29). These prestige Chryslers were expensive, but less so than the really exotic marques, or even the equivalent Packard; in fact they were superb value for what they were. Only the fact of the Depression kept sales down. By now there was a broad range of models from the Chrysler Corporation to suit every pocket.

For 1934, a most extraordinary new model was introduced, both as a Chrysler and as a DeSoto. Dodge and Plymouth were spared the agony of the Airflow: the strangest of risks for a well-established corporation to take. The Chrysler and DeSoto Airflow were, apparently, approved by Walter Chrysler as he trusted the engineers who had helped him build a fine reputation for his cars over a relatively short period. This was a good basis for taking decisions in technical areas but, in matters of style, revolutionary trends need testing.

The Airflow had excellent interior bodyspace, good performance and great strength in its modern unitary structure. Yet its peculiarly conflicting and dumpy lines did not flow as the name implied they should. Since there was no yardstick for acceptance of something so radically new it is, perhaps, slightly unfair to judge the car with hindsight. Who knew, over half a century ago, what the cars of the future would look like?

Other car makers with less imagination followed the Chrysler and DeSoto Airflow line almost slavishly at the time – notably Opel, Peugeot, Toyota and Volvo, all seeking a broader appeal for their products. Airflow production struggled on for three seasons, fortunately with enough money coming in from the more conventional car market to keep the corporation afloat.

In later years, Chrysler gimmicks were more of the 'instant' kind. A classic in this field must have been the 1941 Chrysler Highlander; you tapped the horn button and you got a truncated Highland fling.

In 1946, the Chrysler Town and Country hard-top and convertible brought woodwork to the coupé market. From 1951 the Town and Country name and trim were, wisely, used on genuine station wagons

BELOW LEFT *The 1926 Chrysler 4.7-litre six-cylinder Imperial E80 offered outstanding performance at a reasonable price. Provided by Eric Barfield.*

only. Throughout the 1940s and 1950s, Plymouth (ousted occasionally by Buick) was consistently America's third best-selling marque, well behind Ford and Chevrolet. In 1960, the DeSoto was dropped, but Chrysler, Dodge and Plymouth continued to offer a wide range of popular cars.

Overseas expansion, however, represented a big problem for Chrysler. Taking over the Rootes Group (Hillman, Humber, Sunbeam) and SIMCA (formerly the French FIAT) were short-term ventures. In 1978, Peugeot acquired Chrysler's European interests to enable the corporation to survive. Mitsubishi took over Chrysler works in Australia, and the heavily overdrawn corporation set about putting its own house in order.

In recent years, Lee Iacocca, father of the Ford Mustang, put his considerable marketing talents into restoring the appeal of the Chrysler, Dodge and Plymouth ranges: and he paid off the corporation's very heavy debts to the US government, thus putting the Chrysler name back into a position of strength at home, if not abroad.

CITROËN France

Technically, the Citroën has been a wonder car. As has so often been the case, the penalty for such brilliance was the failure of the marque to stay independent for long. Its success has been the unfailing significance of virtually every model.

The first Citroën car, the Type A, was a tough, straightforward four-cylinder 1.3-litre tourer, designed by Jules Salomon along the lines of his 1916 Le Zèbre. It was ideal for the needs of André Citroën, who was as interested in the methods of mass production as he was in the design of cars. He had worked in the

industry, for Mors, but had left to start his own gear-cutting machine shop just before the First World War. From 1919 to 1921 he used an old Mors factory in which to produce these simple Citroëns at the rate of over 10,000 a year – the first true 'people's cars' to come from France.

In 1921 came additional models, including the famous 'cloverleaf', and the appeal of the Citroën extended to an even wider public. One design, the 5CV, was taken up by the German manufacturer Opel.

Citroën toughness was demonstrated by several pioneering expeditions in Africa and elsewhere, notably the first crossing by car of the Sahara in 1922–3, for which half-track adaptations were used. This modification was the work of Adolphe Kégresse, who had once had to look after the Russian Tsar's fleet and knew what off-road motoring entailed. From 1931, the Yacco oil company sponsored a series of long-distance demonstrations by Citroën cars, all nicknamed 'Rosalie'. 'La Petite Rosalie', a 1.5-litre four-cylinder C4 model, was the most famous. The car was driven at about 93 km/h (58 mph) for over four months of 1933 – 134 days to be precise – covering a distance of 300,000 km (186,400 miles).

It was in April 1934 that the company made one of the most significant announcements of motoring history, with the launch of the Type 7A, to give the legendary *traction avant* Citroën its original designation. There were few manufacturers who did not admire or acquire the new model, which combined front-wheel drive, fully integral body-cum-chassis, independent suspension by torsion bars and unique lines that still looked good decades later. Servicing was also considered: the engine and transmission could be withdrawn forwards from the car, complete and in a fairly short time. Citroëns were made not only in Paris but in locations abroad, including the Slough

RIGHT *Citroën's traction avant, launched in 1934, did not look out of date when phased out over 20 years later, still admired by engineers and car owners everywhere. This 1953* Onze Normale *was provided by Alec Bilney.*

Citroën's magnificent modern white elephant, the SM coupé of 1970, had a four-camshaft Maserati V6 engine. This one is seen where it belongs, in The Patrick Collection, during the construction of this new, living museum at Kings Norton, Birmingham.

trading estate some 20 miles to the west of London.

It was the realization of such a masterpiece as the *traction avant* that cost Citroën its freedom. Michelin, whose tyre development went hand in hand with the evolution of new suspension and transmission characteristics, was the rescuer.

An all-time endurance record (still listed in the *Guinness Book of Records* over 50 years later) for any car was achieved in 363 days of driving between July 1935 and July 1936. Fifty-six-year-old François Lecot, a French hotelier, and his Citroën *Onze Légère traction avant* saloon travelled 400,000 km (nearly 250,000 miles) in that period, incorporating the 1936 Monte Carlo Rally in his mileage for good measure.

The 1934 V8 *traction avant* did not go into regular production, but the four-cylinder models were later supplemented by six-cylinder ones. The smaller front-wheel-drive power train formed the nucleus for the 1939 versions of several famous old French makes: and a new one, the DB, ancestor of the Matra.

By 1939 all conventional Citroëns had been phased out, and a new and brilliant small front-wheel-drive car was well advanced. In the tradition of the original Citroën 'people's car' the 2CV was a practical, cheap, go-anywhere four-seater with an opening top. Its power unit, a 375 cc air-cooled twin, gave enough performance for the loads it was designed to carry.

Independent suspension was interconnected, front to rear. Bodywork was strictly utilitarian. Several more 'civilized' variations have appeared over the years but, in the 1980s, the 2CV in (approximately) its familiar guise is now a cult car, as common a sight in the Champs Elysées as in a French farmyard.

The *traction avant* continued to thrive and was not phased out until 1957. The last series of six-cylinder models featured self-levelling, high pressure, load-sensitive suspension. This had a driver-controlled facility for raising the whole car for rough country, or to aid wheelchanging. It was a suspension system which, to quote one magazine road tester: 'sets new standards of ride which are without parallel in our experience . . . The superlative comfort of (all) the passengers is coupled with the high-speed stability which has for so long been the hallmark of the products of the Quai de Javel.' Those words were published in the spring of 1955. That autumn, the true purpose of the self-levelling hydropneumatic system was revealed, for it proved to be just one outstanding feature of the futuristic DS19: Citroën's breathtaking 1.9-litre saloon for the 1960s. This sleek, sophisticated car featured the mechanical layout of the *traction avant*, plus power-assisted steering, braking and gearchange. Indeed the brake 'pedal' was a somewhat daunting button that could, almost, be mistaken for the dip switch. Soon afterwards the less-automated ID19 was offered, and in due course the cars were designated the ID21 and the DS21, when the four-cylinder engine was given the first of two capacity increases.

More sporting than its predecessors, the ID/DS proved an effective if large rally car; it made headlines when Paul Coltelloni won the 1959 Monte Carlo event and went on to become the only Frenchman of the 1950s or 1960s to be declared European champion. In fairness, though, the most effective Citroën drivers were René Trautmann (twice winner of the *Tour de Corse*) and Pauli Toivonen (father of the 1980s rally star), winner of the 1962 Finnish Thousand Lakes Rally. Toivonen was also declared winner of the 1966 Monte Carlo Rally: somewhat to his embarrassment, since the true (Mini-mounted) victors were among a large number of competitors disqualified over a lighting regulation.

One of the greatest Citroën wins, showing how the car's natural characteristics could overcome its still relatively low power output, was seen in the 1961 Liège–Sofia–Liège Marathon de la Route. This was in effect a race decided on the mountain tracks of Yugoslavia. The winning driver, Lucien Bianchi, very nearly gave the DS21 an even greater victory in 1968. His car was leading the London to Sydney Marathon, all the difficult parts behind it, when a crash on the home stretch with a non-competing car eliminated it from the event.

An unlikely alliance between Citroën and the Italian company Maserati led to the production of an amazing Citroën GT car, the SM. Its dramatic styling, and its hydropneumatic suspension and front drive were all typical Citroën. The 2.7-litre V6 Maserati engine with two camshafts per cylinder bank made it the most powerful Citroën ever produced, and it did win a few rallies. Unfortunately, the high praise it had received at the 1970 Geneva show was silenced by the practical Peugeot people as early as 1975. Peugeot, who took control of Citroën in 1974, was not interested in complex, expensive, low-volume cars.

In that year, the ID/DS range was phased out after 20 years of leadership. Citroën's important new cars for the 1970s were the GS and the CX.

Peugeot has had a certain influence on Citroën design, especially of the smaller cars; but the marque has not lost its character. The 1983 BX and Visa sold on practicality, and on their long intervals between servicing. Citroën cars still carry the double-chevron emblem, as a reminder of the man who originated one of the world's most innovative marques. For the chevrons represent the double-helical gears which André Citroën had started making back in 1913.

RIGHT *The Citroën BX 16 TRS of the 1980s maintains the marque's traditions of excellent ride and futuristic styling.*

BELOW *From a basic design of 1939 through decades as the French countryman's utility vehicle, the Citroën 2CV has become a modern cult car. This 1983 Charleston from The Patrick Collection seems a perfect match for the mural at Raddlebarn Junior and Infant School in Birmingham.*

CLYNO Great Britain

Confidence bred by success led Clyno down the road to ruin. The car was one of numerous Wolverhampton car makers to tackle the 1920s with a will, only to fall foul of the Depression.

Frank Smith began making motorcycles in Pelham Street, Wolverhampton, in 1909, helped by his cousin. The Clyno – a name apparently derived from its inclined belts – went into production in 1911 as a 5, 6, or 8 hp model. During the First World War the larger engines were used to power machine gun-carrying motorcycle combinations.

Work on a prototype car had been started earlier, but the company was still strictly a motorcycle producer when problems of liquidity first loomed large. Frank Smith immediately formed another company, the Clyno Engineering Co. (1922) Ltd, declaring that the main product would now be motor cars. A. G. Booth designed the thoroughly orthodox Clyno 10.8, in which a 1.4-litre Coventry Climax engine transmitted through Clyno's own three-speed gearbox to a rear axle which had no differential gear. (It had to come, in time, of course.)

Even after giving up motorcycle manufacture in 1924, the small factory did not have adequate space for the assembly and partial manufacture of cars.

The Clyno was reliable and uncomplicated, and became very popular. Somehow, production went up by leaps and bounds to meet demand in the period 1924 to 1926, by which time there were several different models. Sometimes over three hundred cars would be made in one week, although half that number was more usual. Sales success made Frank Smith and his colleagues competitive. They even tried to compete with William Morris, but failed. The strategy was to wait until Morris's autumn announcement for the following year's model, then rush around and try to produce something at a comparable price. This led less to paring down of specifications than to unrealistically low pricing.

Clyno was committed to moving into a brand-new factory at Bushbury, just north of the centre of Wolverhampton; and a new small car, the Clyno Nine, was introduced there in 1928. It was at this point that the Rootes brothers, who had been selling Clynos hard, decided to concentrate on the Hillman and drop other agencies (*see* Hillman). This coincided with the news that the new Morris Minor (the Austin Seven's new opponent) would cost £100. Actually, its initial price was more like £125 (a great difference in relative terms), but Smith panicked and brought out a flimsily bodied version of the Nine with minimal comfort or equipment at £112.10s. It did not sell well; nor did the bigger models.

The machine tool giants, Alfred Herbert Ltd, bought the factory from the receivers in the autumn of 1929, at which time A. G. Booth had a straight-8 on the stocks. The parts business was taken on by R. H. Collier Ltd of Birmingham, while AJS of Wolverhampton took over some of the design patents.

AJS, the Stevens family's very well-established motorcycle business, owned Clyno's main body suppliers, Hayward's, and it was decided to try and make the best of a bad job by completing the engineering work on the little Clyno. The result was the neat 1-litre Coventry Climax-engined AJS Nine. It was announced in March 1930 and went to one London motor show. A year later, in October 1931, A. J. Stevens Ltd went the way of Clyno. The car disappeared into Willys-Overland-Crossley, who kept the AJS name going for a year; in 1933, Crossley's Stockport subsidiary collapsed, but at least the AJS motorcycle went on to flourish under Matchless management for some years.

Meanwhile Frank Smith had joined Star, another reputable local manufacturer, recently acquired by Guy Motors. Hardly had he become its works manager when Star production ceased; he left Wolverhampton to run a London garage. A. G. Booth went on to design the Singer Nine before joining Rootes.

The story of the Clyno car company is just one example of what can go wrong with a good but sadly under-capitalized marque.

COOPER Great Britain

The Coopers, father and son, were pioneers in many ways. They led the way to the modern racing car. In their day they were the most prolific manufacturers of racing cars anywhere in the world. Yet they were not dreamers, or even men with a mission. Born in 1893, Charles Newton Cooper had been a Napier apprentice before serving in the army throughout the First World War. Afterwards he began his own garage business from scratch, in a builder's yard in Surbiton, Surrey. He helped some of the leading racing drivers of the day, including Kaye Don. The first two Cooper Specials were made for his son John, born in 1923.

Motor racing was slow to recover after the Second World War. It had never been a hobby for the man in the street. The Coopers now proved otherwise, when they joined the '500' movement. They took two FIAT Topolinos which had been wrecked, but still had their independent front suspensions intact; these units were removed and placed back to back, to form the basis of the new Cooper T2 of 1946.

From then on Coopers, usually with JAP or Norton engines, dominated the 500 cc class in speed events.

RIGHT *Stirling Moss in a Cooper 500 at Castle Combe in 1952. This was one of his innumerable victories in the Cooper 500, and he drove all types of Cooper throughout his career.*

BELOW *Jack Brabham won the 1959 and 1960 World Championships for Cooper, two seasons in which the front-engined Grand Prix car was rendered obsolete. Here he heads for victory at Spa-Francorchamps, Belgium, in 1960.*

One of the first Cooper users, in 1948, was an 18-year-old boy wonder called Stirling Moss. As early as 1949 he was impressing Continental teams with his performances in one of these 'miniature Auto Unions', now fitted with a 1-litre twin-cylinder JAP engine. The first front-engined Cooper (apart from a 1936 'toy') was a Vauxhall-engined sports car. M.G., Bristol and Jaguar engines were fitted to some later ones but, until the Coventry Climax days, Cooper sports cars would always be far outnumbered by single-seaters.

It was the front-engined Cooper-Bristol Formula 2 car that brought world champion-to-be Mike Hawthorn instant fame at Goodwood in 1952.

Use of Coventry Climax engines (designed for fire pumps) set the pattern for the most successful phase of Cooper racing history, starting in the mid-1950s with the 'bobtail' central seater. Then when a new Formula 2 came into being in 1957 the Coopers were ready with their neat, light 1.5-litre T41/43. Driven by Jack Brabham, Bruce McLaren and Roy Salvadori, these cars dominated F2 racing in 1957 and 1958: and they began to make their mark in full-scale Grands Prix, too, although theoretically outclassed.

A 2-litre version of the Coventry Climax Formula 2 engine was installed in Rob Walker's Cooper T43 and raced by Jack Brabham for the first time in the 1957 Monaco Grand Prix. It got as high as third on the twisting Monte Carlo streets before a fuel pump broke off; Brabham pushed the car home into sixth place.

It was Stirling Moss in Walker's T43 who gave Cooper its first Formula 1 championship race win, in the 1958 Argentine Grand Prix. Maurice Trintignant won at Monaco that year with a 2-litre T45, also entered by Walker. In the end it was another great British car, the Vanwall, that won the World Manufacturers' Championship. The champion driver was Mike Hawthorn, who drove Ferrari; but the rear-engine revolution had begun, and the Coopers had started it.

The years 1959 and 1960, the last two of the 2.5-litre GP formula, were Cooper's greatest. Jack Brabham was champion both times, with the Cooper-Coventry

Climax T51; and with help from his team mates (and in 1959 from Stirling Moss in Rob Walker's T51) brought the little Cooper Company of Surbiton the manufacturers' title twice in succession.

First Ferrari then Lotus dominated the five-year 1.5-litre GP formula, introduced in 1961; but Coopers were still very much in the hunt. Suddenly, however, the victories began to stop. Bruce McLaren scored a fine win in the 1962 Monaco GP, but it was an isolated one. Maserati V12 engines were adopted by Cooper for the new 3-litre formula from 1966, but the T81/86 was larger and heavier than its rivals, and achieved only two big victories.

The heart had really gone out of the team when Charles Cooper died in 1964. In addition his son had had a serious road accident. In April 1965 Chipstead Motors, under Jonathan Sieff, acquired the Cooper Car Company. A great deal of effort went into the Cooper-Maserati and a subsequent Cooper-BRM project, but it all petered out fairly quickly when sponsorship became vital but unobtainable. The Cooper name lived on in the Mini Cooper – the high-performance version of the Mini – until 1972. John Cooper left Surbiton when the racing stopped and went to run a garage in Sussex.

CORD USA

The magnificent Cord appeared in two brief spells of American motoring history. The first period was from 1929 to 1932, and the second from 1935 to 1937. During the time in between, E. L. Cord went to Britain under something of a financial cloud because he had a reputation for buying companies on the cheap.

His was a fascinating empire, consisting of two further great marques, Auburn and Duesenberg, plus the Lycoming engine company and a number of other engineering and financial enterprises as well.

Errett Lobban Cord, born in 1894, sold second-hand cars in Los Angeles, California, in his younger days. He already had great plans for Auburn and Duesenberg when he launched a new marque in his own name. The L-29 Cord of 1929 was longer and lower than almost any other American car of the time, two exceptions being Gardner and Ruxton which shared a distinctive feature with the Cord: front-wheel drive. Of the three, only the Cord looked as if it might succeed.

The main inspiration for the first Cord was Harry Miller, who had been making front-wheel-drive racing cars since 1925 (see Miller) and another engineer by the name of Cornelius Van Ranst, who had helped Louis Chevrolet build racing cars in the early 1920s.

The Cord L-29 had a sluggish straight-8 Lycoming engine of just under 5 litres capacity. The weight distribution was poor, and traction and general road behaviour were not good. The (inboard) brakes, the de Dion front axle and the transmission still needed a lot of development work, but Cord would not allow Miller and Van Ranst the time they needed. He wanted the car on the market. Unfortunately, the market did not want the car – although it is said that more than 4000 of them were made. The rate of wear in the front drive train was notoriously high – as was the $3000 price tag.

Those that sold did so largely on looks, which were magnificent, and it would not be until 1966 and the Oldsmobile Toronado that front-wheel drive would be again applied to such a large car.

The second appearance of the Cord was even more spectacular than the first. Where Chrysler's attempt to revolutionize styling with the 1934 Airflow had been such a flop, the new Cord of 1935 was harmonious, modern, and unique: to the extent that the body shape, which featured retracting headlamps, was protected by a patent, taken out by the company on

RIGHT Cunningham C4R-K coupé of C. Gordon Benett and Charles Moran leads Alfa Romeo of Juan Manuel Fangio and Onofre Marimon at Le Mans in 1953.

LEFT The 1936 Cord 810 Westchester had front-wheel drive, independent front suspension, preselect gearchange and many other outstanding features – not least being its brilliant and original styling.

behalf of its styling team, led by Gordon Buehrig.

Beneath the exciting lines was a 4.7-litre Lycoming V8 engine, for which a centrifugal supercharger could be specified, making the new Cord one of the world's fastest four-seater saloons. A much improved front-wheel-drive system and transmission layout meant a better distribution of weight.

The cars were difficult to make and high-priced, and with fewer than 2500 built it is perhaps not surprising that this dream vehicle failed. On the other hand, with investigations into his affairs still pending when he returned to the United States, E. L. Cord's big business career was due to end anyway.

The second series of Cords, the 810/812, is revered today, and there have been several commercial reincarnations of this splendid design.

CUNNINGHAM USA

There were two great Cunningham marques, quite unconnected. James Cunningham of Rochester, New York, was a carriage maker before starting on cars in 1907. In 1916, this Cunningham was one of the first cars to have a V8 engine, and the super-luxury versions of the 1920s and early 1930s were popular personal transport for the stars of show business. That Cunningham disappeared in the mid-1930s. The cars of Briggs Cunningham were made between 1951 and 1955, by which time the losses they made were too great to continue: they were expensive to build and too few were sold. Cunningham's affair with the car has, however, occupied much of his life since then.

Born in 1907, Briggs Swift Cunningham raced M.G.s with the Collier brothers in Westchester County, New York, in the 1930s – when the popularity of European sports cars in America was just beginning. Cunningham's main sporting involvement was in sailing and the America's Cup. He did, however, create a fine special,

the Bu-Merc, which consisted of a Buick engine in a Mercedes-Benz chassis. Later determined to see their country succeed in motor racing — at Le Mans in particular – Cunningham and the Colliers entered two Cadillacs for the 24-hour marathon in 1950. Both finished the race.

Cunningham then took over the Long Island tuning and preparation shop known as Frick-Tappett Motors, specialists in fitting Cadillac engines into Ford chassis, and moved its key personnel to premises of his own at West Palm Beach, Florida. A Healey Silverstone was bought and fitted with a Cadillac V8 engine. It was raced successfully while the first Cunningham cars were being prepared. The very first of these did have a Cadillac engine, too, but General Motors would not cooperate after that and Cunningham switched to a Chrysler unit.

Every year from then on Cunningham poured money into a racing programme that centred around Le Mans, where the team did very well with third places in 1953 and 1954, but never scored that elusive victory. The biggest Cunningham win was in the 1953 Sebring 12-hour in Florida – a particularly notable event in that it was the first race of the first World Sports Car Championship.

The competition cars were big and strong, featuring a de Dion rear axle. Their stubby bodies were the work of Robert Blake who was to join the Jaguar engineering department in Coventry when Cunninghams ceased to be made. A production model was introduced in 1952: a fine-looking GT car with Vignale coachwork. Only 18 were made. From 1955 Cunningham continued racing with other marques, notably Jaguar, Lister, Maserati and Chevrolet. For this activity, he hired the services of Alfred Momo, a wizard of race preparation and tactics as well as a fine engineer. Perhaps one of his most satisfying later results – for Cunningham is a great patriot as well as a great sportsman – was to win the GT category at Le Mans in 1960 with a Corvette.

DAIMLER Great Britain

Daimler

The oldest of British marques, Daimler continues to represent automotive engineering at its best, as it has often done in the past. Nowadays the marque is unashamedly 'Jaguar' in every essential respect, although its fluted radiator cowl serves as a reminder of its heritage.

In the late 1880s, the work of Carl Benz and Gottlieb Daimler became famous around the world, displayed in all the major engineering exhibitions. Another exhibitor at Bremen in 1888 was Frederick Richard Simms, the 25-year-old inventor of an aerial transporter. Daimler and Simms met and quickly established mutual respect and cooperation. Simms became a frequent visitor to Daimler's Bad Cannstatt premises, and saw a wider variety of uses of the internal combustion engine.

The law as it stood made it difficult to promote the idea of the motor car in Britain but Daimler lent Simms a motor boat, which received publicity after its first demonstration on the River Thames in 1891. This led to the formation by Simms of a private company to sell Daimler engines, mainly for river launches: one of the first was a pinnace for London County Council. Simms's new firm, created from his existing engineering consultancy, was registered in May 1893 as the Daimler Motor Syndicate Ltd.

King George V and Queen Mary using the central seats of their Daimler so as to be seen by the crowds, as they take the short ride from Buckingham Palace to Westminster for the state opening of Parliament in 1934. The car is one of five Hooper-bodied sleeve-valve V12s, with the new fluid flywheel transmission, supplied to the Palace in April 1931.

In 1895, the first Daimler-powered cars arrived in England. Among them was a Panhard for the Hon. Evelyn Ellis (who had already bought one of Simms's launches) and a Bad Cannstatt-built Daimler car for which Simms held a press preview at the Crystal Palace in South London.

Here it should be mentioned that the cars of the German Daimler Motoren-Gesellschaft were never adopted by the British company, although Simms worked closely with Gottlieb Daimler and his colleague Wilhelm Maybach on carburettors and other developments. Daimler was an honorary director of the British firm, named out of respect for his engine design, until his death in 1900. Soon after that, German Daimlers became known as Mercedes (*see* Mercedes-Benz).

Panhard and Peugeot were already well under way with Daimler-patent car manufacture by the time Britain was ready to start motoring. Late in 1896, the Locomotives on Highways Act came into effect, permitting cars to run on British roads at up to 12 mph (19 km/h) without being preceded on foot by someone carrying a red flag. Early in 1897, the first British Daimler car was completed, following the Panhard layout of front-mounted vertical engine and chain drive to the rear. Other motor vehicles had been built in Britain earlier, but the Coventry Daimler – made in a former cotton mill – was to be the first made in series.

Various management changes affected early progress; the company was controlled by Harry John Lawson, born in 1852. The son of a preacher, he was a professional floater of companies, one of his aims being to monopolize motor manufacture. It was he who tried to hold a monopoly of all important British patents and who formed the British Motor Syndicate in 1895 to acquire the Daimler rights from Simms. Late that year he arranged the purchase of the cotton mill, and the Daimler Motor Company became effective in January 1896. For a short time, several other makes and types of car besides Daimler were made in, or publicized from, those 'Coventry Motor Mills'. Simms, having sold out as licensee, remained a consultant to Daimler until 1897. Later he made cars under his own name before setting up the Simms Magneto Company in 1911. Simms, often described as the father of Britain's motor industry, died in 1944.

Meanwhile, the British Daimler was quick to prove itself, now that cars could be run legally at 12, rather than 4 mph (19, instead of 6 km/h). One impressive proof came on the steep climb up the Malvern Beacon track. Even more so was the demonstration shortly afterwards, in the autumn of 1897, undertaken by former schoolteacher Henry Sturmey who had founded *The Autocar* magazine two years earlier. He drove a two-cylinder 4 hp Daimler from John O'Groats to Land's End in a running time of 93½ hours. This was the first full-scale proving run of a British car on British roads, and Sturmey handed out cards to people along the way, explaining the exercise as follows:

WHAT IS IT?

It is an autocar. Some people call it a motor car.
It is worked by a petroleum motor.
The motor is of four horse-power.
It will run sixty miles with one charge of oil.
No! It can't explode – there is no boiler.
It can travel at 14 m.p.h. Ten to eleven is its average pace.
It can be started in two minutes.
There are eight ways of stopping it so it can't run away.
It is steered with one hand. Speed is mainly controlled by the foot.
It can be stopped in ten feet when travelling at full speed.
It carries four gallons of oil and sixteen gallons of water.
The water is to keep the engine cool.
It costs less than ¾d. a mile to run.
The car can carry five people. It can get up any ordinary hill.
It was built by the Daimler Motor Company of Coventry and costs £370. We have come from John O'Groats House.
We are going to Land's End.
We are not record-breaking but touring for pleasure.

In 1898, the Prince of Wales (soon to become King Edward VII), who had been given several private motor demonstrations, took a ride by Daimler from Warwick Castle to Compton Verney. The driver was J. S. Critchley, Daimler's works manager, and probably as influential as anyone in establishing a technical identity for the British marque. Although the car needed a push up the steep hill leaving Compton Verney, the Royal enthusiast was impressed and in 1900 he approved the first of many Daimler purchases for the Royal Mews.

The early management problems were for a time overcome by a voluntary winding-up, prior to the formation of the Daimler Motor Company (1904) Ltd. Expansion followed and soon 'The Daimler' was renowned as Britain's premier motor works.

Large, powerful chassis took part in sporting events, usually in the form of sprints 'along the prom' or speed hill climbs. One of Daimler's famous victories was at the very first Shelsley Walsh hill climb – since 1905 the longest-running motoring event in the world with a consistent history. In 1907, Daimler director Ernest Instone won a race during the first-ever meeting at Brooklands racetrack; and the marque was also raced abroad.

A change of direction occurred in 1908, when Daimlers were considered to be crude in operation, in relation to the much more ingenious Lanchester and

ABOVE *This beautiful body by Corsica of London is fitted to a special underslung Daimler Double-Six 50 (V12) chassis. (The car was originally delivered in 1930 with less attractive Weymann two-door saloon bodywork.)*

RIGHT *1925 six-cylinder sleeve-valve-engined Mulliner-bodied Daimler 16/55 saloon, kept in running order in The Patrick Collection.*

The style of the Daimler Majestic followed that of the 1953 Conquest and its successors. The Majestic Major (1960–8) had a 4.5-litre V8 engine designed by Edward Turner, and disc brakes all round. It may not have looked it, but it was one of the fastest four-door saloons of its day. This example, from The Patrick Collection, was photographed in the village of Berkswell, near Coventry.

HIGHLIGHTS

1888: F. R. Simms meets G. W. Daimler at Bremen International exhibition.

1891: Simms runs boat powered by Daimler petrol engine on Thames.

1893: Daimler Motor Syndicate Ltd formed in London, following Simms's acquisition of Daimler engine patent rights for Great Britain and its then colonies (other than Canada).

1895: French Panhard and German Daimler cars (powered by Daimler engines) imported into Britain for demonstration. British Motor Syndicate Ltd, led by H. J. Lawson, acquires Daimler rights from Simms.

1896: Flotation of Daimler Motor Company Ltd, Coventry.

1897: Production of Daimler cars in Coventry 'Motor Mills', together with another make called the MMC (the product of a short-lived Lawson firm called the Great Horseless Carriage Company).

1910: Acquisition by BSA.

1960: Jaguar acquires the company from BSA and retains the Daimler marque name.

the smooth-running Rolls-Royce straight-6. Daimler took up the sleeve-valve engine invented by Charles Yale Knight of Wisconsin. This design eliminated normal valve gear, and featured a pair of perforated sleeves moving between piston and cylinder wall. Daimlers ran very quietly and smoothly from 1909 when the 'Silent Knight' was adapted across the range.

In 1910 Daimler became a part of the Birmingham Small Arms Company. The First World War saw Daimler, which now had two large factories in Coventry, engaged in all kinds of munitions work, from trucks and staff cars to aero engines and aircraft.

In 1927, to remain competitive in the luxury car market, Daimler brought out the 7.1-litre Double-Six – or V12 – of which there were smaller and more efficient versions later. A more important innovation for the 1930s was the combination of preselective gear-change and fluid coupling: a step towards the modern automatic transmission. This became a feature of Daimler buses and coaches as well as cars from that point on.

In 1931, BSA bought the ailing Lanchester Company, and Lanchester and BSA cars were made at the Daimler works for a time in an endeavour to broaden the range of Daimler production (*see* Lanchester).

The late 1930s marked a return to competition work, the enthusiasm being generated largely by the managing director Edward Cooke, the chief engineer Cyril Simpson and Robert Crouch (son of the Coventry car maker of that name). By this time, the sleeve-valve engine, never a great performer, had given way to the regular poppet type, which had come a long way since last used by Daimler. The company was now determined to acquire a sportier image, and Crouch in particular was achieving impressive rally results with the DB18 Dolphin sports when the Second World War put a stop to such activity.

The scout and armoured cars were Daimler's most famous contributions to the war effort; but the company expanded into other premises, known as 'shadow factories', to produce a variety of munitions.

The early postwar straight-8s coachbuilt by Freestone & Webb, Hooper, and others were among the most elegant cars of their day, and throughout the reign of George VI, the Daimler remained the state car of Britain's Royal Family. (In the mid-1980s Queen Elizabeth the Queen Mother was carrying on the Royal Daimler tradition.)

A new, compact Daimler, the 1953 Conquest,

proved one of the most successful Daimlers ever. There were convertible and roadster models, and from 1954 a twin-carburettor version called the Century proved a fine performer in saloon car racing. With these models, Borg Warner automatic began to replace the traditional preselective transmission.

In 1959 came the glass-fibre Daimler SP250 sports car (announced, although never sold, as the Dart because Dodge was using the model name). It had a Triumph-inspired chassis and a superb new 2.5-litre V8 engine. Designed by BSA's Edward Turner, it had a 'big brother' of 4.5 litres which was put into the large Daimler saloon. That Majestic Major of 1960 looked staid, like many earlier Daimlers, but was a real wolf in sheep's clothing.

That other Coventry-based company, Jaguar Cars Ltd, was in urgent need of additional premises in 1960, when BSA was ready to sell Daimler. A fascinating result of this takeover was the 1962 Daimler 2.5-litre saloon, combining Turner's V8 with Jaguar's compact Mark 2 saloon structure.

The V8 engines remained in the Daimler range until the late 1960s. The Jaguar-designed Daimler limousine, launched in 1968, had the dubious honour of being the first new model to be announced after the formation of British Leyland. Since then, all new model Daimlers have been Jaguars in minimal disguise.

The Daimler marque has, since before the turn of the century, represented luxurious motoring in its most British form. Today's Jaguar company wisely retains the name, and markets it shrewdly.

DARRACQ France

Darracq is unquestionably a great marque, but its story is a very complex one.

Born in Bordeaux in 1855, Alexandre Darracq trained as a draughtsman before joining Hurtu and Hautin. (Hurtu then made sewing machines, but the firm later turned to motor manufacture.) In 1891, when the cycle business was booming, Darracq went into independent partnership. The firm, Aucoc & Darracq, was one of the first to produce bicycles economically and in quantity. The machines were given the name Gladiator and soon they began to ease out the British bicycles that were selling so well in France at that time.

After five years, Aucoc & Darracq sold the business to a British consortium, which soon merged with another French firm, Clément. Part of the agreement was that Darracq would make no more bicycles in France, but this did not stop him from doing well in the parts business.

Darracq was adaptable and enterprising. He tried making and selling electric cars and Léon Bollée four-wheelers, before settling for a small and relatively cheap shaft-drive orthodox car of his own make soon after the turn of the century. (British interests in fact controlled the Darracq works for 30 years, from 1905.)

Darracq produced large vehicles as well as small ones. Although his cars did not score in the famous Gordon Bennett races, he did his best to be well represented in the 1904 event. Participating countries had their own ways of narrowing each national entry down to three cars. Darracq saw the potential prestige to be gained by winning. Not only were his cars entered in the French qualifying trials, but he also sent drawings to Opel in Rüsselsheim and to a Glasgow engineering company called Weir so that there could be German and British Darracqs! It was all to no avail; only one car, an 'Opel-Darracq', qualified, but it retired early in the actual race. The most extraordinary part of that story was that the Scots produced three cars from scratch in ten weeks. These Scottish-built Darracqs may not have been very successful, but they did work after a fashion.

By 1905 the big 1000 kg (2200 lb) Darracq was competitive and Victor Hémery won that year's Circuit des Ardennes. The Ardennes races brought success to the light Darracqs, too. The marque won the 650 kg (1430 lb) class in 1903, 1904 and 1905, and the 400 kg (880 lb) voiturette category in 1903 and 1905. Hémery was also victorious in the great American 1000 kg Vanderbilt Cup race in 1905, and Wagner repeated the success in 1906.

By far the most spectacular Darracq car was the 22.5-litre overhead-valve V8-engined special for which a figure of 200 hp was quoted. Hémery set a world record of 176.46 km/h (109.65 mph) with it in 1905; and a British driver, Sir Algernon Guinness, got the monster to average almost 189 km/h (118 mph) for one kilometre during the Ostend speed trials of 1906.

Darracq's Perfecta works at Suresnes thrived on its ability to manufacture good cars cheaply; in France only Peugeot and Renault could be compared with the company for productivity in the opening decade of the 20th century. Income from the Italian Darracq company, whose factory later became Alfa Romeo's home, and from Opel, was just part of a quick accumulation of wealth (see Alfa Romeo; Opel).

The range was broadened and Darracq began to move away from his strictly commercial policy and started experimenting with the unknown. His flirtation with the Henriod rotary-valve engine in 1912 was a failure and he took early retirement later in the year; however, hc continued to be involved in big business during the First World War, and afterwards took an interest in a garage business and a bus service

Darracqs, or Darracqs, in Britain in the hope of avoiding confusion with the British Talbot: an endeavour that was helped by the fact that the products, fortunately, were quite different.

The Talbot-Lago began winning races and in the late 1940s and early 1950s came its most successful period. The engine was now a fine, reliable twin-camshaft 4.5-litre unit, quite capable of giving the marque major race wins when the Alfa Romeo 158 was not around – notably in the 1949 Grand Prix de France at Reims and that year's Belgian Grand Prix with Louis Chiron and Louis Rosier driving. Rosier was champion of France for three successive years. His most famous victory was at Le Mans in 1950: the Talbot-Lago was equally at home in long-distance events. In 1952 the audacious Pierre 'Levegh' would have given Talbot-Lago a second great win in the Le

ABOVE *Several different engine types, including the BMW V8, were offered in the Talbot-Lago America from Suresnes, of which this 1957 example represents one of the last survivors of the historically complex Darracq line.*

on the French Riviera where he had settled to live.

Darracq's successor at the now well-established Suresnes works was Owen Clegg, and the next new Darracq cars were evidence of the latter's Rover engineering background.

From 1920 to 1935, the Darracq identity was rather lost in the Anglo-French complexities of STD Motors Ltd, which consisted of the Sunbeam, Talbot, Darracq, Heenan and Froude, Du Cros and Woodhead companies. One of the British features acquired by the French marque was the Wilson preselect gearbox which Georges Roesch had specified for the Talbot (that is, the one pronounced the English way).

In 1935, with the demise of STD and the advance of Rootes, Suresnes became detached and, under the new management of Antoine Lago, there appeared a fine new series of sporting straight-6s.

The French firm's products were usually called Talbots (pronounced the French way, with the second 't' silent), whereas they were known as Talbot-

Mans 24-Hours, had he not tried to drive the full distance without handing over to his waiting co-driver. With the race in his pocket, he bungled a gearchange and broke the engine in the 24th hour.

Lago kept on trying to win Le Mans again but never succeeded. The last two attempts, in 1956 and 1957, were with Maserati-engined cars which were a total failure.

The road cars struggled on throughout the 1950s and there were some engaging designs to follow on after the Talbot-Lago Grand Sport: probably the most powerful production sports car of the pre-Jaguar XK era. From 1955, the 2.5-litre BMW V8 engine was used, but the very last of the line, exhibited at the 1960 Paris show, was an Aronde-powered coupé. Use of this engine indicated that the company had been acquired by SIMCA which, in turn, was engulfed by Chrysler-Rootes, later Peugeot-Talbot.

There *is* no simple way of recording Darracq history.

DE DION-BOUTON France

This classic marque bridged the gap from steam power to petrol (gasoline) and as such was one of the true French pioneers. It won the first motor race, too – even though it was not awarded the first prize. Yet after the First World War, the marque went downhill faster than most.

The origins of the company lay in the partnership of two brothers-in-law, Bouton and Trépardoux, founded in 1869 in Paris where Georges Bouton had been born 22 years earlier. Bouton came from an artistic family, but his own training had been as a locksmith and as an engineer. Bouton and Trépardoux made steam engines, and the aristocrat and man-about-town Albert de Dion (from Nantes, although the de Dion dynasty had originated in Belgium) became fascinated by a working model of one when he came across it in a Paris shop window, for he himself had experimented with steam power in his youth. The Count de Dion was, in fact, only about 25 years old when he met the partners. Shortly after that, in 1881, he began to sponsor them.

In 1883, de Dion, Bouton and Trépardoux took out their first patent for an easy-to-service boiler. Towards the end of that year (having moved only recently from Clignancourt), the new company transferred from its avenue Malakoff premises to 20 rue des Pavillons, Puteaux, and by 1885 its first compact, four-wheeled, steam-driven roadgoing vehicles were a reality.

In 1887 the editor of *Le Vélocipède* organized a race, for which several vehicles were entered – but only one turned up, that of Georges Bouton. His quadricycle nearly rammed some railings at the finish near the bridge at Neuilly-sur-Seine, but that was the only excitement.

In 1888 there was a duel between Léon Serpollet (another great steam pioneer) and Bouton, which the latter won on his lightweight steam tricycle. However, the first motor race worthy of the name took place between Paris and Rouen on 22 July 1894, and was the brainchild of Pierre Giffard of *Le Petit Journal*. By this time, the company was making large and small steam road vehicles, and the Count took part with an articulated machine! Panhard and Peugeot shared the first prize of 5000 francs. The 2000-franc third prize went to de Dion 'for their interesting steam tractor which draws a carriage like a horse and develops (though with a powerful engine, it must be admitted), a speed absolutely beyond comparison'.

The event was, in fact, judged (to the organizers' best ability) on safety, economy and ease of handling and, although the steam tractor was quickest of all at 18.5 km/h (11.5 mph), it incurred penalties because the driver needed a helper to operate it comfortably.

Steam cars were made for several more years but the coming of the internal combustion engine fascinated Count de Dion (by now thoroughly immersed in the industry, despite family disapproval).

He met opposition from Trépardoux, who remained convinced that there was no future in the high-speed engine, and that they should not experiment with it. Indeed, he is said to have had a heated argument with Bouton. Meanwhile, to avoid further argument at Puteaux, the Count had subcontracted the building of his first experimental engines to a M. Delalande in the rue St Maur. This led to the resignation of Trépardoux, and from 1 January 1894 the company was called de Dion, Bouton et Cie.

From 1895, de Dion-Bouton produced power units in such quantities that it became the world's premier supplier of proprietary engines. The firm produced its own tricycles and quadricycles, too: and from 1899 its own true motor cars, of the voiturette type.

It was also in 1895 that Count de Dion conceived the idea of the Automobile Club de France. In that December he invited Baron van Zuylen de Nyevelt (a great supporter of the automobile movement and an important backer of the growing de Dion-Bouton organization) and national newspaper journalist Paul Meyan to his Paris home on the Quai d'Orsay to discuss the idea, which developed from there. France has been the world centre of motor sport jurisdiction ever since.

The company grew and grew. There was occasional competition participation, but usually only in the smaller-capacity classes. The range of cars broadened rapidly and the supply of engines to other companies continued. But in complete contrast to the early voiturettes, the de Dion-Bouton V8 was powerful and impressive: and in 1910 the first European car to go into series production with that configuration of power unit. One such machine did come fourth in the 1913 Targa Florio, but it was an isolated race appearance. During the 1920s the V8 was continued in updated form, but fours became the usual product. Towards the end of the decade there were interesting innovations, such as servo-assisted brakes and a new straight-8.

For some reason, de Dion-Bouton did not keep pace with motoring in the post-voiturette period, and after 1932 there were no cars despite a late effort to return

ABOVE *In the early 1920s, de Dion offered two V8-engined models and a four-cylinder one. This 1923 example of the latter can be recognized (by such items as the tyres and the flash/park lights) as a working survivor.*

whose de Dion-powered vehicles were the predecessors of the first Austrian Puch.

The money from this work helped finance the first (1906) Delage cars, which were also de Dion-powered. Soon, however, Delage was making his own complete designs.

From the outset, racing was important to Delage, and he produced some magnificent vehicles: the earliest important one was the 3-litre four-cylinder overdrive machines that in 1911 won the 620 km (385-mile) Coupe de l'Auto race at Boulogne. Other early race victories for Delage included Indianapolis in 1914.

Most Delages were sixes, but the Grand Prix cars of the 1920s were not. There were two distinct postwar GP Delages – quite apart from several record-breaking specials, among them a 10.7-litre V12. The 1923–5 Grand Prix formula was for 2-litre cars and there was strong competition between Alfa Romeo, Bugatti, Delage, FIAT and Sunbeam. The Delage, however, did not come into its own until 1925, when its roller-bearing four-camshaft V12 engine ran reliably in

to the popular market. Until 1950, however, there was a limited output of commercial vehicles; the last was a novel form of rear-engined single-decker bus.

The pioneering work of de Dion and Bouton is incalculable (except, perhaps, in the many examples which appear in the annual RAC London-to-Brighton veteran car run). Today de Dion's name is, of course, well known in a practical system for driven-axle suspension. It is ironic that Trépardoux designed that system before leaving the company.

supercharged form and two Grands Prix were won, albeit without opposition from the P2 Alfa Romeos. Had this particular formula gone on, these two marques would have been well-matched, but the 1926 and 1927 Grands Prix were for 1.5-litre cars; and Albert Lory designed for Delage a beautiful dry-sump roller-bearing straight-8 engine to be run supercharged. The gearbox was Delage's favourite five-speed. In those years Delage was dominant, the great Robert Benoist being the team's top driver.

But Grand Prix racing at this level had become an indulgence for Delage and it used up much of the fortune he had amassed – as did his life style. From 1928, however, he concentrated upon building up a fine range of production models; the Grand Prix cars were sold to private owners, who proved for many years just how far ahead of their time Lory's designs had been. As late as 1936, Richard Seaman was still winning with one of these cars!

DELAGE France

ABOVE RIGHT *Francis, the fifth Earl Howe, did not start racing until he was 44, but was successful in a variety of marques. With this ex-works straight-8 Delage (in which he is seen at Shelsley Walsh) he won his class in the 1931 Dieppe Grand Prix. So advanced was this model that it remained competitive in voiturette racing for many years after it was considered obsolete.*

France has produced many great cars that could have been selected for inclusion in this book. There was the de Dietrich (later the Lorraine-Dietrich or Lorraine); there was the de Lavaud, which had automatic transmission as early as 1927, but never went into production; and, of course, there was the Delaunay-Belleville, which some say was the finest car built before the First World War – and many more. There are even French marques that will remain forgotten, simply because there were so many to remember in those early days of the motor car. For example, there can be few people today who even know of the existence of the Turgan-Foy; yet these machines were built in several forms at Levallois-Perret between 1899 and 1906, and included one model with a horizontal flywheel at the base of a vertical crankshaft.

Turgan, Foy et Cie should not be forgotten, however, for that company provided one of its young draughtsmen with the experience he needed to go on to create some of France's finest cars in his own name. After a further learning period testing experimental chassis for Peugeot, 30-year-old Louis Delage set up his own components business in 1905; his main customers were Messrs Levêque and Bodenreder,

ABOVE *Beautifully proportioned, this Chapron-bodied 1930 Delage D8 with 4-litre six-cylinder ohv engine would have been just the car for a quick, comfortable run to the Côte d'Azur.*

In the difficult days of the 1930s, Delage produced truly elegant, luxurious long-distance touring cars, usually enhanced by gorgeous coachwork. The 4-litre straight-8 chassis was lowered and shortened in 1932; but hard times led to a merger with Delahaye in 1935, after which no more eights were made.

The later Delage sixes made good sports-racing cars; they scored a Tourist Trophy victory in 1938 and were runners-up at Le Mans in 1939 and 1949. Sadly, the Second World War spelled the end for many great marques and the Delage was one of them. No more were made after 1954 when Delahaye-Delage became part of Hotchkiss.

DELAHAYE France

The first Delahaye company was formed in 1845 to manufacture brick-making equipment in Tours. The car-building member of the family, Emile Delahaye, followed the early Benz layout from 1894. Before the turn of the century the business was being financed by Léon Desmarais and Georges Morane, and a Paris base was established in the rue du Banquier.

Emile Delahaye had been a railway truck designer originally, and from the outset he recognized the importance of developing commercial road vehicles. Once these were being made, the whole range became somewhat ponderous; but Delahayes did acquire a reputation for reliability.

There was cooperation between the commercial vehicle interests of the Delahaye, Chenard-Walcker, Donnet and Unic companies between 1927 and 1932. Delahaye's return to independence was followed by a distinct modernization of the product, bringing the marque into the high-performance category.

Emile Delahaye had retired as early in the company's history as 1901, but continuity was maintained by his chief engineer Charles Weiffenbach, who set the Paris factory in motion and was to stay with it for over 50 years. The car historian Michael Sedgwick once used an apt description of this strong and serious engineer-turned-manager: he called him the Rip Van Winkle of the rue du Banquier.

All the elements of a high-performance car seemed to exist, and in 1933, with the aid of Jean François, Weiffenbach began to make use of them. At the heart of this project lay an existing six-cylinder truck engine, capable of considerable development. With it came a lighter chassis with independent front suspension, the option of a Wilson epicyclic gearbox (as used by Armstrong Siddeley) and, from the mid-1930s, a Cotal with 'finger-tip' electric change.

In 1935, Delahaye bought up troubled Delage, thus adding a veneer of reflected sophistication to its own quickly improving image, but maybe slightly at the expense of its acquisition.

Sporting accolades began in 1934 with victory in the over 3-litre class of the Alpine Trial by three 3.2-litre 18CV Superlux Delahayes. This led to a 1935 version being called the Coupe des Alpes model, and further rally and race successes began to bring a new level of vitality to the marque.

Lower and lighter models appeared. Some of the touring cars received exotic, futuristic coachwork; the more outrageous of these fanciful concepts, which were to persist after the Second World War, came from Saoutchik, the French stylists. More restrained and British-looking was the coachwork by the French firm of Labourdette, who copied the previous year's new SS saloon, the Airline. (William Lyons of SS either did not notice or did not mind, for the Airline was his own least favourite creation; indeed it was to be his only fastback design until the E-type Jaguar of 1961.)

The Type 135 3.6-litre Delahaye sports enjoyed several fine years of competition work. Second place in the 1936 Monte Carlo Rally was followed by wins in 1937 and 1939; likewise, second in the 1937 Le Mans 24-Hour race preceded outright victory in 1938.

Jean François further reinforced Delahaye's 'new look' by introducing a 4.5-litre overhead-valve V12 racing car, the ugly Type 145. With this car René Dreyfus won the 1938 Pau Grand Prix, beating the lone but troubled Mercedes-Benz of Rudolf Caracciola and Hermann Lang; but it could not really combat the might of Germany on equal terms.

In Britain, the White Mouse Stable of Prince Birabongse Bhanubandh ('B. Bira') of Thailand proved the Delahaye 135 a formidable rival for any other sports car: certainly for all the contemporary British models. By now owned by Rob Walker, this machine won further notable publicity in 1939 after *Autocar*'s

John Dugdale had written a controversial article. He had been out in a supercharged 2.9-litre Alfa Romeo and, suitably impressed, headed his story: 'The Fastest Road Car?' The question mark brought a big response and the outcome was a pair of challenge races at Brooklands. Nine road-equipped sports cars were entered and the Alfa Romeo (driven by its owner Hugh Hunter) won the first race on the Campbell circuit by 0.8 seconds from the Delahaye. Part Two of the challenge was held on the Mountain circuit and was an easy win for the Delahaye, once the Alfa had broken its transmission. Much of this success was attributable to the driver of Walker's car, Arthur Dobson: one of the best of the time and the best by far on that day.

There were more successes in the early postwar years, the most significant being another victory in the 1951 Monte Carlo Rally. The drivers were Jean Trevoux and Roberto Crovetto and the car was the Type 175, 4.5-litre, six-cylinder sports saloon with impressive, rather Italian looks. This model was not a sales success, however, although a detuned version of the engine was offered as an alternative to diesel power in several commercial vehicles. The last Delahaye car was the Type 235 of 1951, a revamped 3.5-litre, disguised by some rather dated full-width bodywork.

A wartime consortium, which also included the commercial vehicle makers Bernard, Laffly, SIMCA and Unic, did not find fortune in peacetime and was disbanded. On release from this Groupe Française Automobile (GFA), Delahaye and Delage were absorbed by Hotchkiss in 1954.

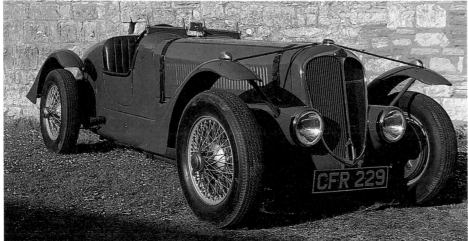

DELOREAN Great Britain

'Would you buy a used car from me?' wryly asked the disarming John Zachary DeLorean as he faced the world's press in 1984. He had just been cleared of narcotics charges in the United States, but was about to face many more concerning his financial affairs.

His problems had really begun three years earlier, when not enough people had been willing to buy a *new* car from him. So much has been said and written about the former General Motors vice-president and his personal life, and about the background to his Northern Irish venture, that this tends to divert attention from his dream car itself – which was intended initially for the North American market.

From 1976 DeLorean had been trying to find a factory and finance. He had visited several countries before the British government decided to back his project to help alleviate unemployment in Northern Ireland. It did not need much assessing to conclude that such a design – assuming quality control and proper service – would delight some enthusiasts and be bought by a proportion of them, but certainly not at the rate the super salesman envisaged and proposed when the factory was built in Belfast suburb of Dunmurry.

There was considerable Lotus technology in the DeLorean DMC-12, which had a 2.8-litre 90° V6 engine from the Peugeot–Volvo–Renault cooperative. The unit was mounted longitudinally behind the cockpit of the purposeful-looking two-seat coupé, the spectacular shape of which had been created by Giorgetto Giugiaro. Like the Mercedes-Benz 300SL of the 1950s, it had gull-wing doors, and it was finished in unpainted stainless steel.

Few cars since the famed Ford 'all-black' period have been marketed in only one colour – and not only that, but with a .surface finish that no customer had ever been asked to accept in a volume-production car. Yet the DeLorean was offered only in unpainted form.

Almost from the outset the original sponsors were beset by doubts, and regrets.

In February 1982, the Official Receiver moved in. DeLorean himself was arrested not long afterwards and the DeLorean Motor Car Company closed its doors for good.

Much more will be written and spoken about John DeLorean. As for the cars, enough were made for the marque to be assured of a place in motoring history and (possibly, one day) of 'classic' status. Although most were built for the United States, a few were made to British specification. An example of each was bought for The Patrick Collection at Kings Norton, Birmingham, which is Britain's newest motoring museum; one of the Collection's cars is shown on page 69.

DKW Germany

Jørgen Skafte Rasmussen was a Dane but his life's work was in Germany. An advocate of steam, with a friend he made steam engine components from 1903, trading as Rasmussen & Ernst GmbH. In 1907 he left to establish the Zschopauer Maschinenfabrik J. S. Rasmussen to make complete steam engines. During the First World War, apart from his munitions work, Rasmussen was given the opportunity to try to overcome the national fuel shortage by making a light steam car, or *Dampfkraftwagen*: DKW for short.

That project was not followed up and the Zschopau works near Chemnitz (now Karl-Marx-Stadt) became famous from 1919 for its motorcycles and engines. Rasmussen obtained the manufacturing rights for two power units, a four-stroke and a tiny two-stroke. The latter was meant for toy-type models and was called *Des Knaben Wunsch* (DKW again), which might be rendered, roughly, as 'Every boy wants one'. It became an industrial unit, too; and then Rasmussen began selling engines to small-car makers, using DKW as his trade name.

Northern European trendsetter, the 1931 two-cylinder 490 cc DKW F1 had front-wheel drive. In 1932, DKW became the 'founder-member' of Auto Union.

SB (Slaby & Beringer) of Berlin made single-seat four-wheeled electric cars from 1920, selling them in London through Gamages, the well-known department store. These tiny cars were made of wood and had no separate chassis. DKW took over the company, and experimented by fitting one of its engines to a little SB. It was not a great success so, in 1927, Rasmussen turned to electric cars himself, making in his Berlin works tall, squared-off taxis and other commercial vehicles called DEWs.

Wooden construction and two-stroke engines were standard features of the first regular production DKW cars of 1928. These were otherwise conventional in that they were rear-wheel-driven. The front-wheel-drive DKW F1 was introduced in 1931 and set the pattern for the future.

Rasmussen's empire was growing, and in 1932 he brought the longer-established Audi, Horch and Wanderer marques into his car-making group in order to withstand the economic crisis. The new combine was called the Auto Union but the four marque names were retained, up to the Second World War. The only cars to bear the name Auto Union in the 1930s were the amazing V16 and V12 rear-engined racers (designed by Dr Ferdinand Porsche and Eberan Eberhorst) which, with Mercedes-Benz, gave the Third Reich complete domination of Grand Prix racing from 1934 to 1939.

The various small DKW cars were to become the most popular of their type in northern Europe, and several Danish and Swedish companies had plans to make their own postwar adaptations of them. (*See* Saab, which was the only one to be developed for modern times.)

All but the Berlin factories of Auto Union came within the Russian Zone (now East Germany) when war ended. The prewar type DKW was produced again in Zwickau as the IFA from 1948 to 1956. After that (with new bodywork) the 2-cylinder models became the Zwickau, now the Trabant; and the 3-cylinder cars replaced the EMW in the former BMW works at Eisenach to become the world's other surviving series-production two-stroke car, for which the name Wartburg was revived. (The motorcycle business was reopened as MZ, which stood for Motorradwerke Zschopau.)

Meanwhile, a new West German Auto Union was formed. It retained the DKW marque name for its 1950 Meisterklasse (0.7-litre two-cylinder) and 1953 Sonderklasse (0.9-litre three-cylinder) two-strokes, produced in Düsseldorf and Ingolstadt. (The latter location had been chosen in 1945 as a central parts depot by former group employees, to serve the owners of surviving DKWs. It was to become the nucleus for today's Audi NSU Auto Union AG.)

In 1958 a 1-litre version of the three-cylinder DKW was introduced; it was named the Auto Union 1000 and was made until 1962. The three-cylinder two-stroke engine was still a fine performer and several Formula Junior racing cars were fitted with this unit. DKWs won

Finance was not a problem for Auto Union and Mercedes-Benz when they monopolized Grand Prix racing from 1934. Here the 1938 three-camshaft 3-litre V12 takes victory at Donington, thanks to the amazing skills of Tazio Nuvolari. Some later DKW models would also be called Auto Union as a marque name.

several rallies, including the 1956 East African Safari and Finnish Thousand Lakes. Biggest successes for the Auto Union 1000 were outright victories in the 1958 Safari and the 1959 Acropolis rallies.

In the late 1950s Daimler-Benz acquired 88 per cent of Auto Union's shares. The motorcycle business was passed to Zweirad Union; this in turn was acquired by former rivals Fichtel & Sachs in 1966, after which the DKW name gradually disappeared from motorcycles.

The last DKW cars to be introduced, the 1958 Junior and its successors, gave the marque a new look which would see it through to the automotive two-stroke's last days in 1966.

The mid-1960s marked a further big change of direction with Volkswagen taking over full control from Daimler-Benz, who had already developed a new four-stroke front-wheel-drive family saloon. For this the dormant Audi name was revived to open a new chapter in German motoring history (*see* Audi).

DUESENBERG USA

'Almost certainly the best automobiles ever made in America, one of the very best ever made anywhere . . . a unique combination of great power and utter luxury . . . as fine in every way as a Rolls-Royce or a Daimler, but much, much faster.'

'Superbly made and very fast indeed . . . America's fastest, costliest and finest white elephant.'

These were the words of Ken Purdy and Michael Sedgwick respectively, both highly esteemed writers and true enthusiasts for their subject.

The vehicles they were describing were the fabled 6.9-litre double-overhead camshaft straight-8 Duesenberg SJ supercharged supercars built from 1932 to 1935, when Errett Lobban Cord's auto empire (*see* Auburn; Cord) was wound up.

The Duesenberg J series deserves all this praise, despite its great size and price, for close on 500 were built and sold, whereas production of Bugatti's legendary Royale never got under way at all.

The story began in Lippe, Germany, in 1876 with the birth of Frederick Samuel Duesenberg. By 1885, the birth year of the car, the Duesenberg family had emigrated to Des Moines, Iowa, in the United States. When the new century began, Duesenberg was making high-grade racing bicycles. Then a local lawyer named Mason began sponsoring Fred Duesenberg and his brother August in a car-making venture. Their first Mason car of 1906 or 1907 was a flat twin with epicyclic gearbox and chain drive. The Mason company stayed in business until 1910, when it was taken over by Frederick Maytag of Waterloo (another Iowa town). Maytag was a washing machine tycoon who soon gave up car manufacture.

The Duesenbergs did not give up. They built racing machines, continuing to use the name Mason until 1914, after which the cars were called Duesenbergs. For some years the Duesenbergs concentrated on marine and racing engines. There was also a relatively brief period in New Jersey during the latter part of the First World War when they put their name to a disastrous Bugatti-designed 16-cylinder aero engine; this had been commissioned shortly after America joined the war in 1917. It ended up costing the American taxpayer nearly $5 million with nothing to show for it.

Racing cars continued to be a Duesenberg speciality. A world record attempt was set up at Daytona in 1920 by Tommy Milton driving a Duesenberg built at Elizabeth, New Jersey. Its two straight-8 4.9-litre engines followed the general layout of the Bugatti military 16-cylinder but it was a crude device in that the units drove separately to the rear axle. Most figures indicate that Milton was the first man ever to average over 240 km/h (150 mph) for the flying mile: but he did it in only one direction, so the record was never ratified.

Much more significant was the famous victory by Jimmy Murphy in the 1921 French Grand Prix at Le Mans. The team of single-camshaft 3-litre straight-8s was sponsored by the Champion Sparking Plug company and the cars were fitted with the first-ever Lockheed hydraulic brakes. The Europeans were startled when the Duesenbergs came first, fourth and sixth. The marque went on to win the Indianopolis 500-Mile race in 1924, 1925 and 1927.

It was in Indianapolis in the winter of 1920–1 that the production of roadgoing Duesenbergs began. Those expensive Model A luxury cars were, in fact, the first straight-8s ever sold to the American public – and they had hydraulic brakes.

E. L. Cord, head of Auburn, took over the company in 1926 and gave Fred Duesenberg freedom to design

1930 Model J dual-cowl phaeton typifies the magnificence of the Duesenberg at the height of its glory. This car from the Briggs Cunningham Museum has coachwork by LeBaron.

the best car possible. The result was the classic Model J: a huge, brilliantly engineered chassis which was light to the touch and therefore easy for an experienced driver to control; 470 were made. Introduced in 1929, the J series included several extra-special variants. It was sad that Fred Duesenberg did not live to see all of them, for the perfectionist car maker died as the result of an accident in 1932. His brother Augie remained involved to the end; he died in 1955.

The first supercharged model was made in 1932, and 36 of them were built during the next four years. In 1935 came the JN with an extra 280 mm (11 in) in the wheelbase, bringing it not far short of that of the Royale: Duesenberg 3.9 m (153 in); Bugatti 4.3 m (169 in). Only 10 JNs were made. That year also saw the production of two short-wheelbase supercharged roadsters, known as SSJs, one for Gary Cooper and one for Clark Gable. 'He drives a Duesenberg', was all the advertisements said, and it was all they had to say.

Such is the glamour, and the mystique, of this marque that it has had many revivals.

held in November 1896 to celebrate the repeal of the 'Red Flag' Act, and the raising of the official British speed limit from 4 to 12 mph (6.5 to 19 km/h). Frank Duryea was quickest, although that fact was not publicized.

In 1900 Frank Duryea went into business with the Stevens Arms & Tool Co. of Chicopee Falls, Massachusetts, where the low-volume, but high-quality Stevens-Duryea range of cars was produced between 1902 and 1927. Thus Charles Duryea became the sole proprietor early on, manufacturing cars in Peoria, Illinois, Reading, Pennsylvania, and Saginaw, Michigan, up to 1913. There were times, too, when Duryea cars, were built under licence in Belgium and England (*see* Daimler).

During the early years of the First World War, Duryea cyclecars were made in Philadelphia, but the marque vanished in 1916. Although their marques were relatively short-lived, the Duryea brothers did much to get the motor car under way in the United States.

DURYEA USA

RIGHT *This car, built and raced by Frank Duryea in 1895, defeated a Benz to win the event sponsored by the* Chicago Times-Herald – *America's first real car race. (The marque does not appear to have any badge or trademark.)*

With the exception of a three-wheeler, made by John Lambert in 1891, the Duryea brothers Charles and Frank can lay reasonable claim to having produced the first practical American car with an internal combustion engine. They began drawing the car in that year and had it running in September 1893. The second Duryea won the famous 1895 race over the snow-covered roads from Chicago to Evanston and back.

The first Duryea motor wagons were made at Springfield, Massachusetts, from 1895 to 1898, and confidence in the Duryea's future was affirmed by participation in the London to Brighton run, the event

ERA Great Britain

As the name implies, English Racing Automobiles Ltd of Bourne, Lincolnshire, made no roadgoing cars (although in the late 1930s the founder, Raymond Mays, did arrange the construction of five Standard V8-powered sports cars named after him). Funded by amateur racing driver Humphrey Cook as a patriotic gesture when British machines were achieving little in international events, the company produced some 20 cars all told: and they proved to be Europe's most consistently successful voiturette (or 'Formula 2') racers by 1937. Virtually all the early machines built between 1934 and 1936 have survived.

Simplicity, sound design and superb response were the ERA's main features. Peter Berthon was the designer-in-chief and he had the help and advice of other fine engineers such as Reid Railton. The engine was a much modified Riley six-cylinder overhead-valve unit which became increasingly more powerful through development. Most often the cars raced in the 1.5-litre voiturette category, but there were 1.1- and 2-litre units for other events.

Four A-types and thirteen similar B-types were built in 1934 and 1935 respectively. They had Jamieson-designed Roots-type superchargers mounted ahead of the engine, and a Wilson preselector gearbox was used. Three cars (numbered R4B, R8B and R12B) were brought up to the C-type specification, which included a Zoller vane-type supercharger mounted behind the engine (over the gearbox) and Porsche-style trailing arm independent front suspension. One of those cars was modified further and became the only D-type ERA (R4D); Raymond Mays ran this particular

machine privately after he left the company in 1939.

'B. Bira', the famous British-based member of the Thai royal family, was the most successful ERA driver of all, taking the top awards of the British Racing Drivers' Club for 1936, 1937 and 1938. Other fine ERA drivers, on their way to greater things, were Dick Seaman, Tony Rolt, Peter Whitehead and Peter Walker.

With so few cars sold, Humphrey Cook found the manning of a works team increasingly costly and in March 1939 it was announced that a subscription fund would be started. This was intended to support ERA in 1940, when it was expected that a 1.5-litre Grand Prix formula would be in force. Despite a poor response, and Mays's departure, Cook kept up what was in effect a 'Racing for Britain' programme in that truncated year of motor sport. The fund had to be wound up and the few subscriptions returned.

After the Second World War Cook made it clear that ERA must have its own profit-making business in future or it would cease to exist. Fellow racing driver Leslie Johnson bought the name and the few assets, which included the disastrous E-type project begun in 1939 for the new formula. The E-type ERA looked purposeful but was a failure and the company, now based in Dunstable, Bedfordshire, began work on a new sports car chassis (see Jowett).

The ERAs continued to shine during the early postwar period. The only new example was the G-type of 1952 but, despite a modern specification and Stirling Moss to drive it, it never began to look a winner. The G-type was sold to Bristol (who had supplied the engine) and reappeared as that company's long-distance sports-racing car, the Type 450, which was campaigned from 1953 to 1955.

RIGHT *Britain's voiturette racing took place at Brooklands, at Donington and at the Douglas road circuit on the Isle of Man. ERA cars won the vast majority, and the 1937 RAC International Light Car Race was no exception, with ERAs in the first five places. Here Pat Fairfield brings the redesignated independent front suspension-equipped works car, R12C, through Onchan Corner, Douglas. He was one of the very best drivers, but in these wet conditions those other two most effective ERA men, B. Bira and Raymond Mays, beat him. (Fairfield was injured fatally at Le Mans less than three weeks later, when his works BMW 328 got caught in a multiple accident.)*

FERRARI Italy

More than any other marque, Ferrari conjures up a picture of the motor car as an art form complete in itself, a harmonious expression of expertise in the processes of design, engineering and production. It is not just the fact that the founder, Enzo Ferrari, still takes an active part in the firm he created. It is because the company continues to move with the times, producing superlative machines for road and race-course. When Ferrari is not winning, it is taking the action necessary to ensure that it will soon win again.

Enzo Ferrari went into the army while still a teenager and served in mountain artillery for the latter part of the First World War. Afterwards he tried unsuccessfully to join FIAT. In 1919 he achieved his first ambition – to enter the rapidly expanding car industry – when his friend Ugo Sivocci, chief tester at Costruzioni Meccaniche Nazionali (CMN), managed to get him a job at this Milanese company. Almost at once he was given the chance of driving a CMN car in competition; but it was a brief appointment because, in 1920, another opportunity presented itself at Alfa Romeo. This gave Ferrari the chance of repaying Sivocci's kindness. CMN would not be long-term manufacturers of motor cars – that was clear. Soon Sivocci, too, was working at Alfa Romeo.

Apart from testing and racing quite successfully, Ferrari became Alfa Romeo's specialist in finding new engineering talent. It was he who brought in Luigi Bazzi and Vittorio Jano; and the latter was followed from FIAT by several disciples.

Despite several excellent results, Ferrari did not reach the heights as a racing driver and his health,

One of the earliest styles of Ferrari, with lightweight body by Carrozzeria Touring, this 2.3-litre 1949 Tipo 195 was the first derivative of the original 2-litre V12 road car. Provided by Peter Agg/Trojan Ltd.

HIGHLIGHTS

1898: Enzo Ferrari born in Modena.

1919: Ferrari joins CMN (Costruzioni Meccaniche Nazionali SA) of Milan, aircraft makers turned car manufacturers.

1920: Ferrari recruited by Alfa Romeo, finishes runner-up in Targa Florio.

1923: Ferrari wins at Ravenna and adopts 'prancing horse' badge.

1924: Ferrari wins Coppa Acerbo for Alfa Romeo.

1929: Formation of Scuderia Ferrari in Modena to run Alfa Romeo racing team.

1938: Scuderia Ferrari taken over by Alfa Corse (new Alfa Romeo works team).

1939: Ferrari sets up machine-tool business in his Modena premises called AAC (Auto Avio Costruzione), and builds two cars for 1940 Mille Miglia.

1947: First Ferrari sports car race victories: Rome, Vercelli and Varese (Franco Cortese); Forlì and Parma (Tazio Nuvolari); and Turin (Raymond Sommer).

1948: First 'Formula 1' win: Farina at Garda.

1949: First of nine Le Mans victories (Luigi Chinetti/Lord Selsdon).

1952: Alberto Ascari wins World Drivers' Championship, and again in 1953.

1953: Ferrari wins first of many World Sports Car Championships.

1961: Ferrari's first (of eight) World GP Manufacturers' Championships.

1985: Enzo Ferrari still going strong at Maranello headquarters, near Modena.

Ferrari 250 GTO, or Gran Turismo Omologato, *the 1962 competition version of the classic 250 GT 3-litre short-wheelbase Berlinetta, both bodied by Scaglietti. The 'GTO' title was revived in the mid-1980s. Car provided by Don Nelson.*

never good since his war service, was always troubling him. In 1929 he decided to maintain his interest in the sport by taking charge of the team (although he did not give up racing altogether until the winter of 1931–2, when his son Dino was born).

The Scuderia Ferrari was to operate independently of Alfa Romeo. The latter would, nevertheless, give its full backing to the new company, which was not only going to race the wonder machines but would also service customers' cars in the Modena area. Ferrari's racing cars carried the emblem of a prancing horse on a yellow shield and this became the badge of the Scuderia Ferrari from its inception. This emblem was dear to Ferrari's heart, for it was borne by the squadron the ace pilot and national hero Francesco Baracca had flown with until he was shot down in 1918. In addition to this, Baracca's father had watched Ferrari win the first Savio circuit race at Ravenna soon afterwards and had presented him with the squadron's badge as a token. It was to appear on every car Ferrari built.

Throughout the early 1930s, the Scuderia Ferrari was Italy's premier race team; and the arrival of Jano's masterpiece, the Alfa Romeo P3 made it the best in Europe – until the Germans came on the scene.

In 1938, Alfa Romeo decided to run its own team and

invited Ferrari back into the fold for this purpose: but the idea could not have worked as he was too used to independence. It was not long before Ferrari was back in Modena, where he renamed his works, situated in the Viale Trento Trieste, the Auto Avio Costruzione.

In 1939, two small sports cars were ordered for completion for the following year's Mille Miglia. These cars bore only a type number, 815, because part of Ferrari's severance agreement with Alfa Romeo was that he would not use his name on any car for a certain period. The 815s (one of which has been resurrected) were designed by Alberto Massimino and incorporated a number of FIAT parts, including a pair of cylinder heads from the ubiquitous 1100 model, adapted to fit on to a special straight-8 cylinder block. (The '815' stood for 'eight cylinders, 1.5 litres'. Alfa Romeo was already using the '158' terminology.)

The rest of Europe was at war when the 1940 Mille Miglia took place in the guise of the Gran Premio di Brescia. Both 815s led their class before retiring.

The first car actually called a Ferrari was conceived during the Second World War, when the Modena works was making machine tools, and announced in late 1946. Like so many later Ferraris it had a 60° V12 engine designed by Gioacchino Colombo and it began

RIGHT *The 1968 206 GT was created as a direct challenge to the Porsche 911 and, as such, was Ferrari's first true production car of the rear- or mid-engine type. Its 2-litre V6 power unit was mounted crosswise behind the two seats, permitting a compact yet beautifully styled body. Soon afterwards (with engine enlarged to 2.4 litres) it became the 246GT – but it was always best known as the Dino, in memory of Enzo Ferrari's son who died young. This example provided by Kay Stubberfield.*

BELOW *Announced in 1984, the 5-litre flat-12 Testa Rossa was called after one of the great sports-racing cars of the 1950s. The name originally derived from the fact that the cylinder head was painted red. The new coupé was clearly in the running to be one of the finest supercars of the late 1980s.*

winning races in its very first season, 1947.

From 1946, the company was called the Auto Costruzione Ferrari; and from 1948 road cars were offered for sale, first with 2-litre, then 2.3- or 2.5-litre V12 engines.

Ferrari's old firm, Alfa Romeo, was dominating early postwar Grand Prix racing and Ferrari could not put a stop to this with his 1.5-litre supercharged single-seaters. Aurelio Lampredi's big unsupercharged V12 engine was the answer and it appeared at Monza in 4.5-litre form for the 1950 Italian Grand Prix; although

it did not win, Alberto Ascari proved the new Ferrari to be a match for the magnificent but obsolete super-charged Alfa Romeos. He retired after swapping the lead with champion-elect Giuseppe Farina. Then he took over from his team mate Dorino Serafini and finished second.

The second year of the official World Drivers' Championship, 1951, saw the 4.5-litre Ferraris win three title races. The beefy Argentinian José Froilan Gonzalez beat his compatriot Juan Manuel Fangio at Silverstone: a result that delighted them both, for it

ABOVE *A classic among classics, the Pininfarina-styled Ferrari 365 GTB4 Daytona coupé is regarded by many as the ultimate front-engined Ferrari road car. Its 350 bhp 4.4-litre V12 engine drove via a five-speed transaxle unit. The tubular frame had independent suspension all round. Car provided by The Patrick Collection.*

was the first big win for Gonzalez, and Fangio was already well on his way to becoming champion. Alberto Ascari defeated the Alfa Romeo drivers at the Nürburgring and Monza. Although they could not come between Fangio and the world title, Ascari and Gonzalez between them pushed 1950 champion Farina down to fourth place in the table.

At the end of the 1951 season, Alfa Romeo pulled out of racing, leaving Ferrari without opposition, and race organizers little option but to switch to Formula 2 for the next two seasons, until the new (2.5-litre) formula was introduced. Ascari was World Champion in 1952 and 1953 with a new Lampredi-designed F2 Ferrari: the marque's first four-cylinder car. The year 1953 was also the first of the World Sports Car Championship, a competition that Ferrari was to dominate almost every year over a long period.

In Grand Prix racing, the return of Mercedes-Benz changed the pattern for 1954 and 1955. In 1956, when the German team withdrew, Fangio won his fourth world championship (of five), driving Lancias modified by Ferrari. Britain's Mike Hawthorn won the 1958 title for Ferrari. (This was the first year of the Constructors' Championship, which was won by the British

marque, Vanwall.) Since then, in the period to 1985, the following Ferrari drivers have been world champions: Phil Hill in 1961, John Surtees 1964, Niki Lauda 1975 and 1977, and Jody Scheckter 1979; and Ferrari has won the Constructors' title a record eight times: in 1961, 1964, 1975, 1976, 1977, 1979, 1982 and 1983.

The roadgoing and competition GT Ferraris from the Maranello works, just outside Modena in northern Italy, have been leaders of their class ever since the first 250 3-litre models appeared in 1954. Significant cars have been the 1959 short-wheelbase 250 GT; the 1969 365 GTB4; and the 1971 Berlinetta Boxer, first of a line of flat-12 rear-engined road cars.

For 1985 Ferrari maintained its place at the top of the supercar ladder when it followed its announcement of a revived GTO (a turbocharged V8, probably the fastest of road cars in the mid-1980s) with the launch of its latest 5-litre flat-12 coupé, the Testa Rossa, named after the famous 1950s sports car.

Although FIAT stepped in many years ago to keep Ferrari solvent, the policy of combining technical variety and sheer beauty with ultimate performance has not changed. Enzo Ferrari's own presence is rock-like and truly legendary.

FIAT Italy

FIAT

The FIAT 500, or Topolino, was the world's neatest new baby car of the mid-1930s. Its 570 cc four-cylinder engine was located well forward, ahead of the radiator. Between 1936 and 1948 it brought motoring to over 122,000 customers, most of whom had not been able to afford a car before. Provided by F. C. Watts.

Almost from the birth of the industry FIAT has been in the forefront, and has created the pattern for popular motoring in Italy. Yet the Turin giant has made many a spectacular oddity, and has also proved itself perfectly capable of winning races and rallies of world class. First called the Società Italiana per la Costruzione e il Commercio delle Automobili Torino, and soon changed to Fabbrica Italiana Automobili Torino, the firm that was to become known simply as FIAT, or Fiat, was founded by 32-year-old former cavalry officer Giovanni Agnelli in 1899. Since then this huge organization has extended into many other types of business, including aviation, and has absorbed many other makes of car.

Agnelli's main colleague in the venture was Roberto Biscaretti, father of Carlo Biscaretti who was to instigate Turin's famous motor museum. It was an uneasy start. Agnelli felt that Aristide Faccioli, the company's first engineer, did not really keep abreast of developments in the new industry and so, in 1901, replaced him by Giovanni Enrico. The new engineer quickly brought out a four-cylinder design and before long FIAT was producing a wide range of vehicles for home and overseas.

Motor racing played a big part in FIAT promotion on both sides of the Atlantic; the original works drivers were Vincenzo Lancia, possibly the fastest driver of the day, and the skilful, reliable Felice Nazzaro. (In later years both were to go into car manufacture on their own account. Nazzaro would return to FIAT after a relatively short absence.) In 1907, Nazzaro won the French Grand Prix in – or on! – a typically massive 16.3-litre four-cylinder FIAT, and went on to victories

in the Kaiserpreis and the Targa Florio. In the following year, Louis Wagner won the first American Grand Prize at Savannah, Georgia. This event was won twice by the American star David Bruce-Brown, driving a Benz in 1910 but a FIAT in 1911. A third Grand Prize went to FIAT in 1912 at a new location in Milwaukee, driven this time by Caleb Bragg. As early as 1910, a company was formed to market FIATs in the United States.

FIAT has made some of the world's smallest production cars – but it has also built some of the biggest. However, only a very few of the large and luxurious 6.8-litre V12 touring cars of 1921 were produced.

A racing revival led to Nazzaro winning the 1922 French Grand Prix, 15 years after his first victory. FIATs also won the 1922 and 1923 Italian Grands Prix at Monza, in the hands of Pietro Bordino and Carlo Salamano respectively. The runner-up both times was the remarkable Nazzaro. The 1922 racer was a 2-litre six, but for 1923 a straight-8 was developed; the latter marked the first successful application of supercharging to a Grand Prix car.

During the 1920s and 1930s, FIAT expanded its overseas activities, with assembly or complete manufacture taking place in many countries, including France, Germany and Spain. Most models had a solid, even stodgy look to them. Others were delightful: for example, the little Balilla Sport was neat and light, a real Italian equivalent of the original M.G. Midget.

It was the first Topolino, or Mickey Mouse, of 1936 that tickled the world's fancy. This tiny car was fashionable abroad, and at home it brought motoring to a much broader cross-section of society than any previous Italian offering. Dante Giacosa and Franco

ABOVE *Launched in the early 1970s, the 1.3-litre FIAT X1/9 is still a yardstick in compact sports car design. Styling was by Bertone, and this 1983 model is a fine representative of the type of modern classic that is singled out for posterity in The Patrick Collection, Kings Norton, Birmingham.*

RIGHT *Another fine example of 1970s cooperation between artist and manufacturer: the graceful Pininfarina-bodied 3.2-litre V6 ohc-engined FIAT 130 coupé.*

Fessia were the two engineers responsible for this beautifully scaled-down 'big' car, the ancestor of a whole line of baby FIATs.

Many small FIAT and FIAT-based sports cars have been built over the years. Strangely forgotten, however, is the 2-litre 8V FIAT coupé of 1952, another sensational Giacosa design. It had independent suspension all round and its performance was on a par with the Aston Martin DB2, but not quite up to the Lancia Aurelia GT, which it postdated. Only 114 of these beauties were produced. Fifteen years later, the V6 Dino (a joint venture with Ferrari) brought FIAT back into the sports car market more firmly. More recently, the Bertone-styled FIAT X1/9 set further new and high standards in compact sports car design.

From 1955, the smallest FIATs were for the first time rear-engined; the six-seater Multipla version of the 633 cc saloon was an interesting exercise in fitting a quart into a pint pot. The 1.1-litre saloon stayed with front engine and rear-wheel drive. Then, in 1969, came the front-wheel-drive transverse-engined 128, based on the 1964 Primula, which was a design from one of FIAT's acquisitions, Autobianchi (formerly Bianchi). The 127 followed soon afterwards.

In the early 1970s, FIAT turned the 124 into a successful rally car; later the 131 was adapted even more effectively for this sport. Consequently, FIAT won the World Rally Championship three times in four years between 1977 and 1980.

Through the statesmanship of Gianni Agnelli, grandson of the founder, FIAT continues to be a major force in motoring: particularly in the small family saloon field, with its thoroughly practical Panda and highly regarded Uno models. In 1984, the famous but abandoned FIAT factory in Lingotto, Turin, was used for the Italian motor show.

FORD USA/Europe/Australia, etc.

Like the Agnellis of FIAT, the Ford family set its sights on world markets from the very beginning. Henry Ford is rightly considered to have been the most influential person in the history of motoring, from the time it became clear that the car was going to be universal.

Ransom Olds (*see* Oldsmobile) sowed the seeds of mass production between 1901 and 1904, but his Curved-Dash Runabout was more a buggy than a car. Henry Ford's Model T unquestionably revolutionized motor manufacture, and from its introduction in 1909 it became the world's biggest-selling car by far.

Henry Ford was born on a Michigan farm in 1863. He was fascinated by steam engines and by the threshing, woodcutting and other machines they powered. He trained as a machinist and a craftsman in his own right. Only the very wealthiest of farmers could afford a roadgoing steam engine. Young Ford wanted to reduce weight and therefore cut costs, and so he experimented.

Then, in 1885, Ford saw an Otto four-stroke gas engine for the first time. Within two years he had built one himself – just to make sure he understood the system. (It was the Otto principle that Benz and Daimler, separately, adapted for their first four-stroke petrol-engined road vehicles of the very same period.) In 1895, Ford went to Macy's store in New York to look at the first imported Benz. He returned home full of confidence, for by then he had already made a car of his own that was lighter and, in his opinion, more practical.

In 1899 Ford designed a car with epicyclic transmission for a new group called the Detroit Automobile Company, and elements of this 'Detroit' design were to be seen in the first Cadillac (the name adopted by Henry Leland for the Detroit company when he took control in 1902, by which time Ford had left to form his own firm).

Even before embarking on regular production, Ford had become famous with his own special by racing and winning in it at Grosse Pointe in 1901. (There were also two later specials to give the new company publicity.)

The first Ford production model of 1903 followed Henry Ford's earlier principle of using a flat-twin

CENTRE RIGHT Ford brought budget-priced V8 motoring to Britain in the mid-1930s on initial cost if not on tax or fuel prices. This Model 60 was built at Dagenham alongside its famous, frugal brother, the £100 Y-type Popular.

BELOW The first of the 'Ponycars' – the 1966 Ford Mustang – was inspired largely by Lee Iacocca. Subsequently he and Ford fell out. Ultimately, however, he went on to become a national hero by injecting lifeblood into a listless Chrysler Corporation in the mid-1980s. Twenty years earlier, his Mustang had shown America that relatively cheap motoring could also be done in real style.

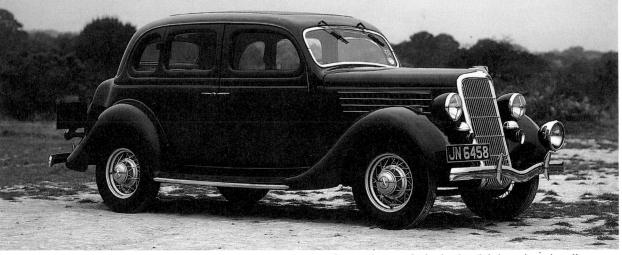

engine underneath the body, driving via epicyclic gears and chain. At first the Ford was slightly more expensive than the similar Cadillac; but as production went up the price came down. Ford also tried his hand at making big six-cylinder cars as early as 1905, but they were not a success. Much planning time was lost by Ford as he fought a battle to rid America of George Selden's patent, a device that sought to make all car manufacture subject to licence. Ford managed to prove in court that a complete vehicle could not form the subject of a single master patent and that an association of licensees (which had been formed by those makers willing to pay) was equally unacceptable. This fight took him until 1911, from which time the American motor industry was freed of the noose which Selden had tried to tie.

The Model T or 'Tin Lizzie' was simple if unorthodox. It had a side-valve four-cylinder engine of just under 3 litres capacity, giving enough torque to enable

ABOVE *In the 1960s, Ford took over saloon car racing where Jaguar had left off – not with just one model, but with many. The Galaxie, the Falcon, the Mustang, the Cortina, the Anglia and other models were raced and rallied in various forms, all being capable of outright as well as class victory. Here Peter Arundell (Lotus Cortina) leads Gawaine Baillie (Falcon) and Jacky Ickx (Lotus Cortina) at Silverstone in May 1966, when Fords filled the first five places with John Whitmore (Falcon) winning from Baillie.*

it to manage with only two forward speeds. Special driving techniques were required to control the epicyclic transmission and in some American states owners had to obtain a separate operating licence. This did not stop the Model T becoming the world's most popular car. During its 18 years the price dropped from $850 to $260.

Ford took a brave risk in 1927 by closing the works completely while retooling for the next new Ford, the Model A. Another landmark year was 1932, when the Ford V8 was launched. Also in 1932, Ford introduced the 0.9-litre Y-type to be made at its new Dagenham plant and designed with the high British rate of horsepower tax in mind. This outstanding full four-seater saloon deflected some attention away from the internal struggle for supremacy between the native British Austin and Morris. In 1935, Ford became the only manufacturer to offer a fully equipped family car on the British market for £100: a price that was held until the Y-type's successor appeared in 1937. By then Ford plants existed in many parts of the world, including Britain, Germany and Australia.

As at FIAT, the founder's grandson took over control of a vast worldwide business. From 1945 Henry Ford II would reign for over 30 years, approving such innovations as the 1955 Thunderbird (which started as a two-seater to compete with the Chevrolet Corvette but grew into something larger); Britain's top-selling family car, the Cortina; and the Mustang.

HIGHLIGHTS

1863: Henry Ford born at Dearborn, Michigan.

1896: Ford demonstrates his first car.

1899: Ford joins Detroit Automobile Co.

1902: Ford leaves to start his own car-making business.

1908: Model T announced.

1911: Model assembly in England (Manchester).

1922: Ford buys Lincoln Motor Co.

1927: Model T production run ends. (Final number built surpasses 16.5 million.)

1932: First mass-production V8. Introduction of small Ford Y saloon at new Dagenham plant in England.

1947: Death of Henry Ford.

1958: 50 millionth Ford produced.

1966: First of four successive Ford victories at Le Mans.

1967: First World Championship Grand Prix win.

1983: 155th World Championship Grand Prix win.

1984: Announcement of RS200 two- or four-wheel-drive rally car.

The last-named was the brainchild of Ford president-to-be Lee Iacocca, an engineer with an unusual grasp of sales technique and public taste. Compact (in American terms), simple and well-styled, especially in 'notch-back' form, the Mustang was successful where the Chevrolet Corvair was not. It had instant appeal and it helped take Ford's annual North American output past the two million mark for the first time in 1965 and 1966. This put it on a par with Chevrolet, and both were far ahead of the opposition.

The Mustang's appearance also coincided with a Ford policy of participation in racing and rallying at the highest level. The British Ford-Cosworth V8 3-litre Grand Prix unit was to be the most successful Formula 1 engine of all, powering the cars of champion manufacturers no fewer than ten times between 1968 and 1981: namely, Lotus (five), Williams (two), and McLaren, Matra and Tyrrell. Ford has won the world Rally Championship on three occasions; but it is for the way in which it tackled the assault on Le Mans with the magnificent GT40s that Ford is most remembered. Encouraged by the success of Carroll Shelby's Ford V8-powered AC-based Cobra, Ford set up a company, Ford Advanced Vehicles, borrowing the services of Eric Broadley, whose Lola GT had been the sensation of the 1963 London racing car show. From this multi-million dollar project Ford achieved its goals of winning Le Mans *and* a new clientele of enthusiastic motorists.

Ford's market research usually has been of the highest calibre; and when occasionally it has not, the company has made up any lost ground quickly.

Ford Sierra XR4i, introduced in 1983, was the top-performance version of the aerodynamic successor of the ubiquitous Cortina. Even more sporting Sierras including a version with four-wheel drive were announced in 1985.

FRANKLIN USA

The 1932 Franklin Airman Six may have been so called because of the aviators (notably Charles Lindbergh) who became regular customers of this highly respected manufacturer. Franklins were also air-cooled, although their radiator grilles suggested otherwise.

H. H. Franklin began making air-cooled cars in 1902 at his Syracuse, New York, foundry and stuck to this principle through thick and thin. The Franklin proved its capabilities early on. In 1904, a four-cylinder model crossed the United States from New York to San Francisco, a road distance of 6600 km (4100 miles), in 30 days. Two years later L. L. Whitman brought the transcontinental record down to 15 days when he covered the distance in the opposite direction. This achievement with a six-cylinder Franklin was used to considerable effect in advertising the marque.

Competition motoring was never undertaken officially by the company after that, although in 1912 R. Hamlin did win the Cactus Derby, a desert road race from Los Angeles, California, to Phoenix, Arizona, at over 45 km/h (28 mph) and there were other demonstrations as further evidence of the Franklin's strength and the ability of designer John Wilkinson's engine to stay cool under adverse conditions.

As specialists in die-casting, Franklin made extensive use of aluminium, and this helped reduce car weights – although only relatively speaking, for the Franklin was to become even more luxurious.

One of the first makes to list a fully closed model, Franklin was noted for its dignity. Its appearance was not as unusual as might have been expected for an air-cooled car, for there was a dummy radiator cowl. On the new 1930 models there were slats which could be adjusted to vary the amount of air that came in. Automatic control of this feature was by a thermostat monitoring the front cylinder temperature. Franklins represented ideal transport for the well-to-do professional person, and were usually produced without the fashionable white-wall tyres or flashy two-tone paintwork.

Steady increases in sales had led to a record output of over 12,000 cars in 1929. Then the money market collapsed and, in 1930, only 6000 were sold. At home the cost of the regular 4.5-litre six-cylinder was $2400; prices were cut by $500 to $600 as matters became still more desperate in 1931. The 1930–1 British equivalents (in L. C. Rawlence's Sackville Street premises in London) varied between £850 and £940. At the same time the cheapest 4.5-litre Bentley was over £1000, for the chassis only. In Britain, the Franklin was more in the price category of the Armstrong Siddeley Special Twenty or a typical Lagonda.

The final fling was a supercharged 6.6-litre V12, priced around the $4000 mark in 1932. In Britain it was more a case of 'price-on application'.

Too late, a return to reality came in 1933. An arrangement was made with Reo (*see* Oldsmobile) to supply virtually complete but engine-less Flying Cloud saloons from the Lansing, Michigan, plant to Syracuse. There an air-cooled six-cylinder unit was installed; the interesting result was dubbed the Franklin Olympic which, at $1400, must have been a good buy. Too many debts had piled up by then, however. When the Franklin factory was forced to close down in the spring of 1934 it could be said that it did so never having made a bad car – and often extremely good ones.

FRAZER NASH Great Britain

The origins of this marque can be traced back to the early years of our century when Ronald Godfrey and Archibald Nash were training together, first as engineering students in London, and then in Rugby with English Electric's forerunners, Messrs Willans and Robinson. In 1910 they went into partnership to make sporting light cars with air-cooled V-twin JAP and other small engines, calling their marque GN; later, when the Austin Seven was announced, the noisier and more spartan GN lost its popularity.

Both men moved on to greater things. Ron Godfrey became a partner in the Halford, Robins and Godfrey (HRG) sports car company in the 1930s. Archie Frazer-Nash (as he now signed himself) called his new Kingston upon Thames company Frazer-Nash Ltd in 1924, combining with William Thomas in 1926 for the bigger premises he needed to make his Frazer Nash cars (without the hyphen).

Thomas left Nash in the lurch when he pulled out, but fresh finance was obtained to form a new company, AFN Ltd, in 1927. In 1928, while Nash was in hospital, his financiers sold AFN (and the right to make Frazer Nash cars) to H. J. Aldington, a salesman and a businessman through and through.

The early Frazer Nashes were characterized by their chain-drive transmission, with a cunning but simple dog-clutch mechanism which was foolproof in that two sets of gears could not be engaged simultaneously. The rear track was kept narrow to reduce the effect of having no differential; a positive effect was the good traction on muddy hills during trials.

At their works in Isleworth in Middlesex, Aldington and his two brothers developed the 'chain-gang' Frazer Nash into a reasonably civilized high-performance sports car. It offered few creature comforts, however,

and they knew they needed something more sophisticated if they were to sell to a broader clientele.

It was while taking part (very successfully) in the 1934 Alpine Trial that H. J. Aldington became aware of his own cars' shortcomings in relation to the excellence of the new BMWs, designed by Fritz Fiedler and no longer remotely reminiscent of the Austin Seven that begat them. After a visit to Germany, he was offered the British import licence for BMW cars. Soon Aldington was importing complete cars and, occasionally, chassis to which bodies were added in Britain. These machines were sold, as Frazer Nash-BMWs, to a different clientele (alongside the traditional Frazer Nash), establishing new and unfamiliar standards of engineering and performance. Aldington himself raced and rallied the exciting 328 sports model in Britain and Germany, as did the brilliant A.F.P. Agabeg ('Fane'), and many other famous drivers including Richard Seaman.

Such was the rapport between Frazer Nash and BMW that, after the Second World War, Lt-Col. H. J. Aldington was able to obtain Ing. Fiedler's release and take him (and considerable technical data) to Britain. BMW's car factory in Eisenach came within the Russian Zone, cut off from the Munich headquarters where car production did not begin until the early 1950s. Aldington did, however, manage to obtain one of the special streamlined BMW 328s which had been made for the 1940 Mille Miglia, and this provided the inspiration for a postwar Frazer Nash.

For a brief period it looked as if Aldington would sell out to the Bristol Aircraft Company, with which he had worked closely in his military role (the first Bristol car was in fact originally called the Frazer Nash-Bristol). From mid-1947 the marques became separate, both using 2-litre Bristol engines created from BMW's prewar drawings. Later that year, Fiedler moved from Bristol to Isleworth.

BELOW *Speedy and spartan, almost every 'chain-gang' Frazer Nash was bought with competition motoring in mind. Here the prototype 1932 TT Replica (first owned by Roy Eccles) is seen taking part in a 1938 event driven by its second owner, Barry Goodwin. Frazer Nashes of this period had Anzani, Blackburne, Gough or (as in this case) Meadows engines.*

The original character of the Frazer Nash was restored in the 1948 High Speed model: a businesslike competition two-seater on a tough, tubular chassis. Former racing motorcyclist Norman Culpan saw it at the 1948 London motor show, ordered one on the spot and entered it for the first postwar revival of the Le Mans 24-Hour race. He invited H. J. Aldington to co-drive and they finished third overall. Thereafter, Le Mans Replica became the car's name, and there followed a whole series of international race and rally successes. Franco Cortese's outright victory in the 1951 Targa Florio must remain the most memorable. New styles named Mille Miglia, Sebring and, of course, Targa Florio were introduced.

In 1952 the Healeys and the Aldingtons exhibited new Austin-powered sports cars at the London show; they knew that the new British Motor Corporation wanted to make a completely new Austin-based sports car. The Healey men won that particular contract (*see* Healey) and Frazer Nash reverted to making very expensive bespoke models as it had always done but production petered out in the late 1950s. By then Aldington, the commercial man, had acquired the Porsche concession; BMW and DKW franchises would follow. The day of the Frazer Nash was done, but AFN was to live on into the modern sports car age – with a new-generation Aldington still at the helm.

GUY Great Britain

At one time there were many Wolverhampton vehicle manufacturers, but Guy Motors Ltd was one of the few to enjoy a long life, with periods of prosperity.

Sidney Slater Guy had been the works manager at Sunbeam before starting his own company at Fallings Park, Wolverhampton, in 1914. Only a few light trucks and buses were made before the factory had to be turned over to wartime munitions work.

In 1919, the return to civilian production included entry into the luxury car market. The 4.1-litre V8 Guy was costly – although not as expensive as (say) a comparable Lanchester or Napier – and it had the unusual feature of fully automatic chassis lubrication, operated by a cam on the steering mechanism every time full right lock was applied. ('I see you have a telephone in every bedroom', remarked someone on seeing the oil-pipe complex for the first time!)

Deliveries of the new car started in 1920. But although this was Britain's first series-production car with a V8 engine, and despite the smart semi-polished tourer body seen at that year's show (and upon which King George V commented favourably), there was insufficient public response once the heady days of the immediate postwar period were over.

Several four-cylinder Guys appeared, including a 1.9-litre saloon called the 13/36 featuring four-wheel brakes. Total output had only just reached three-figure quantities by the mid-1920s when Guy cars were discontinued. At about the same time, Guy Motors took over the long-established Star company, also of Wolverhampton. Star cars and commercial vehicles continued to be made until 1932 when Guy reverted to its own make of trucks, buses and trolleybuses. (Guy was later to buy the Sunbeam trolleybus business.)

One of Guy's suppliers was the famous engine maker Henry Meadows Ltd, whose factory was adjacent. In the 1950s Meadows decided to produce a miniature car in glass fibre. Designed by Raymond Flower, it had a two-stroke Villiers engine and bodywork by Guy Motors, who happened to be introducing glass fibre for truck cabs. This diversion was just one possible reason for Guy being put into the hands of the receiver.

Sir William Lyons, who had been about to reintroduce a Daimler truck, bought the Wolverhampton company in 1961 and his new chief truck engineer, Clifford Elliott, moved from the Daimler to the Guy works. In 1964 came a new range of heavy-duty trucks and tractor units called Big J (or 'Big Jaguar'); it stayed in production until the late 1970s. Even in the mid-1980s the sturdy Guy bus chassis, once called the Victory J, was being built for overseas markets by Leyland at its Farington, Lancashire, plant. The Wolverhampton factory was, however, sold off in 1983 to make way for a supermarket after nearly 70 years of continuous vehicle and component manufacture.

RIGHT *Guy V8 tourer is the 1919 works demonstrator, so who was having the picnic?*

HEALEY Great Britain

Donald Healey, truly a grand old man of motoring, continues in the mid-1980s to live his active and varied life to the full, having given pleasure to thousands of motoring enthusiasts, for he has produced and been involved in many different sports car projects *en route*.

The Cornish garage proprietor first came to fame when, at the age of 32, he won the 1931 Monte Carlo Rally for Invicta. Two years later he moved to Coventry to work for Riley. In 1934 he transferred to Triumph, where he was in charge of Gloria and Dolomite development; later he became technical director and was responsible for selling the defunct company a few weeks before the outbreak of the Second World War (*see* Triumph).

During hostilities Healey was with Humber, and he was planning a car of his own. Typically, he was quick off the mark after the war, acquiring the use of part of a small factory on the industrial estate in the area of Warwick known as The Cape. By the end of 1945 he had established the format of the first Healey car: a rugged but light steel chassis frame, independent front suspension and trailing arms (making high-speed reversing in rally tests all the more dramatic), engine and gearbox from the lively 2.5-litre four-cylinder Riley, and shapely open-tourer bodywork by Westland of Hereford. By late 1946 there was an even more individual close-coupled saloon by Elliott of Reading, Berkshire, which could reach well over 160 km/h (100 mph) and, for a time, could lay genuine claim to being Britain's fastest production car.

Success in competition and high-speed demonstrations followed rapidly, as did new variations. Most famous of these was the stark Silverstone model, with its retractable windscreen. One of the first customers was Briggs Cunningham, who had the Riley engine replaced by a Cadillac V8.

Over 600 Riley-engined Healeys would be made, most of them with smart Abbott or Tickford two-door bodies. In the meantime, however, Healey was looking for more power. He found it while crossing the Atlantic on an engine-hunting expedition. During the trip he met George Mason, the president of Nash Kelvinator, and the Nash-Healey was conceived immediately. It had a 3.8-litre (later 4.1-litre) Nash six-cylinder engine and rear axle fitted to the Healey chassis, and prototypes did well in the 1950 Mille Miglia and at Le Mans that year. (Often with his elder son Geoffrey, Donald Healey continued to take part in road races and rallies well into the 1950s, for he was always an accomplished long-distance driver.) More than 500 Nash-Healeys were built between 1950 and 1954; the later ones had Pininfarina bodies, which pushed the costs far beyond the reasonable showroom price. The original British two-seater Nash-Healey body, relieved of its heavy, grinning Nash grille, was kept in production briefly at The Cape as the Alvis-Healey 3-litre, an attractive if over-priced touring roadster, of which 25 were made.

When the British Motor Corporation came into being, Sir Leonard Lord let it be known in several quarters that he was looking for a new Austin-based sports car. The Jensens were not quick enough to get their 'bargain' sports car to the 1952 London motor

ABOVE *Shapely Elliott-bodied Riley-powered Healey, driven by Tony Marsh in the 1952 Welsh Rally. This was the first definitive Healey saloon.*

show, whereas Frazer Nash and Healey made it. Lord, it seems, had no hesitation in selecting the Healey 100, for it was both beautiful and practical. The Riley unit was no longer available, but the simpler Austin Atlantic 2.7-litre four could do a similar job.

Production of the Austin-Healey 100 began at Longbridge in the spring of 1953. It was Jensen, ironically, who supplied the bodies, and a cheery Donald Healey set off on a North American tour to promote the car he would not have the worry of making. As the Austin-Healey 100-Six, and then as the 3000, that car went on to win great acclaim and popularity and its disappearance in 1967 upset many enthusiasts. Outright victory by Pat Moss and Ann Wisdom in the punishing Liège–Sofia–Liège Marathon de la Route of 1960 marked the car's ultimate achievement.

Meanwhile, the Warwick company developed the 1954 all-disc-braked Healey 100S for competition with Longbridge approval, and in 1957 proposed the small car that became the much-loved Austin-Healey Sprite and was built until 1971. The Healey-Coventry Climax and Healey-Repco Le Mans cars of 1968–70 were less memorable, but the Healey Motor Company was, by then, much more involved in the retail trade, but there was to be another Healey-inspired car (*see* Jensen).

as a worthy make, but not a very sporting one. One exception, as if proving a rule, was the successful sprint car with which ERA and BRM founder Raymond Mays began his racing career.

William Hillman had six daughters, two of whom married ex-army captains John Black and Spencer Wilks. Black and Wilks were joint managing directors at Hillman when the Rootes brothers made their bid in the late-1920s to start a manufacturing group by combining Hillman and neighbouring Humber. Black went to Standard and Wilks to Rover, doing those companies and themselves a power of good.

Large – if never enormous – sales began to come Hillman's way with the launching of the popular and famous Minx in 1932. A delightful variation on this new theme was the 1933 Aero-Minx coupé, which inspired another product of the expanding Rootes empire, the Talbot Ten. Successive models of Minx served the company for many years and post-Second World War variations helped keep Sunbeam and Singer going.

Developed by Michael Parkes, son of the head of Alvis, and built initially at Linwood, near Glasgow, the Hillman Imp of 1963 was a better-looking and less basic small family car than the Mini, and had a 0.9-litre overhead-camshaft power unit of Coventry Climax origin mounted in the rear. It did well in its class in races and rallies, but it was phased out in the mid-1970s, when front-wheel drive had become almost universal for small saloons.

Chrysler had been taking an increasing interest in Rootes and from 1976 the surviving Hillmans (the Hunter and the Avenger) became Chryslers. The Hunter (the Minx's successor) was still being assembled in Iran in the mid-1980s.

It was in 1968, however, that the Hillman had its moment of true greatness when a Hunter won the unique, and extraordinarily tough, London–Sydney Marathon, driven by Andrew Cowan and Brian Coyle of Scotland and Midlander Colin Malkin.

HILLMAN Great Britain

RIGHT *This 1935 Hillman Aero-Minx had an underslung frame and low lines. When Rootes took over Sunbeam and Talbot, its chassis provided the basis for the Talbot and Sunbeam-Talbot Tens.*

William Hillman built a car factory in his big garden at Stoke, Coventry, and was joined by an energetic French engineer named Louis Coatalen, who had previously worked for de Dion-Bouton, Crowden of Leamington Spa, and Humber. From 1907 to 1909, the Hillman-Coatalen was made on a small scale as a luxury car, the range including a six-cylinder model with a capacity of nearly 10 litres.

Coatalen moved to Sunbeam in 1909 and the (plain) Hillman developed into a more modest marque. Throughout the 1920s, the Hillman established itself

HISPANO-SUIZA Spain/France

Messier-Hispano-Bugatti is the name displayed by the French aero industry giant SNECMA on the wall of the old Bugatti factory at Molsheim. It is a long time since Hispano-Suiza took over the remnants of Bugatti, and longer still since the cars of either of these truly great marques could be purchased new.

The name Hispano-Suiza was chosen for the new marque in Barcelona in 1904 because the first model had been the work of a Swiss engineer, Marc Birkigt. King Alfonso XIII was an early customer and allowed his name to be used on a sporting model after it had won a major race. From 1911, there was a French company in Paris and the advanced specification of the aero engines it produced during the First World War set the engineering standards for the magnificent cars that were to follow. Among the Allied aircraft that used Hispano-Suiza engines had been the French Spad. This was the type flown by ace pilot Georges Guynemer, whose squadron's *Cigogne Volante* emblem Birkigt adopted for the elegant prow of his cars.

RIGHT Hispano-Suiza H6, introduced in 1919, had servo-assisted brakes and a 6.6-litre six-cylinder ohc engine. It led to the marque becoming one of the most highly acclaimed in the world.

Probably Birkigt's greatest contribution to motoring was in applying mechanical assistance to the brakes to cope with the high performance of his cars. This was a feature of the new 6.6-litre overhead-camshaft steel-lined aluminium alloy six-cylinder H6 which appeared at the 1919 Paris Salon, and promptly took over from Delaunay-Belleville as 'France's Rolls-Royce'. From 1923 the bore was increased and the capacity was then close on 8 litres.

Royce, Bentley and other great designers paid silent tribute to Birkigt by studying, and noting, what Hispano-Suiza did.

The most exotic Hispano-Suiza was the 9.4-litre overhead-valve V12, which could carry even the most opulent coachbuilt body at well over 160 km/h (100 mph). It was made from 1931 to 1938, when the French company went back to its aero engines. In Spain, the Barcelona firm made its own versions of the six-cylinder models until the early 1940s. Then Emprasa Nacional de Autocamiones SA took over the Barcelona works, making not only trucks but also (from 1951 to 1958) Spain's supercar, the Pegaso.

HOTCHKISS France

Tough, well-made, fast and dependable, these were the lasting traits of the Hotchkiss: the first marque that won that most famous winter event of all – the Monte Carlo Rally – six times. (This record was exceeded by Lancia, but only as recently as 1983.)

Thoroughly French in so many ways, it took its name from Benjamin Berkeley Hotchkiss, a New England industrialist who had gone to France in 1867. The subsequent cars had crossed-gun badges, stemming from Hotchkiss's original activity in St Denis, Paris: providing armaments for the Franco-Prussian war.

When the needs of the French army and navy had been satisfied, Hotchkiss et Cie found itself with too little work for its size – although it did manufacture components for the fledgling motor industry before becoming a significant maker itself, from 1903.

Early Hotchkiss cars were large and luxurious with considerable British influence. This was due largely to the presence of an Englishman, Harry Ainsworth, who became a Hotchkiss draughtsman in 1904 and, within ten years, production director. There were some monster racers, but only a few and not for long.

The First World War saw Hotchkiss back in the gun-making business, besides manufacturing staff cars; by 1917 there were several factories, including one in England, in Gosford Street, Coventry, which Ainsworth managed. When its contract for medium machine guns ran out, Hotchkiss made engines for William Morris, whose earlier suppliers could not meet his mushrooming production requirements. In 1923, Morris took over British Hotchkiss, and Ainsworth went back to France.

Soon the six-cylinder Hotchkiss became recognized as a very special car. The AM80, engineered by Vincenzo Bertarione and first seen at the 1928 Paris Salon, was the basis for all the great rally winners. From the mid-1930s, the regular top-of-the-range capacity was increased from 3 to 3.5 litres.

Competition successes included the Alpine and Paris–Nice trials; the latter gave its name to a high-performance variant. However, it was the Monte Carlo Rally that showed Hotchkiss in its very best light. Hotchkiss cars won in 1932 and 1933, driven by Maurice Vasselle; in 1934, 1939 and 1949 with Jean Trévoux at the wheel; and finally in 1950 – a particularly hard event, won by a prewar car in the hands of Marcel Becquart.

The final 3.5-litre models – the V-screened Anjou saloon and the Chapron-bodied Anthéor drophead coupé – appeared in 1951. Meanwhile, Hotchkiss had become interested in front-wheel drive, acquiring two

Grégoire designs (*see* Tracta): one through assisting the famous but faltering Amilcar light car concern in 1938; the other through buying the postwar Grégoire flat-4. Both were failures and, shortly after Hotchkiss acquired the Delahaye-Delage company in 1954, production of all three marques came to an end.

Hotchkiss had made fine trucks since the mid-1930s and continued to do so. In 1956 Hotchkiss-Delahaye became Hotchkiss-Brandt. There were various other cooperative schemes, notably one with Leyland, but armaments began to take precedence and, in due course, what remained of Hotchkiss vehicle technology was absorbed by Citroën.

BELOW Hotchkiss cars won the Monte Carlo Rally six times, the last occasion being in 1950, driven by Becquart and Secret (illustrated), but these feats did not help sales of these fine saloons which, at 3.5 litres, were just too large to find a market in the early postwar years.

HRG Great Britain

FAR RIGHT Neat, lightweight bodywork of the Monaco Engineering-prepared 1949 HRG Le Mans cars, one of which won its class in the notoriously gruelling 24-hour French road race.

After Archie Nash and Ron Godfrey gave up producing their outmoded GN cyclecars, both set out to make better sports cars. Nash, however, had sold AFN and the Frazer Nash car business long before the HRG appeared.

Once the Aldingtons had created the Frazer Nash-BMW, the traditional 'chain-gang' Frazer Nash seemed more quirky and outdated than ever. To Godfrey and his two partners – ex-Trojan production man Guy Robins and administrator E. A. Halford (a Brooklands racing man) – it seemed there was a need for a no-nonsense sports car; traditional, bespoke where necessary, but orthodox. So it was, that 'H', 'R', and 'G' announced their first car in November 1935.

The HRG was built in small numbers in Oakcroft Road, Tolworth, Surrey. Proprietary components

such as the proved Meadows 4ED 1.5-litre engine and the Moss gearbox were specified. The car was a two-seater sports, light and easy to handle, with the front axle tube well ahead of the radiator to give a relatively long 2.62 m (103 in) wheelbase.

The HRG's performance was good and its reliability excellent. With Archie Scott as co-driver, Halford came second in class at Le Mans in 1937. Peter Clark and Marcus Chambers followed suit in 1938 and went on to win their class in 1939. When Halford left the company, two more racing men, Lord Selsdon and T. A. S. O. Mathieson, joined the HRG board.

The cars were quite expensive in 1939 at £425 (nearly twice the price of a T-series M. G. Midget), but £882 for a 1500 and the £812 for an 1100 made selling HRGs in 1946 an even more formidable task. This was undertaken by Charles Follett Ltd, a firm with great experience in selling specialist machines.

The slowest mover in showroom terms was the 1947 Aerodynamic, with enveloping bodywork by Fox and Nicholl Ltd, who had raced teams of Lagondas and Roesch Talbots in the 1930s. It cost £1246, which might have been retrospectively worth it for the exclusiveness as only 30 were built; but the chassis and the body did not get on well together and few of the latter survived more than one rally.

A few prewar and all the postwar HRGs had Singer engines, and the traditional two-seaters sold quite well during the late 1940s, when all new cars were in short supply. There were even a few left-hand-drive models.

Some of the 'streamliners' were rebodied by their owners. Peter Clark was one of the unofficial racing team, which ran cigar-shaped cars prepared by Monaco Motors, a specialist tuning shop managed by another HRG user: John Wyer, later to become famous as racing administrator with Aston Martin, Ford and Porsche teams. In 1949 an HRG succeeded in winning its class at Le Mans again, driven by Eric Thompson and Jack Fairman; the Belgian 24-hour race produced the same result, plus the team prize.

In rallying, Robin Richards won a coveted Coupe des Alpes in the 1948 Alpine Trial: this was awarded to the few competitors able to complete the course without time penalties. John Gott won a second Coupe for HRG three years later – and there were other successes.

Somehow, the tiny company struggled on into the 1950s, when Singer was planning some major updating which, it was hoped, might be put to good use by HRG: but Singer itself was in trouble. However, the last dozen production HRGs did have the short-stroke SM1500 engine.

Not more than 250 HRGs were made in a lifespan of close on 20 years. After the company turned to general light engineering in the mid-1950s, the occasional promising prototype would appear. The works closed altogether in 1966 but a good number of HRGs remain as a reminder of how traditional-style sports cars have always found at least some customers. This may, more than any other factor, account for today's so-called replica market.

HUMBER Great Britain

'The Daimler' and 'The Humber' were the anchors of Coventry's very early car industry, and in that city those names are still used to indicate the respective Radford and Stoke works of Jaguar and Peugeot-Talbot.

The two firms were famous for the quality both of their products and of their training. Many great men of the industry began their careers with Daimler and Humber. For example, Bill Heynes, the director in charge of every Jaguar engineering project, from the first car of 1935 to the XJ6 more than 30 years later, started out as a Humber man.

Thomas Humber had acquired his considerable reputation as a bicycle maker in Nottingham. He built his late-19th-century motor vehicles there and in Coventry, and he was drawn into Harry Lawson's attempted monopolization of the British car industry (*see* Daimler). Soon it was possible to reorganize Humber as a separate company; its products were influenced to a large degree by young Louis Coatalen before he moved to Hillman. From 1908, production and expansion were centred upon Coventry.

Most Humbers were dependable, coachbuilt, middle-priced cars for dependable middle-class people, although, surprisingly, there *was* some racing activity by Humber in the early Brooklands days.

From 1930, Humber became the prestige marque of the Hillman-Humber combine, created by the Rootes brothers who had been highly successful in the retail trade in Kent, and were moving in on London's West End. They merged the activities of Hillman and Humber (whose factories in Stoke were neighbours in any case). Although often cursed for their ruthless 'badge engineering', William and Reginald Rootes should also be remembered for expanding the industry in Coventry at a time when small businesses were vanishing every week in the wake of the world Depression.

The Rootes Group (as it would become) already owned Thrupp & Maberly, a long-established coachbuilder, and this kept Humber in the luxury car market – especially when it came to 'second string' limousines for state occasions.

Probably the most famous Humbers were the military staff cars of the 1940s. In 1944, General Montgomery's famous tourer *Old Faithful* fell into the sea from a Mulberry Harbour structure during the follow-up to the Normandy landings, but is said to have been in his use again within two days.

The 4.1-litre side-valve Humber Super Snipe was not considered a very potent car, but it was handsome, and it amazed the sporting world when the Dutch driver Maurice Gatsonides brought one home second in the very wintry 1950 Monte Carlo Rally. The last of the bigger Humbers was removed from the Rootes range soon after Chrysler had taken control in the mid-1960s.

However, the Humber Sceptre (a glorified Hillman Minx) soldiered on until 1976. Peugeot-Talbot has not used the name yet, but it is never too late, as recent use of 'Sunbeam' and 'Talbot' has proved. And, of course, Humber Road (like Daimler Road) is still there as a reminder of one of Coventry's great marques.

taken some class records at Brooklands with the Silver Hawk. In 1926, she and a team of drivers covered 24,140 km (15,000 miles) at nearly 90 km/h (56 mph) with a 3-litre Invicta at the Monza track near Milan in Italy, following that exercise with an 8047 km (5000 mile) run at more than 113 km/h (70 mph). For these performances Invicta won the RAC's Dewar Trophy for the motoring feat of the year.

In 1929 Violet Cordery and her sister Evelyn covered well over 48,000 km (30,000 miles) in 30,000 minutes with the 4.5-litre model, to win the trophy for Invicta again. There were more demonstrations, and there is no doubt that the Invicta established a special niche for itself.

William Watson was largely responsible for what was called the '100 mph' model, which was underslung at the rear. It gave this car a purposeful low look; with the 4.5-litre engine now standard, 100 mph (160 km/h) was quite feasible with a light body and with a little tuning. After all, this engine would soon power a Le Mans-winning Lagonda.

The Silver Hawk and the Invicta had always had a distinctive radiator cowl and bonnet shape. As adapted for its 1930 London show début, the new low-chassis Invicta was exciting and eye-catching: and it made the news in the following January when Donald Healey drove one in the Monte Carlo Rally to become only the second Briton in a British car to win the event. In 1932, Healey nearly repeated the achievement, but had to be content to finish second to Maurice Vasselle in a Hotchkiss. There were successes in the Alpine Trial and other events, but attempts to launch new models brought the company to its knees in 1933.

INVICTA Great Britain

Hugh Eric Orr-Ewing (father of Hamish Orr-Ewing, interim Chairman of the new 1984 Jaguar holding company) and N. C. Macklin (father of racing driver Lance Macklin) used their middle names for the light cars they made in a corner of the Handley Page aircraft factory immediately after the First World War. Their Eric Campbell cars had 1.5-litre Coventry Simplex engines, which were forerunners of the Coventry Climax, and did well in sporting events, but soon the partnership broke up.

Macklin retained the right to make Silver Hawk competition cars, along similar lines to the Eric Campbell, near his Surrey home. However, that plan failed, too, and the family went to live in Monte Carlo.

Back in Britain in 1925, Macklin was shown one of the rare and exotic American Doble steam cars owned by a neighbour, who commented how easy it would be to forget how to change gear. Macklin took it as a challenge to make his next car flexible enough to run most of the time in top gear. The result was the Invicta.

The first phase of Invicta manufacture, from 1925 at Cobham, Surrey, saw the 2.5-litre six-cylinder overhead-valve Meadows engine acquire more and more low-speed torque as it went up to 3 and then 4.5 litres. It was also marked by a series of performance demonstrations by Violet Cordery, who had already

The second phase of Invicta, from 1933 until the Second World War, saw the assembly of a few cars in the premises of the service garage in Flood Street, Chelsea, in London, while Macklin created yet another new marque (his fourth), the Railton. This retained the top gear acceleration for which the Invicta had become renowned, but was in reality a Hudson beneath the riveted bonnet and the typically British styling. In 1938, several baby Railtons were made and these were like 'toy' Invictas on Standard 10 chassis. When war came, Macklin was working on marine projects. Watson worked with W. O. Bentley on the postwar Lagonda and was responsible, too, for the third and final Invicta phase. This lasted briefly, as the Black Prince, with its twin overhead-camshaft 3-litre Meadows engine, a totally untried Brockhouse automatic transmission, and independent suspension all round (which was by then a Lagonda feature). By the time the goodwill had been bought by AFN in February 1950, (Sir) Noel Macklin was no longer alive. His son, Lance, was more of a salesman and went to work for Facel-Vega in France.

There have been several users of the Invicta name. In the 1980s, a company in Plymouth, Devon, was experimenting with a mid-engined Jaguar-powered 'Invicta' sports car, the Tredecim, which bore a resemblance to Jaguar's XJ13 project.

ISOTTA FRASCHINI Italy

The first vehicles of Cesare Isotta and the Fraschini brothers, Vincenzo and Oreste, were derived from imported cars and ideas: mostly Renault, Mors and Mercedes. From the beginning of the century the company grew quickly and, in 1905, moved into a full-sized factory in Milan's Via Monterosa.

Two of Italy's top engineers, Giustino Cattaneo and Antonio Chiribiri, joined the company and the Isotta Fraschini was soon second only to FIAT, with a big sales force in the United States. When financial problems arose, Lorraine-Dietrich took over; but the partnership did not work out and the Italian company was soon free again to make cars and buses.

Four-wheel braking was an early feature and the marque was successful in racing on both sides of the Atlantic; 1908 was a special year, with wins by Lewis Strang at Briarcliff and elsewhere, and by Vincenzo Trucco in the Targa Florio.

After spending the First World War on military work, including magnificent marine and aero engines, Cattaneo introduced the classic Tipo B 5.9-litre straight-8 in 1919. This fine car was very expensive and luxurious, but not especially fast until the sporting 7.4-litre came along in the mid-1920s. For a while it sold well abroad – especially to Hollywood stars such as Rudolph Valentino. The newspaper baron William Randolph Hearst bought one, for it was as exotic as any

car on the road, when one of the great Italian or American coachbuilders had added his touch (the Duesenberg J was not yet on offer).

Italian government intervention put a stop to a rescue plan by Ford in the early 1930s. Cattaneo left and new management from Caproni turned the emphasis towards commercial vehicles.

In 1947–9, several examples of the Monterosa, a completely new rear-engined luxury car designed by Fabio Rapi (who had worked with Cattaneo), made their appearance. The rear-mounted V8 engine and long sloping tail were reminiscent of the big Tatras. The company was closed down in 1949, although the great name of Isotta Fraschini was subsequently used by a marine engine business.

ABOVE RIGHT *Elegant example of a Type 8 Isotta Fraschini with Fleetwood coachwork. This one is dated 1924, and was made for the actor Rudolph Valentino.*

JAGUAR Great Britain

Jaguar's recovery and return to private ownership between 1980 and 1984 was a modern success story of British industry. Jaguar under BL had been heading for closure, if not extinction, until Sir Michael Edwardes, then head of British Leyland, allowed the Jaguar and Daimler marques a new autonomy. In 1980 he approved the setting up of a company called Jaguar Cars Ltd (for the first time since 1972) and appointed John Egan to the task of restoring morale and markets. Just over four years later Jaguar was, once again, being quoted on the London Stock Exchange.

One man to whom these events brought particular satisfaction was Sir William Lyons, FRSA, RDI, D. Tech – the much-more-than-honorary Jaguar president, without whom there would have been no company to rescue.

Born in Blackpool, Lancashire, on 4 September 1901, William Lyons had ducked out of his apprenticeship at Crossley in Manchester and was a junior car salesman in his home town when, in the summer of 1921, some new residents moved in, just across the road from his parents' home. A wealthy coal merchant

from Stockport was retiring to the seaside but, somewhat to his displeasure, his 28-year-old son who made motorcycle sidecars had decided to come along, too. Very soon Lyons, a keen (and courting) motorcyclist, began to notice these streamlined, polished alloy sidecars being fitted and driven proudly away from his neighbour's garage by other young enthusiasts. They were a bit expensive, but he bought one himself. The sidecars were called Swallow, and the former warrant officer who made them was William Walmsley.

William Lyons had already decided to create a business of his own. Up to that point he had not made up his mind exactly what form that business might take. He had been thinking of making a modern gramophone but then he saw the Swallow. He liked the product and could see ways of making it more cheaply and in larger quantities without sacrificing its appeal.

Almost reluctantly, Walmsley agreed to go into partnership with Lyons. Their fathers guaranteed them for £500 each at the bank and they were in business early in 1922. On 4 September that year, the day Lyons came of age, the partnership became official by the formation of the Swallow Sidecar Company.

Expansion took place rapidly and in 1927 the first Swallow two-seater car bodies were being built on

Morris Cowley and Austin Seven chassis: the idea was to satisfy the market for an individual form of transport at low cost. Lyons showed his Austin Seven to Henlys, the London dealers, who ordered 500 Swallows – provided a saloon was added to the range. This happened in 1928, and in that November the Swallow Sidecar & Coachbuilding Company moved out of Blackpool because it needed bigger premises. Coventry was chosen as it was near the heart of the motor industry, and there was a cheap old munitions factory there, empty and ready to be leased.

In October 1929, the month of the Wall Street Crash, Swallow took a stand at the London motor show, displaying low-roofed, high-bonneted saloons on FIAT, Standard and Swift chassis. Two years later came the first SS, a long, low coupé built on a modified Standard chassis. The SS marque established a name for its looks and good value, enabling it to secure a strong foothold while less purposeful enterprises struggled for survival.

Walmsley left the business in the winter of 1934–5 and from then on Lyons was master. Lyons's first action was to establish an engineering department under 32-year-old William Heynes who arrived from Humber. Development of Standard's engine by independent consultant Harry Weslake was well under way, and Lyons's ideas on styling were taking a positive form. In September 1935 the first prototype overhead-valve 2.7-litre six-cylinder four-door saloon was unveiled. Its price – £385 complete – was little more than one-third of a 3.7-litre Bentley chassis alone. The SS Jaguar (as it was called) did not pretend to be a Bentley in every way, but its looks and its performance bore a certain similarity to some eyes.

Almost overshadowed by the saloon, the £395 SS Jaguar 100 two-seater sports car was launched simultaneously. Up to that time the SS had developed a reputation for speedy looks that could not be translated into action. Best performance in the 1936 Alpine Trial by Tom and Elsie Wisdom in one of these cars gave the new SS Jaguar a sporting image from the very start and more wins soon followed.

The Swallow sidecar business continued up to and during the Second World War but it was sold off afterwards. The car-making side, SS Cars Ltd, was renamed Jaguar Cars Ltd in 1945. In 1948 a modernized version of the saloon, the Mark V, was introduced. It had a new chassis with Citroën-inspired torsion-bar independent front suspension developed by former 'Bentley Boy' Walter Hassan, who had joined Heynes's small team in 1938. That chassis was to be the basic structure for a new series of Jaguar saloons starting in 1950 with the Mark VII, powered by a brand-new twin overhead-camshaft six-cylinder high-performance engine: the legendary XK unit, which would still be in production for saloons, limousines and military vehicles in the late 1980s.

The Jaguar XK engine, produced by the team of

The two-seater E-type roadster and fixed-head coupé models made their sensational début at the 1961 Geneva motor show. Their shape and general structure were race-bred, as were all-round disc brakes – a feature that had helped Jaguar gain four of its five Le Mans victories – yet they were as docile to drive as they were dramatic to the eye. Both these cars were provided by Will Athawes.

HIGHLIGHTS

1901: William Lyons born in Blackpool on 4 September.

1920: William Walmsley makes first Swallow sidecars in Stockport.

1921: Walmsley moves to Blackpool and sells sidecar to Lyons.

1922: Lyons and Walmsley become partners in Swallow Sidecar Company.

1927: Swallow Sidecar and Coachbuilding Co. makes first special bodies for popular cars.

1928: Swallow moves from Blackpool to Coventry.

1931: First SS car announced.

1935: First SS Jaguar announced.

1945: Company becomes Jaguar Cars Ltd.

1951: First of five Jaguar Le Mans victories.

1952: First race wins with Dunlop disc brakes. XK 120 coupé averages over 160 km/h (100 mph) for a whole week.

1956: Jaguar wins the two great classics – the Monte Carlo Rally and Le Mans 24-Hours race. William Lyons knighted.

1960: Jaguar acquires Daimler for expansion and diversification.

1966: Jaguar-Daimler combines with BMC to form BMH.

1968: XJ6 announced; British Leyland formed.

1972: Sir William Lyons retires.

1975: British Leyland centralized and nationalized.

1980: Jaguar Cars Ltd re-established under John Egan.

1984: Independence restored; record production year.

1985: Death of Sir William Lyons, 8 February.

Heynes, Hassan and chief designer Claude Baily, has been the heart of the Jaguar success story. It was first used in the XK 120 sports car, styled by Lyons and produced at short notice for the first postwar London motor show, in October 1948. The show car was not in fact fitted with a working engine; but in the following spring it was demonstrated at 213.4 km/h (132.6 mph) on a specially closed section of the Ostend–Brussels motorway. Soon afterwards the XK 120, although intended as a touring sports car, won the first Silverstone production car race and the seeds were sown.

International motoring competitions were properly under way by the 1950s, but foreign teams were winning all the main events. Lyons always said he would rather not compete than compete poorly, but a tentative run with near-standard cars at Le Mans in 1950 convinced Bill Heynes and Raymond England, the company's new service manager, that a Jaguar could win. Lyons was persuaded and in 1951 the new XK 120C ('competition' model) did win Le Mans at the first attempt. The C-type and its successor the D-type provided Jaguar with a total of five victories in that 24-hour race for which they were designed – plus numerous other successes, despite being quite unsuitable for some circuits.

Racing provided prestige for the Jaguar, which thrived on the exports it needed (mostly to the United States) to expand as Lyons wanted. The roadgoing Jaguars proved fine rally winners, too. And, when touring car racing became popular, Jaguar immediately dominated it, capitulating only to the great Ford onslaught of the 1960s. The outstanding touring car was the 3.8-litre Mark 2, a high-performance development from Jaguar's first postwar compact, the 1955 2.4 saloon. The Mark 2 was well-suited to high-speed

BELOW *1981 Jaguar XJ12 HE, featuring the world's only volume-production 12-cylinder automotive engine. Still going strong in the year of the motor car's centenary, this model offered an unrivalled combination of quietness, refinement and performance. 'A special kind of motoring which no other car in the world can offer' was once a Jaguar slogan; it would be equally appropriate today. In the mid-1980s, Jaguar and Daimler cars were enjoying a higher sales rate than ever before.*

rallies such as the Alpine and the Tour de France: its last major accolade came at the end of 1963 when Peter Nöcker of Germany was declared first European touring car champion. (Twenty-one years later, Tom Walkinshaw was to repeat that achievement, driving an XJ-S.)

In 1961 came two significant new models: the classic E-type (one of Lyons's most inspired cars) and the Mark X, which would become the basis, much later, for a new Daimler limousine. This was a time for acquisition; Lyons bought Daimler from BSA in 1960, Guy Motors of Wolverhampton in 1961, and Coventry Climax Engines in 1963 – moves that made the Jaguar Group one of the strongest in terms of specialist engineering knowledge. The ultimate expression of this expertise was the Jaguar XJ6 saloon, launched in 1968 and, with relatively minor changes, still being produced and praised in the mid-1980s.

In the meantime, however, Sir William Lyons had merged his company with the British Motor Corporation, in a deal arranged personally between him and Sir George Harriman. Within two years, however, British Motor Holdings was the underdog in the formation of British Leyland.

In 1971, Jaguar's new 5.3-litre engine (the world's only volume-production overhead-camshaft V12) was introduced and in 1972, after half a century at the helm, Sir William retired, having appointed former racing chief Raymond ('Lofty') England as chairman in his place. Before long, however, Jaguar Cars Ltd ceased to exist as an entity. Raymond England retired under pressure in 1974 and the nationalization of British Leyland followed.

It was to take more than five years for Jaguar (with Daimler) to emerge from this position and become, once again, one of the world's finest cars – as well as the most refined. Sales were again at such record levels that the company, through its US associates and the Robert Tullius Group 44 Racing Team, even permitted itself the luxury of a return to Le Mans in 1984. The car involved was the specially built V12 XJR-5, a reminder of the Coventry-built mid-engined XJ13 designed for Le Mans 20 years earlier but never raced. Although the 'American' Jaguar did not win, it did go well and the starved fans loved it: but there were few illusions. Having made this comeback, everyone at Jaguar realized that, once at the top, there are only two ways to go. All-time record production and sales figures for 1984, the year of Jaguar's return to independence, indicated a determination to succeed.

JENSEN Great Britain

Patrick Motors Ltd was, very nearly, named Patrick Jensen; for Joseph Patrick used the expertise of Alan and Richard Jensen to start up in coachbuilding in order to augment the Patrick garage business (still a family concern today). The Jensens had already created neat two-seater bodywork on an Austin Seven and this had led to the prototype Avon Standard Special. Avon of Warwick and, from 1931, Patrick of Birmingham, carried on coachbuilding – but without the Jensens, who had been asked to leave the Patrick board once their takeover hopes were known.

William James Smith, a coachbuilder of Carter's Green, West Bromwich, was the Jensens' next port of call. Old-fashioned but reputable (for the quality of its truck and van bodies), W. J. Smith was soon taken over by the brothers, very much in the way they wanted.

Alan Jensen kept the commercial vehicle side going while Richard instigated a car body section, and in 1934 Jensen Motors Ltd was formed. By then, the Jensen name was becoming quite well known, largely through an order from actor Clark Gable for a Jensen tourer body on a Ford V8 chassis. It was a good-looking machine and more were made for Bristol Street Motors, the well-known Birmingham Ford dealers.

As William Lyons had done several years earlier, the Jensens began ordering special chassis, to suit the lines of the bodies they wanted to make: as opposed to fitting up other manufacturers' existing chassis. The result was the first true Jensen car, the long and graceful S type (saloon or tourer) of 1936.

Some early Jensens were powered by Ford V8 and Lincoln V12 engines. However, the definitive prewar Jensen was the classically styled 4.2-litre straight-8 Nash-engined model.

The forward-control JNSN, a truck/van, and the Invicta Black Prince bodywork figured among the company's immediate postwar activities. In addition there was the new Jensen PW series, which Austin 'borrowed' to create the Sheerline. By way of apology (having first said he would put Jensen out of business), Leonard Lord volunteered to supply Austin's 4-litre power unit to replace Jensen's troublesome new Meadows engine!

The Austin relationship became closer when Jensen's Eric Neale came up with the A40 Sports body design; it was not only accepted but Jensen got the job of producing it. The contemporary Jensen Interceptor was, in effect, a scaled-up version of this design. In 1952 Jensen made a prototype two-seater, but it was not ready in time for that year's motor show. That was where Sir Leonard Lord was won over by the Healey 100 which, in due course, Jensen had the consolation of bodying.

A year later, in 1953, the attractive Jensen 541 coupé made its bow. It still had a large proportion of Austin components but the handsome and well-made glass-fibre body was entirely original and largely the work of Eric Neale and Richard Jensen. In 1956 it became the first four-seater to have Dunlop's disc brake system fitted all round, beating Jaguar by several months (even though the Coventry firm had been racing with these brakes for five seasons).

Now in bigger premises at Kelvin Way, West Bromwich, the company was sold to the Norcros finance group, relieving the Jensens of some of the responsibility as they got older.

In 1962, the once-pretty 541 was restyled as the somewhat ungainly C-V8. Specifications including a 5.9- (later 6.2-) litre Chrysler engine made it the fastest Jensen ever. The styling problem was later

BELOW *The Jensen 541 of 1956 was Britain's first four-seater saloon to be fitted with disc brakes all round, and the finish on its attractive glass-fibre bodywork was to a high standard.*

RIGHT *Reintroduced on a small scale in the early 1980s, the impressive Jensen Interceptor had been originally announced in 1966. The FF version represented an important step in the development of four-wheel drive for production cars. Styling was by Vignale.*

RIGHT *After the war, despite two outstanding new cars which proved themselves in racing and rallying – the Javelin and the Jupiter (seen here) – Jowett could never get out of the vicious circle of those austere times. It was not able to export enough cars to qualify for a sufficient allocation from the authorities of the steel it needed to produce more of them. Less than 1000 Jupiters had been built by 1954 when the main factory in Bradford began producing International Harvester tractors.*

rectified professionally by Vignale of Italy, and the new Chrysler-powered Interceptor was an impressive débutante at the London motor show in 1966. The FF version, with Ferguson four-wheel drive and Dunlop Maxaret anti-lock braking, deserved all the accolades it received. But it could not stem the tide as the costs of meeting US regulations and of further developments rose, especially after Austin-Healey production ceased, and that income was lost.

Norwegian-born, American-based Kjell Qvale was one of several would-be rescuers. For a time, his Jensen-Healey (a cheaper sports car, conceived by Donald Healey and his sons) staved off the receiver, but that was only from 1972 to 1976. Jensen closed down, but it did not die, and a new enterprise reintroduced Interceptor production on a very small scale in the early 1980s.

Bradford. This also provided the basis for the 1950 prototype of a Danish 'people's car', the Sommer S-1, which looked like a miniature Armstrong Siddeley Hurricane but did not come to anything.

It was the very bold, advanced Javelin that took Jowett into uncharted territory. First seen in 1946, it had been conceived as early as 1942, when a young draughtsman, Gerald Palmer, had moved north to Bradford and begun working on a light four-door family saloon. The production Javelin had a powerful flat-4 1.5-litre engine made of die-cast aluminium, with wet cast-iron liners. It had independent front suspension, rack and pinion steering and a streamlined body. It won its class in the 1949 Belgian 24-hour race and several other events. Although the Javelin's niggling problems were, largely, cured in the end this outstanding car ultimately failed because the body supplier, Briggs, had had to stop manufacture while Jowett resolved its own difficulties. By the time Jowett wanted more bodies, Ford had bought Briggs which, in any case, was too big to cater for the stop–go production of Jowett.

In 1950 there was a sports car, too: the Jowett Jupiter, which had the basic Javelin mechanical components, and a sturdy tubular chassis designed by Robert Eberan-Eberhorst at ERA in Dunstable. The Jupiter did well in its class at Le Mans and in the Monte Carlo Rally, and a lightweight version appeared in 1953; but the brave little company had to close down shortly afterwards, after nearly half a century of very positive car making.

JOWETT Great Britain

The Jowett publicists loved to put over a cosily down-market image in their motor show advertisements of the 1930s, and there was certainly a kind of coy homeliness about the little Yorkshire cars that seemed to make friends everywhere.

From 1906, Jowett made utilitarian twin-cylinder machines for private and commercial use. A flat-4 was used for the Hillman Minx-style Ten of 1936, but the two-cylinder models were continued as the practical postwar vans and station wagon models known as the

LAGONDA Great Britain

Although its character has changed several times over the years, the Lagonda car has always been recognizably British. Its originator, however, was an American, Wilbur Gunn, and the name he chose for the products of his Staines, Middlesex, factory was based upon the Shawnee Indian term for his local river in Ohio.

The first Lagonda tricycles and motorcycles were made from around the turn of the century. Cars came next and these proved themselves in reliability trials. As with so many small companies, Lagonda existed on

BELOW *Earlier Lagondas were elegant, if somewhat spartan. This 1929 3-litre was provided by the Nigel Dawes Collection.*

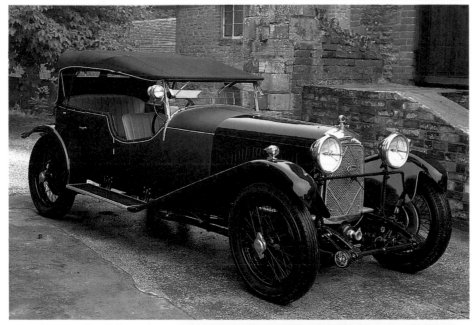

RIGHT *The 4.5-litre LG6 and V12 of the late 1930s filled a role comparable to that of the modern Lagonda: very stylish and very expensive, but worth it for those who wanted something different from a Rolls-Royce. This fine LG6 is in The Patrick Collection.*

a financial knife edge, both before and after its founder became ill and died in 1920, at the age of 61.

The cars became more sporting during the 1920s and, from 1928, Lagondas raced regularly at Le Mans. From 1933 the Meadows 4.5-litre six-cylinder engine, basically the unit made previously for Invicta, put the Lagonda M45 firmly into the top performance bracket; in effect it became the natural successor to the 'pre-Rolls' Bentley. This image was enhanced in 1935 when a 4.5-litre Lagonda M45 Rapide, prepared by Messrs Fox and Nicholl, and driven by Luis Fontes and John Hindmarsh, broke Alfa Romeo's four years of domination at Le Mans.

Victory at Le Mans was not enough to keep Lagonda in business, however, and from 1935 the company was pointed in a different direction by a new head, Alan Good. With W. O. Bentley in charge of design, Lagonda made substantial improvements to the overhead-valve 4.5-litre Meadows engine and introduced a magnificent V12 engine of similar capacity. The Lagondas of the late 1930s were high-speed touring cars of considerable elegance and only the coming of the Second World War stunted their progress. However, in 1939 two V12-engined Lagonda sports cars took part successfully at Le Mans, finishing third and fourth, running well within their capacity.

During the 1940s, Bentley, and a team including Donald Bastow and former Invicta man William Watson, designed a completely new Lagonda with 2.6-litre twin overhead-camshaft six-cylinder engine and independent suspension all round. Several prototypes had been made by 1947, when David Brown acquired Lagonda shortly after taking over Aston Martin. The new 2.6-litre Lagonda was put into limited production (although not with a Cotal gearbox as intended) and its 'Bentley' engine was soon adopted for the Aston Martin DB2. From 1953 to 1957 the same chassis was used for a new model, the 3-litre, with the engine capacity increased and a more modern, if less distinctive, body style.

Brown used the Lagonda name for an unsuccessful 1950s sports-racing car, the V12, and in 1961 for a few examples of a revived Rapide. The latter was a 4-litre luxury saloon with de Dion rear suspension; it was based on the DB4 but never developed properly for series production.

Sir David Brown's last Lagonda was, in effect, a four-door Aston Martin DBS V8. A few replicas were made under the new management: Brown sold Aston Martin and Lagonda in 1972. The marque very nearly ceased to exist soon afterwards when the fuel crisis changed the face of motoring.

DBS stylist William Towns was also responsible for the spectacular shape of the new (1977) model, which was still one of the world's most cyc-catching cars when displayed at the 1984 British motor show as a long-wheelbase Lagonda Limousine: a fully equipped supercar in the £100,000 class, from a company that still needed to practise internal frugality to stay in business.

LAMBORGHINI Italy

BELOW *Still the world's way-out production car, the Lamborghini Countach was introduced back in 1971.*

BOTTOM *The Miura: a transverse engine behind the seats permitted styling freedom. Provided by Michael Gertner.*

With a fortune amassed through manufacturing tractors (and central heating and air-conditioning equipment), Ferruccio Lamborghini sought to make a better grand touring car than any type he had ever owned – including Ferrari and Maserati. He built a new factory for the project at Sant'Agata Bolognese near Modena, and among his early recruits were the young engineers Giampaolo Dallara, from Ferrari, and Paolo Stanzani.

The first Lamborghini, the 350GTV, was displayed at the 1963 Geneva motor show, proudly wearing the now famous bull emblem. It had a 3.5-litre four-camshaft V12 engine and independent suspension all round, and was developed at Cento, Lamborghini's tractor works, before completion of the Sant' Agata factory. The unusual two-seater coupé body was by Scaglione, but for series production the coachwork was made by Touring of Milan and there were Spider and Zagato coupé alternatives.

In 1966, the engine was enlarged to 3.9 litres for the 400GT 2+2: the last production model before Carrozzeria Touring closed. A more powerful version of this engine was placed crosswise behind the two seats of a new coupé of classic beauty which also made its début in 1966. This magnificent Bertone-styled masterpiece was called the Miura and, without doubt, it must go down as the most aesthetically pleasing machine in Lamborghini history.

Other exciting designs were to follow, including the unusual Espada. However the most famous was the one known as the Countach, which is the equivalent (in its Piedmontese pronunciation) of 'Phew!'. Its amazingly low bodywork did not share the simple and delightful curves of the Miura and vision rearward was strictly limited, but as an exercise in spectacular design it stood the test of time and it was still being made in the mid-1980s, having been launched in 1971. The latest 5.2-litre four-valve V12 engine, longitudinally mounted in the rear, was said to provide a maximum speed approaching 300 km/h (190 mph): yet neither this nor any other Lamborghini was ever developed for racing, unlike most supercar marques.

Ferruccio Lamborghini's personal commitment to the company began to falter when a large order for tractors was withdrawn following a change of power in Bolivia in the early 1970s. Over a two-year period he sold his shares in the car factory, and before long in all his other businesses, and retired to Umbria and winegrowing.

There was one bright hope in the mid-1970s, when it seemed that Lamborghini might make the BMW M1 coupé; but that contract was cancelled and, for a brief period, Lamborghini came under state control. Dallara had already left and Giulio Alfieri came from Maserati to become technical chief of Nuova Lamborghini which, in May 1981, assumed private status as part of the Patrick Mimram group.

The Countach was joined in 1982 by the Jalpa, a smaller and more orthodox Bertone-styled coupé; and at Lamborghini there was also considerable mid-1980s activity in high-speed cross-country vehicles and marine engines.

LANCHESTER Great Britain

Frederick Lanchester, a man of genius in several fields, accomplished in Britain what Carl Benz had done in Germany ten years earlier: he built his country's first truly original, fully engineered vehicle worthy of the (retrospective) name of motor car.

In 1893 Lanchester made a single-cylinder engine for his employers, the Forward Gas Engine Co. of Birmingham, and, with help from his brothers George and Frank, constructed a flat-bottomed craft which would (in 1894) become the first all-British motorboat. This was spare-time work, often done on Sundays, and the brothers became known as the 'Unholy Trinity' because of it. At this stage Lanchester was also studying the theory of powered flight, and he was to present erudite and prophetic papers on the subject.

The Lanchester car of 1895 was a design exercise and it ran on the road (illegally, of course) early in 1896. It had a single-cylinder engine but this was soon replaced by a twin; both units were air-cooled. This car was preserved, only to be destroyed in the air raids on Coventry in the Second World War. The second, 1897, Lanchester is in the Science Museum, London. One of its features was the use of two contra-rotating crankshafts and flywheels to give smoothness of running. It also had mechanically operated inlet valves, modern ignition and carburation, epicyclic gears, worm drive and tangent-spoked wire wheels fitted with pneumatic tyres.

In 1899 the Lanchester Engine Company was formed in Birmingham and by 1901 Lanchester cars were being produced for sale. The layout was designed for stability, with all passengers seated well within the wheelbase. When a vertical four-cylinder engine appeared it was placed between driver and front passenger; and the unit construction of the chassis

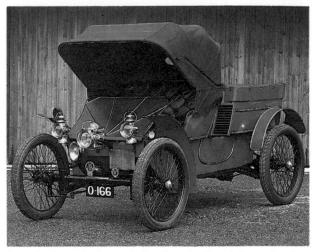

foreshadowed that of the Lancia Lambda and other outstanding cars. This layout was retained for many years and was seen as increasingly nonconformist when long bonnets became fashionable for Rolls-Royces and other high-quality cars.

The early production cars were the creations of Frederick Lanchester, while his brother George was in effect works manager, as well as being a particularly intrepid motorist. Besides taking part in competitions himself, George Lanchester was, from 1901, an active founder-member of the Midland Automobile Club. (He was one of the creators of the famous hill-climb course at Shelsley Walsh, near Tenbury Wells, which has been in continuous use since 1905 and is therefore the venue for the world's longest-running speed event.)

Unfortunately Frederick Lanchester could not stand the interference of his fellow-directors. In 1909 he reduced his involvement to that of consultant to the company that bore his name – and to other companies, notably Daimler whose eternal gratitude he earned when he resolved the early development problems with the Knight sleeve-valve engine. At that stage there was, however, no other connection between the Daimler and Lanchester companies.

George Lanchester became the technical chief, and at first he had to accede to boardroom pressure. As the *Automobile Engineer* said in 1913, it was a pity that the company did not seem able 'to educate its customers to an appreciation of Lanchester Principles' – a comment made following a company edict that stated that there must be a new model with a conventional long bonnet. There were other concessions to orthodoxy, including a return from overhead to side valves in the 1914 Lanchester Sporting Forty. Only six were made, to George Lanchester's lasting glee, for the First World War then intervened. After several busy years of munitions work he was able to develop the Lanchester Forty into a car of Rolls-Royce quality in every way, except for a complex system of geared auxiliary drives which was somewhat noisy on tick over. The 6.2-litre six-cylinder overhead-camshaft engine could propel even the heavier-bodied luxury models at well over 120 km/h (75 mph).

BELOW *1930 Straight 8 Lanchester, a fine product of a company about to be swallowed up by BSA-Daimler. Provided by Stuart Best.*

LEFT *The most original of Britain's early production cars was the Lanchester, which bristled with innovation. This 1901 model had an integral chassis and a beautifully balanced air-cooled twin-cylinder engine.*

HIGHLIGHTS

1868: Frederick William Lanchester born.

1889: Lanchester joins Forward Gas Engine Company.

1895: First Lanchester car built and car-making syndicate formed.

1899: Lanchester Engine Company formed.

1900: First production models incorporating many unique features.

1904: Reconstruction of finances to form Lanchester Motor Co. Ltd.

1909: Frederick Lanchester resigns but remains consultant, to be succeeded by brother George.

1919: Lanchester Forty overhead-camshaft model introduced.

1928: Lanchester Straight 8 introduced.

1931: Takeover by BSA-Daimler.

1946: Death of Dr Frederick Lanchester.

1956: Lanchester marque dropped by Daimler.

1960: Lanchester College of Technology opens in Coventry.

ABOVE *Originally created for tyre testing at Brooklands by Lionel Rapson, this single-seat Lanchester Forty lapped the Surrey track at nearly 175 km/h (110 mph) in 1926 driven by the man in this picture – the legendary Parry Thomas.*

RIGHT *A miniature Daimler since the 1930s, the proud Lanchester marque came to an end in 1956 with this neat Sprite saloon, fitted with the promising Hobbs automatic gearbox. This survivor from the handful ever completed is owned by John Ridley.*

George Lanchester was allowed to retain the now traditional cantilever springs, but only at the rear. The company always had its own coachbuilding department as the brothers preferred to design complete cars. At the first postwar motor show, in 1919, the overhead-camshaft Lanchester Forty made its début in the form of an unusual, rounded two-door saloon with an interior of black leather surrounded by silver fittings, silk blinds and even inlaid marquetry. George Lanchester must have known he had overdone it, but was never ashamed to repeat what King George V observed to him on the stand: 'Very fine – but more suited to a prostitute than a prince, don't you think?' In fact, most Lanchesters were the epitome of good taste and the Duke of York (later King George VI) was to become a devotee. George's younger brother Frank had a natural charm which helped sell Lanchester cars by the fleet to a number of royal households in other countries.

From 1923 a smaller Lanchester, the Twenty-One, supplemented the magnificent Forty. Several cars were adapted for racing and record breaking at Brooklands, where they showed great stamina over long distances.

The last of the great 'independent' Lanchesters was the 4.4-litre overhead-camshaft Straight 8 of 1928: entirely elegant but with a performance to overcome its considerable weight, and the excellent ride and handling of its forebears.

In 1931, George Lanchester was already well under way with a new medium-priced chassis design, the 2.5-litre six-cylinder 15/18, when, as the Depression deepened, the Lanchester Motor Company's assets were acquired by BSA, one of its great rivals and proprietors of Coventry Daimler. Lanchester worked for a while with Laurence Pomeroy, his opposite number at Daimler, to produce this car with the new Daimler fluid flywheel transmission. This enabled it to

THP 476

perform with grace at the lowest possible speed and thus win the first-ever RAC Rally in March 1932 on the basis of its capability in the slow running test.

Soon afterwards George Lanchester joined Alvis to develop military vehicles and the Lanchester marque became an often poor relation of Daimler – although it did avoid having to have a sleeve-valve engine. The Duke of York and an Indian potentate stayed loyal, forcing Daimler to make several of its luxury models as Lanchesters, but it did not stop a general loss of pride for the great marque.

The pretty little Lanchester Tens of the 1940s came at a time when small luxury saloons seemed to have a reasonable market potential, but the face of motoring was changing too rapidly for these overweight, underpowered machines to be a success.

The 1950 2-litre four-cylinder Fourteen (later called the Leda) was a most attractive medium-sized saloon, but the definitive six-cylinder version became the Daimler Conquest and immediately overshadowed it. A coachbuilt version remained a prototype.

There was a final fling in 1954 when the Lanchester Sprite created much motor show interest – not for its dumpy four-door body, but for its use of the Hobbs fully automatic gearbox, the first such application in a small car. Restyling for 1955 was not a remedy and only a handful of these last Lanchesters appeared. The marque ceased to exist after 1956. When Jaguar acquired Daimler four years later, most Sprites had either been destroyed or converted into pick-ups for ignominious tasks around the works.

Coventry's Lanchester Polytechnic is a reminder of what should be one of Britain's proudest names. It is unlikely, however, that any small Jaguar will be called a Lanchester. The marque was misused for far too long by Daimler, which is the main reason why the Lanchester name is not often given its deserved place among the finest cars of its era.

LANCIA Italy

CENTRE RIGHT *Famed for its advanced design, the V4 Lambda brought the Lancia marque world renown. This 1922 tourer was provided by Gerald Batt.*

Success in racing and rallying, plus fresh thinking in road-car design: these are the hallmarks of the great marque Lancia.

Vincenzo Lancia was almost certainly the fastest of all road racers when he drove for FIAT. He scored several fine victories, including the 1904 Coppa Florio, but more often trouble would intervene as he was poised to win. He took steps to start his own company, in association with Claudio Fogolin, in 1906, but a factory fire prevented the new Turin marque from appearing on the roads until 1908.

Light weight and the use of narrow-angle V engines were early Lancia characteristics. Most spectacular was the V12 6-litre prototype of 1919, but it was the 1921 Lambda that first marked Lancia for greatness.

Although the early Lancias were not designed to be particularly sporting, their many inventive features made them fast and outstanding to handle. Indeed,

there seems to be a certain parallel with Lanchester in this respect, although there was no actual connection. Both marques eschewed convention to follow purer engineering theories. This led both of them to pioneer unit construction, to place a wheel at each corner and to seat all passengers within the wheelbase. Frederick Lanchester put his engine between the front seats; Vincenzo Lancia did not need to do that because his engine was very short anyway: a V4 of 2.1 litres (later enlarged to 2.4 and 2.6 litres). The Lambda had grace and poise and simplicity, without the weird, stubby look that had put the uninitiated off buying the prewar Lanchesters.

Because of Lancia's own racing background, his cars were always drivers' cars and the Lambda was fitted with a very effective suspension system: independent at the front, by coil springs and telescopic dampers, and orthodox semi-elliptic springs and friction dampers at the rear. This brilliant design was continually updated during nearly a decade of manufacturing and its features were developed in each succeeding model.

The next big leap forward for Lancia was the 1936 Aprilia, a compact, smooth, four-door family saloon which made extensive use of aluminium and had independent suspension all round. Moreover, its price, as well as its design and specification, put it in a class of its own for value. In Britain in 1938, for example, at £330 it was cheaper than most Rileys and on a par with the Rover Fourteen.

The Aprilia was reintroduced after the Second World

War and over 30,000 had been made by the time the last one was built in autumn 1949. In the following spring came yet another superb new car, the 60-degree V6-engined Aurelia saloon. It was supplemented from 1951 by the Aurelia GT two-door coupé, a delight to the eye and the first of a long line of new-generation race and rally winners.

Vincenzo Lancia had died in 1937 and the Aurelia was largely the responsibility of his son, Gianni, together with the great Vittorio Jano who had done so much for Alfa Romeo, whence he had been eased out in the late 1930s; Alfa Romeo's loss was Lancia's gain. The

BELOW *The Aurelia B20 – introduced in 1950, and largely the work of Gianni Lancia and Vittorio Jano – is generally considered as the starting point for the modern Gran Turismo car.*

BOTTOM *The Stratos coupé was purpose-built for rallying. These two are owned by Ian Fraser (Car magazine) and Nick Mason (Morntane Engineering).*

Aurelia GT proved a race winner, not only in its class but in outright terms, taking first, second and third places in the 1952 Targa Florio. Lancia then gave Jano the go-ahead to develop a sports-racing car which won the Targa Florio and the Carrera Panamericana in Mexico the following year. In 1954 the Targa Florio was won yet again by Lancia, but the culminating achievement was to beat Ferrari in the Mille Miglia. The driver was the reigning world champion, Alberto Ascari Jr. In that year, too, the Aurelia GT scored its first big rally victories in the Monte Carlo and the Sestrière events. Jano's crowning glory was the 1954 V8 Lancia D50 Grand Prix car. Ascari won two races in

HIGHLIGHTS

1881: Vincenzo Lancia born, the son of a soup manufacturer.

1898: Lancia joins Ceirano as commercial apprentice.

1899: FIAT takes over Ceirano.

1900: At around this time Lancia becomes tester and race driver for FIAT.

1906: Lancia sets up his own car works in Turin.

1921: Announcement of unitary construction Lancia Lambda, with independent front suspension.

1936: Announcement of Lancia Aprilia.

1937: Death of Vincenzo Lancia.

1950: Lancia Aurelia introduced.

1951: Aurelia GT sets worldwide *gran turismo* fashion.

1954: Sports-racing car wins Mille Miglia; Grand Prix car introduced.

1955: Lancia passes its racing team to Ferrari.

1956: Juan Manuel Fangio is World Champion driving Lancia D50 as modified by Ferrari.

1960: Lancia Flavia introduced with front-wheel drive.

1969: FIAT buys Lancia company.

1974: Mid-engined Lancia Stratos rally car launched.

1983: Lancia wins Monte Carlo Rally for seventh time (beating Hotchkiss record of six victories); also Manufacturers' World Rally Championship for the fifth time.

ABOVE *In a sense replacing the FIAT 130 coupé (see page 79), the Lancia Gamma had a twin-cam flat-four 2.5-litre engine. This coupé from The Patrick Collection is shown at Kenilworth.*

ABOVE RIGHT *The Lancia Rally, winner of the 1983 World Rally Manufacturers' Championship. This Patrick Collection car is the rare road version.*

1955, but then he suffered a fatal accident (not in a Lancia) which put the organization into disarray. This, and financial problems, led to the sale of the racing assets to Ferrari and, ultimately, control by FIAT.

FIAT Topolino designer Franco Fessia was responsible for taking Lancia down the front-wheel-drive road, with an adaptation of his flat-4 Caproni, which was first seen in 1947, but was still an advanced car for the 1960s as the Lancia Flavia. Lancia's mainstream saloons have had front-wheel drive ever since.

The dramatic mid-engined Stratos of the 1970s, designed specifically for rallying, was followed by more roadgoing and competition coupés. The early 1980s saw Lancia excel in sports-car racing and rallying.

Indeed, the Lancia Rally was the last of the really effective two-wheel-drive rally cars. It managed to beat the Audi Quattro for the 1983 Manufacturers' Championship, and Walter Röhrl's victory in that year's Monte Carlo meant that Lancia had at last beaten the Hotchkiss record of six wins in the most famous rally of them all.

If the Lancia saloons seem more and more like FIATs, the competition models retain the special individuality which was the Lancia's original appeal. From 1979, Lancia and Saab were engaged in technical collaboration, and the outcome was the impressive 1985 Thema: a replacement for the Gamma, Lancia's highly individual businessman's express.

LEYLAND Great Britain/Australia

Parry Thomas at the wheel of one of Leyland's few production cars – potentially one of the finest vehicles of the 1920s, but only a small number was constructed.

Like Guy Motors of Wolverhampton, the Lancashire firm of Leyland Motors was, briefly, diverted from its bread-and-butter work of bus and truck production to make luxury cars.

Leyland's chief engineer, J. G. Parry Thomas, and his project engineer, Reid Railton, used torsion bars to assist the work of the springs of their massive chassis, which had a 7- (later 7.3-) litre straight-8 engine. The vast and handsome – although hardly beautiful – open touring car at the 1920 London motor show was priced at over £3000, making it the most expensive car on the British market.

Huge amounts were, inevitably, invested in this magnificent monster. In 1921 Thomas wrote to *The Autocar* (in reply to a number of readers who expressed views as to what was the best car) saying that the Leyland Eight could be compared only with a Rolls-Royce. Of his masters he said their intention was, 'to produce the most perfect car it is possible to design and manufacture'. He added that the car would not reach the public until 'next year'; 1922 did, in fact, see the Leyland Eight's last Olympia showing. By then Leyland's directors realized the postwar boom was over and they put a stop to production with fewer than 20 cars built. As a result Thomas left to live the life of a hermit at the Brooklands track, racing his Leyland-Thomas and other specials with great success.

No more Leyland cars were made in Britain, although the formation of British Leyland meant that there was a strong likelihood of the name being used again. As it was, by the time Lord Stokes (of Leyland) was out of office, with the nationalization of BL in 1975, the name Leyland Cars was in use.

Before then, in 1972, the corporation's Australian company had introduced the Leyland P76, a large car to compete with the bigger 'internationals', Ford and GM-Holden. As their predecessors had done 50 years before, the policy makers performed an about-face and the second true Leyland car was shelved. In fairness, it might be said that the trend towards smaller and more economical cars virtually coincided with the launching of the Australian car.

Because of what happened between the creation of BL by Sir Donald Stokes in 1968 and the beginning of its decentralization under Sir Michael Edwardes a decade later, the Leyland name as applied to cars will always be somewhat tainted; Parry Thomas's great white elephants are the honourable exceptions.

TB 9205

LINCOLN United States/Canada

Hardly had Henry and Wilfred Leland resigned from Cadillac when they were back in the car-making business, this time naming their product after the famous American president. Their first Lincoln V8 cars went on sale in 1921. It was not long, however, before Henry Ford – in search of a quality marque – took an interest. This was the sixth car company to call itself Lincoln, but the appeal for Ford was the knowledge that the Lelands had a fine reputation and that now (in 1922) they were having some trouble financing their new company's development. They did not stay for long after the Ford takeover, but left a legacy of fine engineering which Edsel Ford was to be responsible for developing.

Lincoln made its name initially with V8s; then, from 1932, came a mighty 7.2-litre V12 which seemed to fly in the face of the Depression. However, there was a huge void between its price and that of the newly introduced Ford V8. The answer was the Zephyr.

In 1934 (the year of the disastrous Chrysler–DeSoto Airflow) an attractive rear-engined prototype by the Briggs body company was shown at the World's Fair in Chicago. Its designer John Tjaarda adapted it, with the help of Ford's styling department, to become an orthodox but modern-looking car with a front-mounted

RIGHT *Announced in November 1935, the 4.4-litre Lincoln Zephyr was a successful exercise in modern styling and the world's first popular-priced V12-engined car. Provided by Fred Spong.*

BELOW *7.5-litre V8 Continental with Rolls-Royce overtones dates from 1974. Although it originated as a Lincoln luxury model range, 'Continental' is used as a marque name, too, as part of North America's complex approach to marketing.*

V12 engine based on the Ford V8. The appeal of a reasonably priced V12, plus superb styling (which looked right in all the places the Airflow had looked wrong) gave the Lincoln marque a passport which would last from November 1935 through to the 1940s.

The Lincoln was always the Presidential marque, however, and the company continued to produce top models. Another Lincoln line, from 1939 to 1948, and then again from 1956, was the Continental. This name was being maintained in the mid-1980s for a 5-litre V8 range of somewhat more compact dimensions than its predecessors, with the option of a smaller six. It was still also possible to buy a big town car with a separate chassis frame. Lincoln was still competing strongly with Cadillac in the state car stakes.

LOTUS Great Britain

The Austin Seven has inspired several great marques, including BMW, Jaguar and Lotus. Anthony Colin Bruce Chapman made his first Austin Seven-based trials special in the late 1940s while completing his engineering degree course. After a brief period in the Royal Air Force he returned to civilian life at the end of 1949, aged 21, to follow more gainful employment while still building specials.

Lotus Engineering was formed as a spare-time occupation in January 1952. The first production Lotus was actually the Mark 6 Chapman sports car. (The Mark 7 was to be the longest-lived development of Chapman's original theme of lightness and efficiency; it was still being made under licence as the Caterham Super Seven in the 1980s.)

The Mark 8 of 1954 was the first Lotus with an aerodynamic body. This was designed by Frank Costin, and he played a major role from that time. Sports-racing cars were the main product but the beautiful little Coventry Climax-engined glass-fibre Elite (or Mark 14) coupé, which stole the 1957 London show, was a pointer to a future of fascinating roadgoing GT models. At the same time, the first single-seater racing cars began to appear.

Success in Formula One racing came with the first rear-engined Lotus, the 1960 Mark 18. By that time Chapman had established a particular rapport with a previously unknown Scottish border farmer, James Clark, who would provide four years of domination for Lotus in Grand Prix racing: he took the World Drivers' and Manufacturers' Championships in 1963 and 1965, and only failed to do so in 1962 and 1964 because his Coventry Climax engines let him down at crucial moments.

In the 1960s Lotus and Ford cooperated in creating the Lotus-Cortina, with a twin-camshaft engine developed from a regular Ford unit by Harry Mundy shortly before he joined Jaguar. That engine was used in a new and very popular road sports two-seater, the Elan. Soon afterwards came the first mid-engined road car, the Europa, powered by a Renault engine.

After the arrival of the Ford-Cosworth V8 GP engine, Lotus was to win five more world crowns in 1968, 1970, 1972, 1973 and 1978. During the 1960s and 1970s there were innumerable 'firsts' for Lotus GP

RIGHT *Contrasting classics from the Chapman stable: braking for the Goodwood chicane during an early 1960s club race are a Lotus Elite coupé and a Lotus Seven.*

BELOW *Introduced in 1981, the turbocharged version of the futuristic mid-engined Lotus Esprit (shaped five years earlier by Giugiaro) developed 210 bhp.*

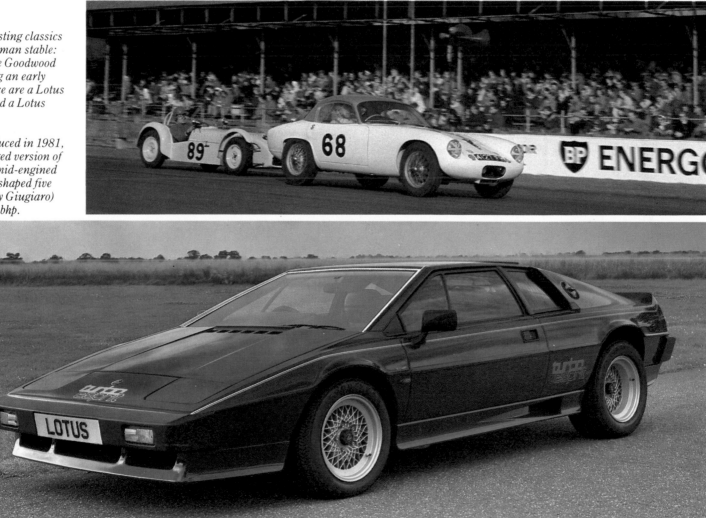

racing cars, including the use of gas turbine engines and monocoque construction, plus continual innovation in chassis design. Colin Chapman's genius kept him ahead of the opposition more often than not; his sudden death in 1982 came just as the company was beginning to win again after going through one of racing's inevitable lean periods.

Since 1975, the Lotus road cars have moved up a league with the Giugiaro-styled mid-engined Esprit and front-engined Eclat and Excel. The Norwich-based company faced the future squarely without its founder, under the solid technical leadership of Jaguar-trained Michael Kimberley. Lotus came to the 1984 British motor show full of exciting plans for the future, including a high-speed four-door limousine project, and looked set to maintain the sparkling image that Chapman had given it from the start.

MASERATI Italy

TOP RIGHT *The Giugiaro-styled Merak SS, introduced in 1975, had a new version of the V6 engine created by Maserati for its French masters, Citroën. Provided by The Patrick Collection.*

RIGHT *The magic of Juan Manuel Fangio and a Maserati 250F in full flight are captured in this French Grand Prix photo taken at Rouen-les-Essarts in 1957. He went on to win his fifth and final world title that year.*

In May 1975 it looked as if the Maserati would disappear for ever, for the famous company was put into liquidation. Shortly afterwards, in conjunction with Italian national interests, the expatriate Argentinian racing driver-turned-industrialist, Alejandro de Tomaso, took control and production of new Maserati models began again.

The start for Maserati coincided with the closure of Diatto, vehicle assemblers and constructors of Turin. The company's racing car development was undertaken by Alfieri Maserati at his sparkplug works in Bologna and, when Diatto was closing down, its 1.5-litre straight-8 racers became the first Maseratis. The name stepped into history when Maserati won his class in the 1926 Targa Florio with one of these cars.

There were six Maserati brothers, all of whom (like Alfieri) had been involved in cars, motorcycles and motor racing from an early age. Mario was an artist, Carlo became ill and died in 1910, and the other three – Bindo, Ettore and Ernesto – ran the company between them after Alfieri Maserati's untimely death in 1932.

Serious production of road cars never got under way during the 1930s when the Maserati marque built up a steady reputation as a race winner. Industrialist Adolfo Orsi put money into the company in 1937 and gave the brothers a ten-year consultancy contract; they left the Maserati works (now situated in Modena) in 1947 and returned home to Bologna to make OSCA sports cars.

Adolfo Orsi and his son Omer built up the Maserati business after the Second World War, but it was not until they brought in Gioacchino Colombo (of Alfa Romeo and Ferrari fame) to improve their six-cylinder racing car that Maserati hit the heights. The classic front-engined 250F Grand Prix car began winning at the start of the new 2.5-litre Formula One in 1954, and attained crowning glory for Juan Manuel Fangio by bringing him his fifth and final World Championship in ·1957.

In that year, however, the Maserati sports-racing car team was virtually wiped out by a series of accidents. The cost was enormous and Maserati gave up works participation. The association with racing was not lost, however, and Maserati's engineering chief Giulio Alfieri was responsible for a number of projects that produced solid victories, notably the 'birdcage' sports car – made up from a multitude of small-diameter tubes – which won the 1960 and 1961 Nürburgring 1000 km races, and the V12 3-litre engine which brought the British Cooper team its last

HIGHLIGHTS

1924: Alfieri Maserati's factory contracted to build a Grand Prix car for Diatto.

1926: Before Diatto closure, Maserati takes over the design. Alfieri Maserati wins class in Targa Florio.

1930: Borzacchini wins Tripoli GP in Maserati.

1937: Adolfo Orsi takes over, and moves Maserati from Bologna to Modena.

1939: Wilbur Shaw wins Indianapolis 500 in Maserati (he won again in 1940).

1957: Fangio is World Champion, with Maserati 250F.

1968: Beginning of link with Citroën.

1975: Citroën drops Maserati; De Tomaso takes over, in conjunction with GEPI.

1982: Maserati sets new trend with compact Biturbo.

important Grand Prix wins in 1966 and 1967.

Meanwhile, the development of road cars had progressed well under Giulio Alfieri and new ground was broken in 1963 with the introduction of the 4.1-litre (later 4.7-litre) four-camshaft V8 engine in a saloon. The Quattroporte could well have laid claim to the title of the world's fastest four-door car. There were magnificent coupés, too.

Still struggling for survival, Maserati passed out of Omer Orsi's control and into Citroën's. The V6 Maserati-powered SM was the most exotic Citroën ever, but it was phased out when Peugeot took over: at which point, in 1975, Maserati was out in the cold.

Under de Tomaso (already a manufacturer of bespoke cars with American engines), the Maserati GT range was rationalized. This meant dropping in 1984 such fine cars as the Khamsin, the Kyalami, and the mid-engined V8 Bora and V6 Merak, following the departure of Giulio Alfieri to Nuova Lamborghini. On the plus side, the mid-1980s saw the great V8 engine still being fitted to the Quattroporte III in Modena, while de Tomaso's Nuova Innocenti factory in Milan was turning out increasing quantities of the compact two- and four-door Biturbo saloons: real little wolves in sheep's clothing. So it seemed that Officine Alfieri Maserati SpA was in as strong a position as it had ever been, with more new models on the way for 1985.

MATRA France

The origins of this specialist marque can be traced to Champigny-sur-Marne, where Charles Deutsch and René Bonnet began making Citroën specials in the late 1930s. These were called DBs, and this marque name was applied to the partners' successful post-Second World War Panhard-based competition and miniature GT cars.

In 1961 Deutsch left to pursue the Panhard theme elsewhere, while Bonnet stayed on to produce the René Bonnet; his Renault-powered Djet formed the basis of a new marque when he was bought out by Engins Matra, when that company wanted to become better-known in public. Matra (short for Mécanique Aviation Traction) had already 'carried' Bonnet for some time; now, in 1965, the Bonnet team helped produce the first Matra Formula Three car.

The Matra quickly established itself as France's most successful Grand Prix car, with Jackie Stewart winning ten Formula One races to take second and first places respectively in the World Championships of 1968 and 1969. In the latter year, Matra took the constructors' title too, although Stewart's cars were powered by Ford-Cosworth engines and entered by the British Tyrrell team. The works Matras, powered by an 'in-house' V12 engine, were never to win a championship Grand Prix, although they would come

close. Subsequent racing activity netted Matra the world sports car trophy for 1973 and 1974. There was a hat trick of Le Mans victories (1972 to 1974) in which Henri Pescarolo shared each time.

From 1970 the Matra car division was under the control of SIMCA (originated in 1934 to make French FIATs) and this virtually coincided with SIMCA's absorption by Chrysler. This meant not only a parting of the ways between Tyrrell and Matra-Simca, but a change in Matra road cars, too, for they had been fitted with German Ford power units.

Known as the Bagheera, the new car of 1973 was a small but broad coupé with three-abreast seating and a central 1.3- (later 1.4-) litre SIMCA engine mounted crosswise. The name Matra was used in 1977 for the Rancho station wagon.

By the 1980s, Chrysler had withdrawn to America, selling SIMCA to Peugeot who brought back the marque name Talbot for use in France and Britain. All the same, the Bagheera's replacement was essentially a Matra; the Matra Murena was a very pretty little coupé, retaining the three-seat and transverse mid-engine layout, with a choice of 1.6- or 2.2-litre units familiar to the Peugeot-Talbot service network.

In 1984 Automobiles Peugeot released Matra, who restored the old bond with Renault by developing the futuristic car-cum-caravan called the Espace. Matra, it seemed, was determined to continue in the field of fashionable motoring after all.

BELOW *Pretty yet practical, distinctive yet compact, the Matra Murena of the early 1980s had three-abreast seating and mid-mounted engine. Provided by Nicholas Storrs.*

MAYBACH Germany

Maybach is a very important name in motoring history. Wilhelm Maybach worked on the internal combustion engine with Gottlieb Daimler at Deutz in Cologne, and afterwards at Bad Cannstatt. It was Maybach who pushed Daimler towards the wider application of his engine and had inspired the steel-wheeled car of 1889. As chief engineer and designer at Daimler, he was responsible for the first Mercedes of 1901, regarded by many as the prototype for the purpose-built motor car. After 61-year-old Maybach left the company in 1907, its founder's son, Paul Daimler, took over as Mercedes' head of engineering.

Most Maybachs would have chauffeurs, and they had to learn.

To celebrate Count Zeppelin's 1929 round-the-world air voyage, the new V12 models were called Maybach Zeppelins. A 7-litre came first in 1930, followed by an 8-litre a year later. During the 1930s, several smaller engines (3.4, 3.8 and 4.2 litres) were produced, but the marque remained the most exclusive of all German luxury vehicles.

Maybach did not make its own bodies, the majority being the responsibility of the Hermann Spohn Karosseriebau at nearby Ravensburg. In general, the Maybach was beautifully proportioned, belying the great size of the beast. The occasional fanciful 'streamliner' would, however, give the game away.

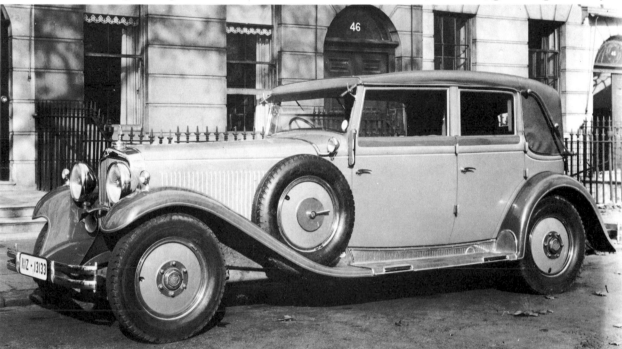

Most examples of the mighty V12 Maybach Zeppelin (like this one from 1931) were so well-proportioned that their great size was not obtrusive.

Together with Count Ferdinand von Zeppelin, Maybach went into the aero engine business, first at Bissingen and then at Friedrichshafen on Lake Constance, where the airships were based. Karl Maybach joined the new company, gradually taking over from his father.

After the First World War, Karl Maybach opened an automotive division. The Maybach 5.6-litre six-cylinder engine did not find a ready market as a proprietary unit (although some were sold to the Dutch Spijker company), so he began making complete cars. The first Maybach was called the W3. A big, luxurious tourer, it made its début at the 1921 Berlin show.

A Maybach speciality was the use of complex transmissions, the most famous being the *Doppelschnellgang*, a dual-range overdrive system giving eight forward and four reverse ratios. The clutch was needed only to engage first gear in either range; for most changes the driver preselected the appropriate gear and 'dipped' the throttle to engage it. Lagonda bought a few but customers remained nonplussed.

Rather more than 2000 Maybach cars were made between 1921 and 1941, by which time military vehicle production was in full swing. In 1950 Spohn came up with new designs, but there was no harmony whatsoever in their looks and it was clear that the great coachbuilder had lost its former artistry. The company also made some crude modifications to American cars for the occupying forces: good practice, perhaps, for the day when the Ravensburg works became a toy factory.

In 1960 Maybach began producing Mercedes-Benz diesel engines at Friedrichshafen, by then rebuilt after 70 per cent of the factory had been destroyed by the Allies in the Second World War, but the definite plan to reintroduce the noble name of Maybach was never followed up. However, the 4.2-litre overhead-camshaft engine from a Maybach scout car did form the basis for the very effective Maybach Special with which the Australian Stan Jones (father of racing driver and 1980 world champion Alan Jones) won the 1954 New Zealand Grand Prix.

MAZDA Japan

MAZDA

ABOVE *Rotary-engined Mazda RX7 with Elford turbocharger conversion: one of Japan's (and the world's) most individual cars. Provided by The Patrick Collection.*

In terms of modern production engineering it may be said that the Japanese have some of the world's greatest marques. No other Oriental manufacturer, however, has scaled such technical and aesthetic heights as Mazda: the only firm to have adopted the rotary-piston engine for long-term production. Felix Wankel's light and compact power unit dispensed with the usual number of reciprocating components and was first used in Germany (*see* NSU), but it was Mazda who persisted with the design.

The Toyo Kogyo Company of Hiroshima, manufacturer of the Mazda, was making lightweight three-wheeled commercial vehicles as early as 1931, but did not embark on private car production until 1960 with its miniature R360 model.

It was in 1967 that Mazda hit the motoring headlines with the announcement of its twin rotary-engined 110S GT model. Other Wankel-engined cars followed and by 1970 the marque was proving its reliability in long-distance races in Europe. By 1980, more than 100,000 rotary-engined Mazdas had been produced and the latest sports coupé, the attractive RX7, was making its mark in competitions. In North America it was a regular winner of the IMSA GTU championship, and Winston Percy took major British titles with the car in 1980 and 1981. Probably the most important individual race victories for the RX7 were those in 1981 by Tom Walkinshaw: in the Belgian 24-hour race (with Pierre Dieudonné) and the Tourist Trophy at Silverstone (with Chuck Nicholson). In the mid-1980s a turbocharged RX7 was the scene-stealer of one of Japan's most distinguished marques.

MERCEDES-BENZ Germany

From 1901 to 1926, the marque name was plain Mercedes. Earlier still, it was Daimler. The retention of the name Daimler for Britain's first series-production cars in 1897 was misleading. If the Daimler Motoren-Gesellschaft of Bad Cannstatt had not accepted the marketing proposals of Emil Jellinek, it is likely that the British marque name would have been different.

Jellinek was a wealthy Austrian who lived in Nice in France when motoring was in its infancy. He was a Daimler enthusiast and the technical chief at Cannstatt, Wilhelm Maybach, responded to his ideas for a more modern car than the 1899 Daimler Phoenix.

Jellinek used his daughter's name, Mercédès, as a pseudonym for his motor racing activities. From 1901, Mercedes became the German Daimler's marque name, for Jellinek was so impressed by the new design that he undertook to buy a large quantity: in return for the selling rights in several European countries and in the United States. Gottlieb Daimler had died in 1900 – but in any case the change of name was not done out of any lack of respect. One of Jellinek's arrangements was to set up, via Charley Lehmann, an agency in France where a French-sounding name would be much more acceptable than a German one. (Panhard et Levassor, who held Daimler engine patent rights, were unsuccessful in taking legal action over the new business.) The French connection is the most likely reason for the general acceptance of the name Mercedes.

It was as if a new marque had been born. Maybach's 1901 Mercedes featured a 35 hp four-cylinder engine with mechanically operated inlet valves. It had a strong and rigid steel chassis (as opposed to the traditional armoured wood) which ensured good handling, possibly for the first time, and its mechanical layout and controls were of the pattern still in use today. Probably the feature that made it look so much more like a motor car than its contemporaries was its large vertical honeycomb radiator.

An experimental Mercedes was raced for the first time by a Briton, Lorraine Barrow, at Pau in February 1901, but all kinds of mechanical trouble intervened. A month later, however, the works driver Wilhelm Werner took everyone by surprise when, with the relatively small and quiet-running car from Cannstatt, he was the clear winner of the 400 km (250-mile) Nice–Salon–Nice road race.

The commercial vehicles kept the Daimler name, as did the Austro-Daimler cars, products of the Österreichische Daimler Motoren AG, founded in Wiener-Neustadt in 1899, where the early technical director was Gottlieb Daimler's son Paul. (The Austro-Daimler marque name was dropped in the 1930s, following the establishment of the Steyr-Daimler-Puch combine.) A further complication was the acquisition of MMB (Motorfahrzeug- und Motorenfabrik Berlin AG, Marienfelde), which led to the construction of Daimler-Marienfelde commercials and also their British-built counterparts, called Milnes-Daimlers up to 1914.

Very quickly, the Mercedes name became synonymous with quality of engineering and manufacture. After Maybach's departure to join Count Zeppelin, Paul Daimler took over as technical chief. He was succeeded at the Austrian works by Ferdinand Porsche. When Daimler retired in 1922, Porsche became technical director at Mercedes.

Meanwhile the Benz company had been making progress, inspired by Mercedes' success, and had acquired the South German motor works of Bergmann at Gaggenau. Benz and Mercedes were engaged in technical and commercial cooperation throughout the early 1920s, each seeking strength from the other during a difficult economic period for Germany. Having preferred to keep their autonomy originally, the mutual decision to merge led to the formation of Daimler-Benz AG in 1926. From then on, the cars and commercial vehicles became known universally as Mercedes-Benz, and adopted the Mercedes three-pointed star as a unifying symbol of excellence.

Porsche stayed with the company for three years and, like Maybach and the younger Daimler before him, kept it in the forefront in car manufacture and racing. Then, in 1930, after a year with Steyr, Porsche set up his own engineering consultancy in Stuttgart. One of the earliest contracts came in 1933, when he was commissioned to design a Grand Prix car to be made at the Auto Union Horch factory in Zwickau. This was half of Hitler's successful plan to put the Third Reich on a pinnacle in Grand Prix racing. The other half was Mercedes-Benz. Between them, the two state-sponsored teams were virtually unchallenged for more than five seasons until 1939.

The 1934 Mercedes-Benz W25 Grand Prix car, the first of the famed Silver Arrows, was the responsibility of Hans Nibel, formerly of Benz. After Nibel's untimely death at the age of 54 at the end of 1934, Fritz Nallinger and Rudolf Uhlenhaut were to carry the Mercedes-Benz banner higher still. Rudolf Caracciola and Hermann Lang were the most successful drivers for the works team.

After the Second World War, Daimler-Benz AG pulled itself together again quickly and the diesel-powered saloon, which had been introduced in 1936,

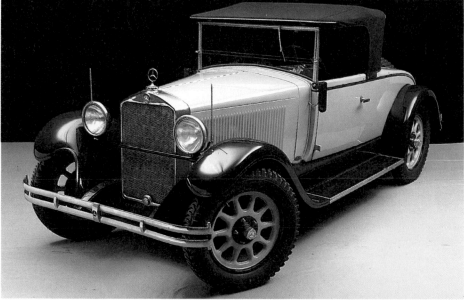

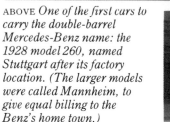

ABOVE *One of the first cars to carry the double-barrel Mercedes-Benz name: the 1928 model 260, named Stuttgart after its factory location. (The larger models were called Mannheim, to give equal billing to the Benz's home town.)*

RIGHT *The supercharged straight-8 Mercedes-Benz 540K of 1937 developed up to 180 bhp, giving a maximum speed of more than 160 km/h (100 mph). Both cars shown on this page are from Daimler-Benz's own museum.*

the W196, brought Mercedes-Benz two great seasons, this time dominating Grand Prix racing in 1954 and 1955. In the latter season the 300SLR showed similar superiority in sports-car racing. The best drivers of that era, Juan Manuel Fangio and Stirling Moss, were chosen to get the most out of these magnificent but not-too-easily handled machines. The company did not return to these specialized fields of competition afterwards, but maintained its reputation by occasional participation in touring car racing and rallying, in which Walter Schock and Eugen Böhringer were to prove exceptional assets. A return to rallying was announced in 1980, only to be cancelled when Auto Union Audi NSU made its intentions clear for the four-wheel-drive Quattro rally car.

That Mercedes-Benz is always capable of producing dramatic and definitive new designs was demonstrated clearly in 1969 when a triple-rotor Wankel engine was fitted into an exciting new coupé called the C111. A quadruple-rotor version appeared in 1970; but these machines and their relatives were never offered for sale once they had demonstrated their technical feasibility.

Evolution, as opposed to revolution, has typified the progress of Mercedes-Benz production models. They

TOP *First sold in 1954, the 300SL was famous for its 'gull-wing' doors, an idea later adopted by DeLorean. Provided by Peter Parsons.*

ABOVE *Typically elegant mid-1980s Mercedes-Benz 500SEC coupé, with 5-litre V8 engine. Provided by The Patrick Collection.*

played a major part in the recovery of the Mercedes-Benz marque.

The ability of Mercedes-Benz to overcome adversity and regain technological supremacy has been shown on many more occasions since then: notably in 1952 when the 'gull-wing' 300SL, although not the fastest sports-racing car, showed great reliability to come second in the Mille Miglia, before going on to win the Le Mans 24-Hour race and the Carrera Panamericana as the hares ran out of breath. Again a new racing car,

possess a special classlessness that permits a diesel-powered taxi to come from the same stable as some of the world's most elegant and desirable coupés and saloons, with fuel-injection V8 engines of the utmost efficiency and performance capability.

With commercial and cross-country vehicles, too, the Mercedes-Benz marque remains the supremely excellent product of the most experienced motor manufacturing house in the world. It may have its rivals – but it has no peers.

M.G. Great Britain

ABOVE *1933 M.G. J2, with 850 cc overhead-camshaft engine, established the classic Midget shape. Provided by Paradise Garage.*

The M.G. was, for many years, the most successful of popular sports cars, with a very strong identity.

In 1980, the famous Abingdon-on-Thames factory (part of the former Pavlova leather works) was closed down after more than 50 years of M.G. tenure, despite a late bid by Aston Martin to acquire it. That could have spelled the end for one of the best-loved of all great marques; happily it did not. Soon after the launch of the Metro, in May 1982, BL revived the name M.G. for a high-performance version of BL's new small family saloon. Since then, Austin-Rover's Maestro and Montego have made similar use of the renowned octagonal symbol. Ironically, the return of the M.G. coincided with the gradual demise – complete by 1985 – of the marque that begat it (*see* Morris).

William Morris was in the cycle trade before entering the car-making business strongly with his 1913 'Bullnose'. Quite apart from this great enterprise, he had converted some stables in Longwell Street, Oxford, as early as 1911. The premises were known as The Morris Garage and from 1913 (after further expansion) as the Morris Garages. From 1922, this retail business was managed by Cecil Kimber. It would have been fairer if the marque had

been named not M.G., after Morris Garages, but after its creator Kimber, for it was he who gave it its personality.

The M.G. was to bring prestige and, in due course, export sales to Britain on an unprecedented scale. Sadly Kimber would not live to see those boom years.

The first M.G.s were mildly modified Morrises, complete with 'bull noses'. In 1926, the 'flat nose' was adopted universally by Morris and by Kimber, too. However, the 1.8-litre side-valve four-cylinder M.G. 14/28 and 14/40 were not yet true sports cars. For a fairly brief period (1928 to 1933) there was a 2.5-litre overhead-camshaft six-cylinder Morris-engined M.G. of commendable performance; but it was not to be typical of the marque in the long term. The car that set M.G. on its road to fame was the mighty Midget.

It was the coming of the Morris Minor in the autumn of 1928 that gave Cecil Kimber the chance to produce a real 'people's sports car'. The 850 cc overhead camshaft-engined Morris was designed as a competitor for the Austin Seven, but it also formed the ideal basis for the first of the legendary M.G. Midgets, the M-type. 'A little gem of a car, fit to take two people and their luggage anywhere, happy as could be.' That was *Motor Sport*'s conclusion, on seeing the prototype at the London show. By the spring of 1929, production of the £175 boat-tailed, fabric-bodied eye catcher was well under way and at that year's show it was joined by a delightful little coupé at £245. An early export order of note was placed by the Ford company in 1930. The customer was Edsel (son of Henry) Ford, who ran his M.G. for three years before passing it on to the Ford museum: where it is still on display, clear evidence of its importance to history (which, surely, was never considered absolute bunk by anyone).

Over the next few years further four-cylinder Midgets were developed, together with the six-cylinder Magna and Magnette, all powered by overhead-camshaft engines. During the early 1930s Sir William Morris (Lord Nuffield) approved a racing programme which put M.G. on the international map. There were victories in three successive Tourist Trophy races and many other important road and track events. The most significant achievement was, perhaps, to take the team prize in the 1933 Mille Miglia with three of the new supercharged K3 Magnettes, which had Wilson preselect gearboxes and could outrun the Maseratis in the 1.1-litre class.

Kimber was essentially an enthusiast; Morris was not. It is probable that the acclamation and renown won by the M.G. marque was not to Morris's liking. Maybe the reason was simply economic, but the Nuffield Organization began to take a much more controlling interest in M.G. in 1935. Official race participation was halted, as was overhead-camshaft engine development.

It is a measure of the excellence of its original concept that the Midget theme was continued with success from 1936 right through to 1955: 'Maintaining the Breed', as the advertisements quite reasonably claimed in later years. There were several attractive tourers and saloons in the late 1930s, too, but they were slow to appear and were eclipsed in their particular market sector by the new SS Jaguars, which no one had taken seriously enough in the first place.

Privateers continued to race, rally and break records with M.G.s, notably Lieutenant-Colonel A.T.G. Gardner, whose well-streamlined Railton-bodied car exceeded 320 km/h (200 mph) in 1939.

ABOVE *M.G. Midget in 1931–2 racing form. This C-type, or Montlhéry, model had a 750 cc engine. The SU carburettor, ahead of the radiator, serves the supercharger hidden beneath the cowl. Provided by Allan Bentley.*

RIGHT *The 1950 model M.G. TD was a great success – despite some diehards opining that, with its independent front suspension and less spartan interior, Midget motoring had gone soft. This one, provided by Alastair Naylor, is owned by Jack Tordoff.*

ABOVE *Ugly front-end treatment on the last (1980) series of MGB roadsters could not spoil the otherwise lovely lines of this delightful sports car, which had made its début 18 years earlier. Provided by Performance Cars Ltd.*

HIGHLIGHTS

1922: The Morris Garages, Oxford, start modifying Morris cars, under direction of Cecil Kimber.

1924: M.G. octagon motif appears.

1928: First M.G. Midget announced.

1930: M.G. production moved from Oxford to Abingdon.

1935: Competition programme halted in mid-season, following several brilliant years of success. Overhead-camshaft engines discontinued.

1941: Cecil Kimber resigns, under Nuffield Organization pressure.

1952: Nuffield and Austin groups merge to form BMC.

1955: MGA sports car launched.

1962: Introduction of MGB sports car.

1967: Launch of MGC sports car.

1973: MGB V8 introduced; it had Rover's 3.5-litre ex-GM engine.

1980: Last MGB and Midget production; Abingdon works closed.

1982: M.G. reborn as Metro: turbocharger optional.

1985: Strong rumours of plan to bring back the Midget – the world's best-loved sports car – in modern guise.

Under the successive thumbs of Leonard Lord (later to run Austin) and Oliver Boden, Kimber was able to keep some semblance of independence for his beloved M.G., and it was not until the Second World War that this autonomy was finally crushed. By then, Miles Thomas had been appointed to coordinate the efforts of the Nuffield Organization. Kimber had already obtained separate war contract work for M.G. and Thomas did not like this. A quiet word from him and, late in 1941, Kimber was gone, much to the silent misery of his loyal team at Abingdon.

Cecil Kimber had no difficulty in finding work, organizing war production for several companies. It was early in 1945, and he had given up the idea of returning to the kind of business he had loved – making sports cars – when he was one of only two passengers fatally injured in a freak and totally avoidable low-speed railway accident at King's Cross, London. It is tragic that Kimber never saw the spectacular new growth of his marque that followed so soon afterwards. Between 1945 and 1955, some 50,000 Midgets (TCs, TDs and TFs) were produced at Abingdon, the vast majority going abroad. These two-seaters were supplemented by the neat, taut 1¼-litre Y-type saloon which, in 1953, was replaced by a blander model for which the Magnette name was resurrected. The last Magnette saloons, built until

1968, were Farina-styled badge-engineered Austins or Morrises (or Rileys or Wolseleys): for the merging of Austin with Nuffield led to some of the least discriminate use of marque names ever perpetrated.

On the sports car front M.G. fared better and there was an active BMC competitions department in the late 1950s and early 1960s. The M.G. Midget was revived again, in the form of an Austin-Healey Sprite variant; but it was the MGA and, even more so, the MGB that kept the marque sparkling into the modern era of sports cars. By 1980, however, the MGB was getting old, with retrograde facelifts, and in that year Abingdon was closed down.

The only front-wheel-drive M.G.s were the 1100 and 1300 cc saloons, discontinued in 1971. Just over a decade later came a natural successor, the MG Metro, and in 1984 Austin Rover announced a four-wheel-drive rally version of it. In the mid-1980s, every basic Austin (except the Mini) was being offered as an M.G. once again. There is no M.G. company as such – that is, perhaps, too much to expect – but when the Austin-Rover Group makes another value-for-money sports car, it is hard to imagine it as anything but an M.G. even if it has Oriental overtones.

MILLER USA

The genius of Harry Armenius Miller, the son of a German immigrant to Wisconsin called Müller, has far too often been ignored, or omitted from history books, simply because his cars and his engines were built strictly for racing. Another reason is that Miller's machines shone at a time when racing cars needed sponsorship; and so, very often, a Miller would run as a such-and-such 'special' with its benefactor's name attached.

As early as 1916, Miller was producing four-cylinder engines with desmodromic – that is to say positively closed – valve operation, based on a Peugeot design.

The most famous Miller engine was the straight-8, created by Leo Goossen, Fred Offenhauser and Miller. Its first big victory was in the hands of Jimmy Murphy in a Duesenberg chassis at the 1922 Indianapolis 500-Mile race. Murphy had won the previous year's French GP for that company (*see* Duesenberg), then bought the car and fitted Miller's engine. At Indianapolis he shattered the race record. From then on Miller engines, usually in Miller cars, dominated the 'Indy 500' right through to the Second World War.

Some of the race winners had front-wheel drive. Miller's combination of de Dion tube and inboard brakes with front-wheel drive was adopted for the Cord L-29 road cars (*see* Cord).

Miller cars driven by Frank Lockhart came close to taking the world land speed record. George Stewart, who raced as 'Leon Duray', took a pair of Millers to Europe and managed the fastest lap against the cream of the Grand Prix machines at Monza in 1929. Although he did not win that race, he had no trouble in doing a barter deal with Jean Bugatti afterwards. The Miller straight-8 engine undoubtedly inspired the Type 50 and subsequent double overhead camshaft Bugattis.

Harry Miller died in 1943, but his technology lived on, for Goossen and Offenhauser continued to produce Indianapolis-winning engines until the mid-1960s. Miller was inventive and meticulous in all his automotive work, to the extent that he is often described as 'America's Bugatti'.

George Stewart ('Leon Duray') with one of the two front-wheel-drive Miller 91 twin-cam racers he brought to Europe in 1929, which were acquired for study by Bugatti.

MORGAN Great Britain

The Morgan is unique in that it is not just a copy of the traditional British sports car. It *is* a traditional British sports car, built where it has always been built, by the same small company, with the son of the founder at the helm.

H. F. S. Morgan was 25 years old when he left his job as a Great Western Railways draughtsman and started a workshop and a local bus service at Malvern, Worcestershire. He bought a Peugeot two-cylinder motorcycle engine with a view to making a machine of his own. The vehicle he made was a three-wheeler; the Morgan story had begun.

With capital provided by his father, the Revd H. G. Morgan, the tiny firm acquired its first machine tools and extended its premises, and by 1910 the Morgan was in production, now with engines from the JAP (J. A. Prestwich) company. The Morgan Motor Co Ltd was actually formed in 1912, and in that year one of the diminutive machines covered only fractionally less than 100 km (60 miles) in an hour at Brooklands. H. F. S. Morgan (who, like his son Peter, competed in many rallies and speed events) was the driver on that occasion. Many competition successes followed.

The first four-wheeled Morgan prototype appeared in 1935 and from then on the three-wheeler was gradually ousted. Independent front suspension had always been a feature of the three-wheelers and this was retained. The engine was a 1.1-litre Coventry Climax. Later, a 1.3-litre Standard unit was used; it was replaced soon after the Second World War by the 2.1-litre Standard Vanguard unit.

The competition successes continued, Morgans winning the three-car team award in the first postwar RAC Rally, in 1951. Peter Morgan, who had joined the company as development engineer in 1947, was runner-up in the rally as a whole, beaten only by Ian Appleyard (Jaguar XK120). The same trio (Morgan, Goodall and Steel) won the team event again in 1952.

Sophistication in the Morgan car has been minimal, yet it still appeals to sportsmen and women around the world – maybe for that very reason. A controlled production programme of about ten vehicles a week ensures a constant demand for these hand-built sports machines, which have become even more exciting in modern times with the availability of a 3.5-litre V8-engined model. Part of the charm of every Morgan is its strictly vintage ride and handling.

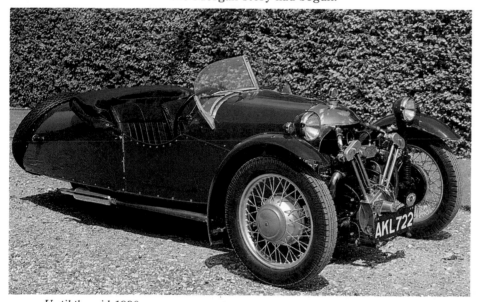

ABOVE *Until the mid-1930s, all Morgans were three-wheelers. One of the most delightful was this 1933 Super Sports with 1.1-litre JAP engine: a model which was being recalled 50 years later in the Norwich-built Guzzi-powered TriKing. In the 1970s and 1980s imitation was, in the case of many historic cars, proving to be the sincerest form of flattery.*

RIGHT *No need for imitations here! The Morgan four-wheeler has kept its original style for decades. Only the wheels suggest that this one was built in modern times.*

MORRIS Great Britain

The story of Morris Garages has been told earlier (*see* M.G.). The tale of the Morris car itself is very different.

By 1985, the Morris marque name had been dropped from the Austin-Rover (formerly BL) car and light commercial vehicle ranges. Maybe they had a mundane name, but Morris cars were the first to be mass-produced by a British company and, for many years, the Cowley works at Oxford surpassed Austin of Longbridge in sheer volume. Moreover, several models of Morris endeared themselves to the British family car owner: not least the original 'Bullnose', of which more than 150,000 were made.

The secret of the Morris philosophy was to find good components at good prices, no matter where, and to create a cheap and straightforward car from them. William Morris had already withdrawn from several manufacturing and selling businesses in Oxford when he decided, in 1910, to start his own car factory. With sponsorship from the Earl of Macclesfield, Morris acquired a disused military college in the Cowley district of Oxford, and from there the first Morris was dispatched in March 1913.

The first Morris Oxford had a 1-litre four-cylinder side-valve engine built in Coventry by White & Poppe, and a worm-drive rear axle supplied by Wrigley of Birmingham (where Cecil Kimber, founder of M.G., worked for a while). In 1914, despite the outbreak of the First World War, Morris switched to America for the supply of cheap engines and gearboxes, and the result was the Morris Cowley, with a Continental unit. In spite of the war, the Morris car gained a strong foothold. Afterwards, however, engine supply became a problem.

The reason was that the Continental Motor Manufacturing Co of Detroit had decided to stop making its 1.5-litre engine, which was too small to sell well in the United States. White & Poppe, the old supplier, was too busy on other contracts; but another company in Coventry, Hotchkiss, was in quite the opposite situation. This French firm had been making armaments in its British factory but, now the war was over, its days looked numbered. Morris had retained the

BELOW *This 'Bullnose' was built during the First World War, when William Morris bought his 1.5-litre engines from Continental Motors of Detroit. The Morris was Britain's first example of true mass production.*

HIGHLIGHTS

1877: Birth of William Richard Morris (later Lord Nuffield).

1913: W. R. M. Motors Ltd formed at Cowley, Oxford; W. R. Morris wins gold medal in London–Edinburgh trial in one of his own 'Bullnose' cars.

1927: Wolseley acquired.

1931: Morris Minor tourer offered at £100.

1938: Purchase of Riley.

1948: Introduction of Issigonis-designed Minor.

1952: Merger of Nuffield Group with Austin to form BMC.

1959: Introduction of Issigonis-designed Mini-Minor.

1963: Death of Lord Nuffield.

1968: British Leyland formed.

1971: Morris Minor production ends.

1984: Morris marque discontinued by new Austin-Rover Group, but 'Mini' types still produced.

PA 7788

right to make the Continental engine, and Hotchkiss jumped at the opportunity to produce it. Full production began in the autumn of 1919.

A year later the postwar market boom ended and car sales dwindled rapidly. In 1915 the Continental-engined Cowley had been listed at under £165; five years later, the equivalent Hotchkiss-engined car was up to £465.

While others lingered indecisively, watched the opposition, or gave up altogether, Morris took the kind of risk that only the greatest industrialists are able to contemplate. In February 1921 he slashed his prices. The £465 Cowley, for example, came down to £375. But he did not stop at that. In October, despite being more fully equipped for that year's Motor Show, the same model was offered at £299! The effect was to increase Morris's annual sales from 2000 to 3000 cars in 1921; then to nearly 7000 in 1922 and 20,000 in 1923. Morris left other British car manufacturers standing, and exceeded 60,000 (more than a third of the British market) in 1929.

Along the way, Morris acquired other firms, usually his suppliers, such as Hotchkiss at Coventry and E. G. Wrigley in 1923; the latter concern became the Birmingham base for Morris-Commercial. He also acquired the Léon Bollée works at Le Mans in the mid-1920s, in the hope of avoiding French import duties. However, he sold out to a short-lived syndicate during the Depression.

ABOVE *Six-cylinder side-valve 1935 Morris in rare sports-tourer form.*

RIGHT *First exhibited in 1948, the Morris Minor gained a reputation for good performance later in its life. Despite a final engine size of 1.1 litres, it was still called the Minor 1000. This 1967 four-door is from The Patrick Collection.*

Meanwhile, in 1927, Wolseley was acquired. M.G., which was becoming an entity at this time, was allowed to follow its own course for a time, but in 1935 it was made to knuckle under as the Nuffield Group grew (Sir William Morris had by now been raised to the peerage with the title of Lord Nuffield). He still admired and followed the American way of progress, and it was by arrangement with the US firm Edward Budd that he set up the modern Pressed Steel body plant at Cowley.

From 1922, the Austin Seven had filled the need for a real car in miniature (as opposed to the once popular, but very basic cyclecars), and in 1928 Morris countered with the first Minor. This model made history in the Depression when another, although less drastic, price-cutting spree made it the first car to be offered in Britain for £100. The specification was pared to a minimum, but it was clever marketing in that it helped sell the more expensive versions. Indeed, relatively few £100 two-seaters were sold.

After the Minor came the Eight which, in its £128 'E' series of the late 1930s, was the first mass-produced British car to have its headlamps built, American-style, into the front wings. The same 0.9-litre side-valve engine was used for the 1948 Minor (first produced in the early 1940s as the Mosquito), although its designer, Alec Issigonis, had originally planned to employ a flat-four. Independent front suspension by torsion bars, plus rack-and-pinion steering, gave the car modern behaviour. Later, overhead-valve engines made the Minor 1000 the outstanding British small car

of the pre-Mini era. Several attempts to update the car failed (although one was successful as a Riley, a marque taken over by Nuffield in 1938). The much-loved Minor lived on into the 1970s.

In 1959 the Mini-Minor, the second of the great Issigonis Morrises, was launched simultaneously as an Austin 'Seven', for BMC had been in existence seven years by then. Perhaps renaming the car as a Mini spelled the end of the Morris as a marque? Or was it the thoughtless badge engineering perpetrated by BMC, and by its successor BL? Lord Nuffield's former lieutenant, Sir Leonard Lord, had become his hardened rival as boss of Austin, and the younger man was the victor in the personal battle to form BMC in 1952. Thereafter, the Austin had tended to be the senior marque, and by the 1980s all Austins had front-wheel drive, while the only Morris was the obsolescent Marina. Later, this was simply dubbed the Ital for the work that was done by Giugiaro and Ital Design to prolong it. The Marina had been created in 1970. In many ways it fulfilled the need for a simple, sturdy four-seat saloon, but it incorporated a number of Morris Minor features that were outdated by then; and despite improvements the Marina had to suffer a lot of criticism from a sophisticated press. The model did well to survive until 1984, when the demise of the Morris went unmourned. The classic British volume car had been overtaken by modern technology, and the introduction of the 1980 Metro as an Austin only was the final nail in the Morris's coffin.

NAPIER Great Britain

The London firm of D. Napier and Son was founded early in the 19th century by David Napier, the son of the Duke of Argyll's blacksmith at Inveraray Castle. The company's most celebrated early product was the excruciatingly named Nay-Peer printing machine. Precision engineering made the firm's reputation, and equipment for banks and mints around the world was among Napier's specialities.

In the 20th century, Napier marine and aero engines have been among the most respected. It should be mentioned that Napier Lion 12-cylinder triple-bank units powered Sir Malcolm Campbell's early *Bluebird*, Sir Henry Segrave's *Golden Arrow*, and John Cobb's *Railton Mobil Special* – all holders of the world land speed record. John Cobb's famous 24-litre Lion-engined track car, the Napier-Railton, holds the Brooklands lap record at over 230 km/h (143 mph).

Such great feats on land, sea and in the air have tended to overshadow Napier's car-making period, in the first quarter of this century.

Thousand Mile Trial, Britain's first important motor competition. Then in 1901 the legendary American Charles Glidden began his series of pioneering long-distance tours which would take him to every part of the world. Where roads did not exist, he fitted his Napier with railway wheels. But it was S. F. Edge's victory in the Gordon Bennett Trophy in 1902 that gave Napier an undisputed claim to be Britain's first successful competition car. The Gordon Bennett races of 1899 to 1905 were the predecessors of the original Grands Prix and, as such, became truly international during their short lifespan. Edge's victory was, in fact, achieved by keeping going as the opposition broke down, but it did bring the British car to the attention of all.

Most famous of all Napier racing cars was the 15-litre L48, subsequently nicknamed 'Samson'. In 1904 Arthur Macdonald drove it at over 168 km/h (105 mph) to claim 'fastest on land' for a brief period. Driven by Clifford Earp the same car completed the 1905 Gordon Bennett race, but its fine performance was kept in check because it had only a two-speed gearbox, hardly adequate for the very mountainous

RIGHT *In 1905, the great racing Napier L48 might have finished higher than ninth in the final Gordon Bennett Cup race if its potential had not been restricted by a two-speed gearbox. Here Clifford Earp takes a breather while he is held at the Laqueuille control point in the Auvergne: one of several established to prevent the cars closing up and getting in each others' dust.*

It was one of the founder's grandsons, Montague Stanley Napier (1870–1931), who took the family firm into the automotive world in 1899, when he designed and made a new engine for the three-year-old Panhard owned by the sporting salesman Selwyn Francis Edge. The subsequent relationship between Napier and Edge was rather like that of Royce with Rolls: one was a technical perfectionist, the other an entrepreneur and racing driver. Edge's enthusiasm was just one factor that led to Napier becoming a manufacturer of quality cars and commercial vehicles.

In 1900, Edge took an early production car on the

Auvergne circuit in France. 'Samson' continued to appear with spectacular success, mainly in the sprint events, its huge six-cylinder engine ultimately displacing fully 20 litres. (A painstakingly created replica of this magnificent beast emerged in the early 1980s.)

For a while, Napier production averaged three to four cars a day, the models varying from a two-cylinder taxi to exotic sixes. Edge, who still claimed sole selling rights for all Napiers (including truck and bus chassis, a basic point of misunderstanding), could not cope with the volume and had to give way. Napier bought out Edge's company in 1912, and part of the arrangement was that Edge would stay away from the motor trade for seven years.

A victim of the 1920s decline, the superb new Rowledge-designed 40/50 had an overhead-camshaft six-cylinder alloy-block 6.2-litre engine and close on 200 of these fine touring cars were made between 1919 and 1924. Napier, however, had already decided to concentrate on aircraft engines.

When Bentley went into liquidation in 1931, there was a serious attempt by Napier to acquire the company and the man himself, W. O. Bentley. The company's great rivals, Rolls-Royce, successfully outbid Napier, however, using a third party as a decoy.

There was a return to commercial vehicles in 1932, when Napier pioneered the three-wheeled tractor unit, or 'mechanical horse'. The prototype was sold to Scammell, however, and the production versions (from 1933) used the Scammell name.

NISSAN Japan

NISSAN

In the early 1980s a policy decision was taken to standardize the name 'Nissan' (from Nihon Sangyo), although in Europe and other territories 'Datsun' had become a more familiar label for the Japanese motor industry's number two marque.

The Nissan Motor Company's origins can be traced back to the very beginning of the Japanese industry. There had been a handful of imports soon after the turn of the century, but the car did not become a way of life in Japan until long after it had done so in many other countries (see Toyota).

Tobata Imono, dating from 1910, was a foundry and (later) motor parts firm that in 1931 absorbed Japan's first car group, the DAT company, and re-formed it in Osaka. (The first prototype DAT had been made by

Kwaishinsha of Tokyo in 1912: 'DAT' was formed from the initials of the second names of Kenjiro Den, Rokuro Aoyama and Meitaro Takeuchi, its three creators.)

The Datson 91 was the first new product after this reorganization, but its name was changed to Dat*sun* within a couple of years. To complicate matters further, the Tobata group created a new company in Yokohama. This in turn underwent an early name change – to Nissan Motor Company – in 1934. Nissan continued to make Datsun light cars, but in 1937 it used American tooling (ex-Graham Paige) to build its first big model, which it called the Nissan 70.

The postwar Datsuns were also based on overseas designs. In 1960, Nissan set up a North American subsidiary, and in the same year made its first sale to Europe. This was the Datsun Bluebird, based on the Austin A40/A50, which the company had been manufacturing under licence since 1952. (Nissan would come under Japanese control again in 1955.)

Since 1960, Nissan has become thoroughly international, recognizing from the outset the technical and sales advantages of taking part in competitions.

Unashamedly European in style, the Datsun 240Z ('a Jaguar E-type with Porsche dimensions') epitomized Japan's emergence as a nation ready to emulate others and translate an idea into a successful production technique. The 'Z' series was to become the world's best-selling sports car, with over half a million made between 1969 and 1978. Nor was it just a pretty design; this Datsun was tough and practical enough to win the East African Safari twice. (In that demanding event, Nissan products have scored more victories than any other make of car.)

The expansion and technical development of Nissan during and after the world fuel crisis of the 1970s and the subsequent recession are graphic illustrations of Japan's industrial resolve.

In only one area does the Japanese industry still suffer to some extent in comparison with others – despite the precedent set by the Datsun 'Z' series. This is in 'individuality', an attribute that in this context is easier to spot than to define.

For this company the change of marque name was probably the biggest hurdle of all to get over, a development that really called for some shrewdly

BELOW Rauno Aaltonen (one of the original 'flying Finns' of rallying) and Britain's Tony Fall at a service point during the 1972 East African Safari, in which they came sixth. Similar Datsun 240Z coupés won this harsh event outright in 1971 and 1973.

LEFT *Modern mobile holdall, the Nissan Prairie. Provided by The Patrick Collection.*

prepared publicity. Yet in the mid-1980s, Nissan's advertising still lacked copywriting flair, to say the least. It would, for example, instruct the customer to compare the 3-litre Maxima SE ('a high-powered rebuttal to high-priced European sport sedans') with the equivalent Audi, BMW, Mercedes-Benz and Porsche. One 1984 advertisement said: 'Computers, robots, and lasers combine with the painstaking care and sensitivity of honoured craftsmen to bring you the best of transportation.' Whatever the words – and every manufacturer struggles with them sometimes – Nissan will continue to penetrate every sector of world markets; that is certain. It is claimed that the Maxima SE has an 'understatedly aggressive image'. If this means that Nissan is punching its overseas competitors on the nose without their noticing, then it is a good description. By the mid-1980s Nissan – following close on the heels of its compatriot, Honda – was assembling vehicles in the United States.

NSU Germany

Audi is now the scene-stealer of the group known as Audi NSU Auto Union, but NSU has a longer history.

NSU is a contraction of Neckarsulm, the name of an old town of Lower Swabia. Rivers provide power, and in April 1880 Christian Schmidt, a maker of knitting machines, bought a former timber and gypsum mill near the confluence of the Neckar and Sulm rivers so that he could have an instant power source for his machines. Most of Schmidt's knitting machines were sold to Austria and when that country imposed prohibitive import taxes, the Neckarsulm factory needed another product at short notice. Therefore Schmidt began making bicycles. His company's entry into the motor industry would be as a supplier.

The Neckarsulmer Fahrradwerke AG collaborated technically with Wilhelm Maybach and Gottlieb Daimler in 1888, and provided the steel wire-spoked wheels for their first true motor car the following year.

BELOW *The Wankel rotary-piston engine was pioneered by NSU, whose Ro80 of 1967 (seen here) was the brave attempt to bring this new technology to the high-performance saloon car market.*

Motorcycles were the logical development for NSU.

It was not until 1905 that NSU began making cars itself and even then they were Belgian Pipes, built under licence. In 1906, the first indigenous NSU light cars appeared. By 1923, having survived the First World War, NSU was producing three motorcycles an hour and a car every two hours. Within a decade however, following the American stock market's collapse, NSU sold its car business to FIAT, together with its new Heilbronn assembly plant.

The result of this sale was to be the production of NSU-FIAT and Neckar cars until 1967, in which year the NSU connection was dropped altogether and Heilbronn went over to the assembly of Italian-type FIATs only.

Meanwhile, NSU at Neckarsulm had concentrated upon motorcycle production, although in 1934 three experimental Porsche-designed 'people's car' prototypes had been made. During the 1930s an Englishman, Walter Moore, formerly of Norton, was in charge of NSU motorcycle design. Among the leading racers of NSU machines were Hermann-Paul Müller and Bernd Rosemeyer, both of whom also joined the élite band of drivers capable of making the unwieldy Auto Union Grand Prix car a race winner.

The Neckarsulm works were virtually destroyed by Allied bombs during the Second World War, but motorcycle production soon began once again. The early 1950s saw NSU machines breaking many records before the company switched from motorcycles back to cars. Then the two-wheeler manufacturing equipment (apart from that for mopeds) was sold to Yugoslavia (Pretis of Sarajevo), while Neckarsulm introduced its all-independently sprung air-cooled twin-cylinder rear-engined NSU Prinz saloon car for the 1958 season. Soon afterwards came the attractive Bertone-styled Sport Prinz coupé.

It is for the first practical application of Dr Felix Wankel's rotary-piston engine that NSU qualifies, unreservedly, as a truly great marque. First run on the test bench at Neckarsulm in 1957, the single-rotor engine made its production début in the NSU Spider (an open version of the Sport Prinz) in 1964, and soon licences were sold to a number of other manufacturers; Mazda of Japan was the only one to follow through and achieve high-volume production.

The rotary-piston engine runs smoothly and is compact and light, with relatively few parts. Precision machining is essential in its manufacture, but the main reason for what may be considered its failure was that in its early forms it consumed excessive petrol *and* oil. NSU's customers also paid the penalty of being, to some extent, guinea pigs.

The NSU Ro80 of 1967 was the true production pioneer of the twin-rotor engine. It was the first four-door saloon to feature the Wankel principle, and it was unusual in other ways. It was one of the first of the high-performance front-wheel-drive saloons, with power-assisted rack-and-pinion steering, disc brakes and independent suspension all round, and

semi-automatic transmission. It was very advanced.

From 1972, the smaller cars were removed from NSU catalogues, leaving only the Ro80. Rotor seal wear took a long time to overcome, however, and owners were without their cars frustratingly often as bemused dealers sought to serve them.

It was too much for NSU to bear. Following a link, in 1969, with Audi (and therefore with Volkswagen), the Ro80's replacement – a similar concept, the K70, but with orthodox engine – was sent to help ailing VW.

Rather more than 37,000 NSU Ro80s, a sadly uneconomic quantity, had been made in the decade up to March 1977, when production of this outstanding model came to an end. Since then, the Audi has taken over as a prestige marque, although the name NSU is retained in the company title.

OLDSMOBILE USA

From 1887 Ransom Eli Olds experimented with steam, petrol and electric propulsion before settling upon the design that preceded Henry Ford's Model T in bringing motoring to the people of America. His Curved Dash Runabout had a single-cylinder petrol engine; one of these cars was said to be the only survivor of a factory fire, which had the effect of changing a multitude of ideas into a one-model policy.

That was in 1901. In four years, over 12,000 'Merry Oldsmobiles' chugged their way from Lansing, Michigan, into the hands of the American public at the knock-down price of $650 a time. Simplicity was the keynote and the Olds, so like the familiar horse-drawn buggy in layout, was the best-selling car of all in the 'pre-T' era.

Like so many other great men, Olds argued with his colleagues and in 1904 he left the company to form

RIGHT *1903's best-selling Oldsmobile curved-dash runabout.*

BELOW *A best-seller of the 1980s was the medium-sized Oldsmobile Cutlass range. This is a 1984 Ciera.*

another firm, this time using his initials as its name. The first Reo was an underfloor-engined buggy similar to the Olds. The later models were attractive and well-equipped, but the Wall Street crash led to final closure of the car business in 1936. Reo commercial vehicles fared better, and from 1957 they were produced by a division of the White Motor Co; in 1960, White bought Diamond T, and Diamond-Reo trucks were produced for many years.

Back in the 1900s, the Oldsmobile struggled for several years to find a new identity, and in 1909 it became part of General Motors. It took a long time, but eventually Oldsmobile established a niche for itself: above Chevrolet and Pontiac in the GM customers' pecking order, but below the Buick and LaSalle.

The Oldsmobile was often the first GM marque to offer cars with new features, such as semi-automatic transmission in 1937 (not a success), Hydra-Matic transmission in 1939, then the modern short-stroke V8 engine for 1949. That was the first full year of NASCAR (National Association for Stock Car Auto Racing) events, and Oldsmobiles won more than half of them. The marque dominated this type of racing until the Hudson Hornet came onto the scene in 1952. It was probably the 1950 victory by Hershel McGriff and Ray Elliott, in the first of the high-speed road races known as the Carrera Panamericana, that established the

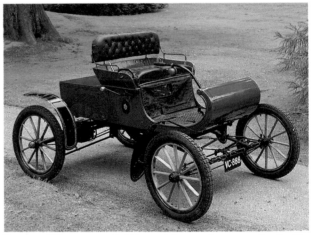

Rocket V8-powered Oldsmobile as the most desirable high-performance car of early postwar America. In 1964, the first McLaren sports-racing cars had modified Oldsmobile engines.

The modern classic from this fine marque is the Oldsmobile Toronado, introduced for 1966. For years American cars had been powerful, but they had not always had the road behaviour to match. The Toronado was the first regular production model (unless the very special prewar Cord can be counted) to combine front-wheel drive with the features of a typically large and high-powered American car. Its acceptance as a luxury car concept was illustrated a year later, when it could be obtained as a Cadillac – GM's flagship marque.

The Toronado led the way, and is still going strong. More to the point is the fact that rear-wheel drive is an increasing rarity in all American car ranges.

OPEL Germany

OPEL

ABOVE GM's top European coupé, the Opel Monza GSE, photographed in the heart of Birmingham not far from its adopted home – The Patrick Collection in Kings Norton.

RIGHT The Opel 400 was the last two-wheel-drive car to give its driver the World Rally Championship (Walter Röhrl in 1982). This 1983 picture shows a Manta version taking part in the San Remo Rally.

The Opel of Rüsselsheim is a marque that has acquired more personality in modern times than it possessed in its earlier days.

From 1863, Opel sewing machines became famous throughout Germany. Bicycles followed, all five Opel brothers being two-wheel racers. It was at the first German car show, in Berlin in 1897, that the decision was taken to make cars at Rüsselsheim. Just three makers were exhibiting: Benz of Mannheim, Daimler of Bad Cannstatt, and Lutzmann of Dessau. Lutzmann had been making Benz-like cars since 1893, and now Opel bought the manufacturing rights.

From 1898 to 1902 the Opel-Patent-Motorwagen, System Lutzmann, was produced in limited numbers. A more successful car was the French Darracq, and Opel-Darracqs supplemented Opel's own designs. A fire in 1911, and the First World War three years later, disrupted Opel's early development.

Mass production was the Opel plan, and the work of André Citroën was admired and copied. The 1924 Opel Laubfrosch ('Tree frog') was a neat copy of Citroën's 5CV, and Opel cars soon accounted for more than one-third of home market sales.

In 1929, anticipating financial problems, Opel approached General Motors who bought the majority shareholding in a reorganized Opel company. GM took full control in 1931 and within a few years Opel was Europe's biggest single producer. Most popular in the mid-1930s was the integral Olympia: a small, unitary construction family saloon which was to provide the

tooling for Russia's postwar Moskvich. The effects of the Second World War made a return to production a daunting prospect. However, GM, who had naturally 'dropped' Opel at the start of hostilities, decided to reinvest in its German offshoot.

Despite the American influence, the Opel soon gained a style of its own. There had been a number of sporting successes in the old days, and even experiments with rocket propulsion. With lines similar, perhaps, to the Chevrolet Corvette, the Opel GT set a trend among compact sports cars when it first appeared in 1965, and the company has been making attractive coupé models alongside its nicely proportioned saloon car ranges ever since.

The rally variants, notably the Ascona 400 of the early 1980s, proved that a conventional (two-wheel-drive, front-engined) machine could still defeat the supercars. In 1982 Walter Röhrl won the World Rally Championship, Tony Fassina took the European title, and Scotland's Jimmy McRae (runner-up in Europe) was British champion – and all drove Opels. The outstanding single result for the Ascona 400 was Ari Vatanen's victory in the 1983 East African Safari.

While the bigger Opels retained their fine combination of dash with dignity (in this they are comparable in many respects with their national rivals, BMW and Mercedes-Benz), the Ascona and Kadett moved into

the front-wheel-drive field in the 1980s, to be joined (in 1983) by the diminutive but thoroughly practical Corsa, all being available in 'go-faster' guise as well. The new-look Kadett hatchback (the British version is known as the Vauxhall Astra) was voted Car of the Year for 1985. In its 1.8-litre 115 bhp GTE form, the 1985 Kadett/Astra had a drag coefficient of 0.30 – best in class – and could touch 200 km/h (125 mph) in reasonable circumstances. The Opel image may once have been humdrum – but not any more.

PACKARD USA

In the early 1950s, America's Big Three – Chrysler, Ford, and GM – were engaging in fierce battles for a market in which price and instant appeal meant more to the buyer than anything else. This situation spelled danger for the 'second echelon' car makers, which in any case had become vastly reduced in number during and after the Depression years. Kaiser, Frazer and Willys (1955), and Hudson and Nash (1957), were early casualties as mainstream car makers. Only their ghosts hover above today's American Motors/Jeep factories, which owe their survival to a nationalized French company, Renault.

Sadder still is the story of the Packard, which was kept on 'life support' until 1958. The fact is that the once glorious marque, which had operated profitably on military contracts between 1942 and 1945, was set on the wrong course once the Second World War was over. Instead of being allowed to seek its place among the top prestige models, the Packard was sent downmarket where it did not belong.

In 1897, bicycle builder Alexander Winton began making cars, and very fine some of them were. It was Winton's challenge that sparked off international racing, in the form of the 1900 Gordon Bennett Cup event. Winton eventually stopped making cars; his subsequent diesel engine business would become part of General Motors. Back in 1898, however, one of Winton's first machines was bought by the owners of an Ohio cable company, the brothers James and William Packard.

There are several parallels in Packard and Rolls-Royce history, and the first of these is the manner in which the cars were born. Just as Henry Royce was to create his first cars out of dissatisfaction with one he had bought – in his case a Decauville – so the Packards sought a better machine than the Winton. The first Packard car was completed in 1899, and the Ohio Automobile Company was formed soon afterwards, in conjunction with Henry Bourne Joy, to make it commercially. Joy was in fact the 'Royce' of the company, which became the Packard Motor Co in 1902 and transferred to Detroit the following year. James Ward Packard, inspirer of the whole project, lost interest in 1909 and handed over the reins to Joy, who brought in Alvan Macauley soon afterwards to run the company, assisted by Jesse Vincent.

Most early Packards, the production of which built up quickly, had four cylinders; but from 1911 the six-cylinder became increasingly popular. However, the Twin-Six of 1915, fitted with the first V12 engine ever offered for general sale, was the car that made Packard a household name. Over 30,000 of these early 12-cylinder Packards had been made by 1923, when Macauley (who had taken over on Joy's resignation during the First World War) introduced a replacement engine. This time the unit was a straight-8, which kept the Packard at the top of the automotive tree throughout the 1920s as the unostentatious car for responsible people. ('Ask the man who owns one' was an oft-quoted advertisement catch line.) The reputation of solid quality was enhanced still further in 1927 when Packard opened the world's first full-scale in-house proving ground, including a high-speed track.

Coincidental with his similar work for Cord, Cornelius Van Ranst designed a front-wheel-drive Packard for 1931 but, like the straight-12 Packard of the same year, it was destined to remain a one-off.

Packard returned to a V12 for its top-of-the-range models from 1932 and the marque's somewhat staid, although eminently respectable, image was given a youthful look by such 'prima donnas' as Ray Dietrich (who styled the Packard Twelve Sport Sedan which won all the prizes at the 1933 'Century of Progress' Exhibition in Chicago) and Howard Darrin, who knew how to make big cars look rakish yet not silly.

All the time, Packard was making lower-priced models which were snapped up by professional people of more modest means, proud to be identified with the sharply sculptured radiator cowl and little red hexagon in the wheel centres.

A 5.9-litre straight-8, with nine main bearings (like the earlier 'eight'), became the top engine again in 1940 and there were to be more delightful body styles: the last of their kind. One of these fine shapes was to re-surface in Russia, for Packard sold a set of body tools for the manufacture of ZIS (later ZIL) limousines.

Typifying the end of the greatest Packard era, the One Eighty Sport Brougham by LeBaron was to be mirrored in miniature, almost curve for curve, by Nuffield's postwar Morris Six and Wolseley 6/80. The sad demise of Packard is covered in the Studebaker section.

1930 (or Seventh Series) Packard 734 Speedster, the rare sporting version of this magnificent range of straight-8s.

RIGHT *Last of the Panhard line was the neat and modern front-wheel-drive 24CT, made from 1964 until 1967 when Citroën discontinued this illustrious marque.*

PANHARD France

Edouard Sarazin was a Belgian and trained with the Cockerill engineering company of Liège. In 1886, when he lived in Paris, he was astute enough to acquire the patent rights for Gottlieb Daimler's engines, which he had observed and admired in their early development stages. Sarazin showed the drawings to Emile Levassor, with whom he had worked at Cockerill. Levassor was now a partner of René Panhard, owner of a machinery manufacturing company. This concern specialized in band saws but was in need of a new product: the Panhard & Levassor (previously Périn & Panhard) factory was becoming under-utilized. Its new product would be the world's first true production car.

Sarazin died at the end of 1887, but his widow Louise remained the catalyst, obtaining a written agreement from Daimler and the hand of Emile Levassor in marriage. Panhard and Levassor continued to experiment, completing their first practical car in 1891. The first Panhard catalogue was published in 1892, and showed on the cover a four-wheeled vehicle with its power unit in front of the occupants (rather than underneath or behind them): in other words, this was a purpose-built motor car, available for public sale.

Levassor was not only a technician. In 1895 he drove single-handed from Paris to Bordeaux and back in under 49 hours, to win the first real motor race on record. In 1896 he was hurt in an accident in another race and, although his injuries at the time seemed slight, his death at his drawing board the following year was attributed to that event. By then the Panhard car was truly established.

Not all Panhards were particularly exciting, but they were widely copied. Like the British Daimler, and the Belgian Minerva, Panhard later adopted the Knight sleeve-valve engine, and most of the company's cars retained this type of power unit through to 1939.

The late 1930s saw some of the most unusual Panhards produced. The Dynamic, launched in 1937, was meant to look modern: but it curved in too many directions at once and, although unmistakable, its ugliness alone made it difficult to sell. Customers did not like its central driving position either, and it was not long before Panhard reverted to a choice of left- or right-hand steering wheel.

The Second World War saved Panhard from the immediate problem of obsolesence. Afterwards the company bought the front-wheel-drive Aluminium

Française Grégoire design (*see* Tracta) which placed Panhard, suddenly, in the high-performance small car class. The Panhard Dyna formed the basis for a number of successful small sports-racing cars, the most famous being the DB (Deutsch and Bonnet). Panhard made its own small sports car, the Junior, and in the early 1950s there was serious consideration by loss-making Daimler of Coventry to take up manufacture of these cars. It would have been a strange alliance if the two longest-established Daimler patent holders' had found themselves making the same sporting flat-twin! But it never happened.

There were new variants of the Panhard Dyna, including the Tigre – a top-performance version of a roomy but ugly saloon – and, finally, the pretty 1964 24CT coupé. Soon afterwards, Citroën's owners were in control, and the Panhard marque of such wonderful heritage was allowed to die quietly in 1967.

PEUGEOT France

To follow Panhard with Peugeot could not be more appropriate for, if Panhard was first, Peugeot was a very close second in the car-making business. By arrangement with Emile Levassor, Armand Peugeot obtained his first Daimler-type engines from the Panhard company in 1890 or 1891.

Based at Valentigney near Belfort in eastern France, the Peugeot family businesses were concerned largely with farm equipment and general hardware, and often traded with Panhard. From 1885 there were Peugeot bicycles, and in 1889 came the first Peugeot steam car, with a power unit supplied by Léon Serpollet.

The first Daimler-powered Peugeot quadricycle was driven successfully to Paris, then on to Brest and back in company with competitors in a race for safety bicycles (won by a Humber). Before the end of 1891, petrol-engined Peugeots were being offered for sale to the public. Success in racing was immediate, and in 1895 it was a Peugeot that was the first car to race on Michelin pneumatic tyres.

With such a well-established business base, Peugeot

One of the most popular family cars of postwar France, still often seen in use in rural areas, the Peugeot 203.

was soon able to make its own engines and expand production, and in 1897 the car company headquarters were transferred from Valentigney to a new plant at nearby Audincourt. By the turn of the century there was already a wide choice of Peugeot motor vehicles. In 1902 another factory began production in Lille.

For several years from 1906 Robert Peugeot built a rival marque, the Lion-Peugeot, in the original Valentigney factory, but this family rift was soon healed. The lion is still the Peugeot house symbol.

The year 1912 was very important for development; that was when manufacture of the Bugatti-designed Peugeot Bébé, a classic among light cars, started. At the other end of the scale was a superb new racing car inspired mainly by Paul Zuccarelli, who had worked with Hispano-Suiza. It had a 16-valve four-cylinder double overhead-camshaft power unit. Panhard and Peugeot had dominated the early motor races; other French marques, notably Brasier, Mors and Renault, had then taken over. By this time, however, foreign makes such as FIAT and Mercedes were showing clear superiority. The 1912 Peugeot redressed the balance, winning many important events – but, *most* important, the French Grand Prix itself, with Georges Boillot at the wheel, in both 1912 and 1913. The great American Miller engines of the 1920s and 1930s owed much of their technology to Peugeot.

Peugeot's continued prosperity involved acquisition of some companies, and cooperation with many more. The combination of individuality and performance made Peugeot's sporting family cars bestsellers. The trend started with the ugly Type 402 of 1936, but the postwar 203, 403, 404 and 504 saloons were all good-looking as well as tough, fast and practical. They were rally winners, too.

Cooperation with Citroën began in 1964, and soon afterwards came the first Peugeot to follow the 'Mini' principle of transverse engine and front-wheel drive: the 204. In 1974 acquisition of Citroën (the owners of Panhard by then) was complete. There was a combined Peugeot-Renault-Volvo engine project in 1975. Chrysler's European operations were taken over in 1978 by Peugeot, who reintroduced Talbot both as a company and a marque name in France and Britain.

If the image of Peugeot seemed to suffer at this stage, it was soon restored by the successful evolution of the 305 and 505 series and, most of all, by the little 205. In its GTi guise, the 205 invaded the equivalent Volkswagen and GM high-performance market and proved that, even in the mid-1980s, a small hatchback could still be charming and original. Two hundred special, turbocharged, mid-engined, four-wheel-drive rally versions were produced, as if by magic; and the self-deprecating Ari Vatanen, who won three major 1984 rallies including the notorious British RAC event, told reporters that this model was his 'favourite toy'. The 205 certainly put the sparkle back into the famous Peugeot name – the oldest in the industry of today.

RIGHT *Highly modified Group B four-wheel-drive Peugeot 205 Turbo 16 makes its sensational début in the 1984 Corsican Rally, driven by Ari Vatanen of Finland and Ulsterman Terry Harryman. They crashed out of this event but went on to win the Finnish, Italian and British championship rallies before the year was out; and they began 1985 in sparkling form with further victories in the Monte Carlo and Swedish events. These were followed in March by Timo Salonen's great win in Portugal.*

PIERCE-ARROW USA

ABOVE *1919 Pierce-Arrow 48 touring car, with characteristic headlamp treatment and steering wheel on the right.*

This marque was an early entrant into the American car industry. George Pierce, bicycle maker of Buffalo, NY, started building de Dion-engined cars in 1901.

The company grew, as did its reputation. So did the cars themselves, and from 1904 the name Great Arrow was used. In 1909, the marque name itself was changed from Pierce to Pierce-Arrow. A styling option from 1913 was the use of built-in headlamps, ultimately to be an almost universal feature of production cars.

The Pierce-Arrow became renowned as a rare and desirable marque. Some of the finest artists of the day were employed to produce evocative paintings, worthy of the cars' class, for use in publicity; and advertising copy was either minimal or non-existent: the picture told the story, one of unashamed wealth. When words were used, they sometimes had an almost literary quality, for example: 'Expectancy of good service soon ceases to be expectancy and becomes conviction'; or 'The Pierce-Arrow differs from other cars in three ways – in its engine, in its body, and in the way the two are combined to make the most thoroughly artistic, comfortable, and dependable car ever built'.

Like Rolls-Royce and other top car makers, Pierce-Arrow introduced a medium-sized luxury model in the 1920s. However, there was not a big enough market to sustain a company like Pierce-Arrow (which did not have other strings to its bow). Nor was it alone, for it was one of the 'Three Ps'. Peerless was to shut down first, in 1931, and turn to brewing. Packard was the strongest of the trio, and survived the longest. The third 'P' was the Pierce-Arrow, perhaps the most prestigious American car of all.

The Pierce-Arrow Motor Car Company was bought by Studebaker in 1928. This was a period when aspiring motor corporations either invented prestige marques or took them over. In 1929, the Packard formula of a sweet-running nine-bearing straight-8 engine was adopted; this, with the Pierce-Arrow's acknowledged ease of handling and good road behaviour, kept the marque in the top bracket. To meet the challenge of the multi-cylinder trend (begun by the Cadillac V16) Pierce-Arrow came out with a V12 engine in 1931; but deadly rival Packard did so too! (Possibly the unluckiest of all at this time was Marmon of Indianapolis who, with Cadillac, was alone in offering a 16-cylinder car to the public; but it did not have the backing it would have needed to survive the 1930s.)

Studebaker went bankrupt in 1933 and reduced some of its financial problems by selling Pierce-Arrow to a group of businessmen in the marque's home town, Buffalo, and in that year considerable publicity was gained from two events. One was the taking of long-distance speed records (by Ab Jenkins), and the other was the announcement of the Silver Arrow: a streamlined show car, of which only five were built. Its lines were adapted more conservatively for some of the last Pierce-Arrows. But the revival was short-lived and, despite genuine excellence, there was no place for the marque even in American society after 1938.

RIGHT *The Pontiac Firebird and Chevrolet Camaro were GM's strong response to the Ford Mustang. This 1971 Formula 350 Firebird was provided by John Poole.*

PONTIAC USA

BELOW *Mid-engined American: the cleverly conceived Pontiac Fiero – GM's popular sports car for the late 1980s.*

During the 1920s, the American corporations were in the habit of introducing new marques to fill price gaps in their ranges. In General Motors this tendency was rife. Marquette was a cheaper form of Buick; LaSalle was a cut below Cadillac; the Viking was intended as an upmarket Oldsmobile; and the Pontiac was meant to be the keenly priced Oakland.

The difference in the last case was that the Oakland itself had been phased out altogether by 1932, whereas the Pontiac has gone from strength to strength! GM's other three 'companion' marques, on the other hand, are long forgotten.

The early Pontiacs developed along orthodox American lines and were, incidentally, mirrored in certain Volvos (notably the PV60). Only in more recent times has the Pontiac, named after the Oakland's home town in Michigan, developed its own distinct place in the GM divisional ranking order.

Such names as Grand Prix, GTO (which was first used by Ferrari), Bonneville, and Grand Am conjured up visions of speed, but the first of Pontiac's true performance cars, the 1967 Firebird, was comparatively unostentatious.

Styled, as was the Chevrolet Camaro, by William Mitchell and his staff, the Firebird was and still is considered to be one of the best-looking of the new breed of smaller four-seat 1960s American coupés known as 'pony cars' (because Ford's Mustang was first). It is also noteworthy that the Pontiac has always tended to be the favourite GM car among Canadians.

While taking its usual place in the GM market place, Pontiac was given its head in 1983 with a unique and (initially at least) exclusive mid-engined sports model called the Fiero. Despite having a somewhat unexciting 2.5-litre four-cylinder engine, this beautiful little two-seat coupé sold very well throughout 1984 and before the year's end a 2.6-litre V6 was being offered. Critical *Road & Truck* magazine, among the first to try it, concluded: 'The debate is over. The Fiero isn't just a nice, two-seat, commuter car any more. It's a world class sports car.' Coinciding as it did with the arrival of Japan's first mid-engined production sports car (*see* Toyota), the Pontiac Fiero was a brave departure, but an opportune one.

PORSCHE Austria/Germany

In 1948, two Austrian families began commercial production of rear-engined sports cars with Volkswagen mechanical components. Wolfgang Denzel made his Denzel cars in small numbers (and helped conceive the BMW 700), but reverted to the selling and servicing of vehicles from 1960. His son runs the family business in Vienna today: end of Denzel story.

Ferdinand ('Ferry') Porsche, born in 1909, has been the central figure of a more famous dynasty which, since 1948, has progressed to technological heights and competition success on a scale it would have been difficult to foresee: except, perhaps, by the firm's founder. Ferdinand Porsche, senior, was of course a legend in his lifetime, and the cars that bear his name are a just tribute to him, for his earlier design influence throughout Europe was unparalleled. Born in Bohemia on 3 September 1875, he worked for Jacob Lohner in Vienna and then for Austro-Daimler in Wiener Neustadt where his son Ferry was born. Later he became technical director at Mercedes in Stuttgart and, after an equally influential period under contract to Steyr in Austria, he set up his own consultancy in Stuttgart in Germany in 1930. Most famous of his many projects were the 16-cylinder Auto Union Grand Prix car and the Volkswagen 'Beetle'. In 1933, Ferry Porsche joined his father in the business.

During the Second World War the Porsches, now under military contract, moved back to Austria to continue with tank development work, well away from most Allied bombing. After the war they were interned by the French; Ferry Porsche was freed first, and was able to return to Austria once more to set about reorganizing the business. The first new contract was for the design of a Cisitalia Grand Prix car. It had a flat-12 engine at the rear and four-wheel drive; but there was not enough cash to finish the job properly, and the marque's sponsor, Piero Dusio, emigrated

BELOW *1955 Porsche Speedster, a variation of the 356, mainly for the American market. Provided by Ray Wright.*

HIGHLIGHTS

1875: Ferdinand Porsche born near Reichenberg (now Liberec, Czechoslovakia).

1909: Ferdinand ('Ferry') Anton Ernst Porsche born in Wiener Neustadt, Austria.

1930: Porsche design consultancy created in Stuttgart, Germany.

1935: Ferdinand ('Butzi') Alexander Porsche born – eldest of four sons, and stylist of Type 911.

1937: First pre-production batch of definitive Porsche-designed Volkswagens produced; Porsche drawing of sports car concept completed.

1939: Porsche-designed VW streamlined specials built for (cancelled) Berlin–Rome event.

1948: First Porsche cars built at Gmünd, Austria.

1950: Transfer to Stuttgart, West Germany.

1951: Death of Ferdinand Porsche the elder; Porsche 356 wins class at Le Mans.

1962: Porsche flat-8 Formula One car wins French Grand Prix (Dan Gurney).

1963: Type 911 first seen at Frankfurt show.

1969: Porsche takes world sports car race title for the first time, with Type 917.

1970: Porsche achieves Monte Carlo Rally hat trick of victories (Type 911) and wins Le Mans outright for the first time (Type 917).

1984: Porsche-engined McLaren cars win Formula One World Championship.

number on the list of consultancy undertakings.

Normal business took a long time to re-establish in occupied Germany and Austria, but one piece of luck for the Porsches was the interest shown by a Swiss businessman, von Senger, who bought the first few cars and helped get supplies to Gmünd: for Volkswagen was back in business and already exporting to Switzerland.

Facilities were nevertheless inadequate at Gmünd, and in 1950 a return to Stuttgart was made. The first German Porsches were built in the Reutter coachbuilding works in the suburb of Zuffenhausen, part of the deal being for Reutter to make the coupé bodies. The founder celebrated his 75th birthday that autumn, before setting off for the Paris Motor Show where the first serious talks were to take place on the subject of selling Porsche cars in the United States. Soon afterwards Charles Faroux visited Porsche, successfully persuading him that the neat, smooth, lightweight coupés should take part in the 24-hour race at Le Mans.

In November 1950 the old man paid his only visit to the Volkswagen factory – by now well on the way to turning the 'Beetle' he had designed into the most

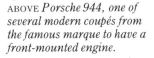

ABOVE *Porsche 944, one of several modern coupés from the famous marque to have a front-mounted engine.*

RIGHT *Dominating World Endurance Championship sports-car racing in the early 1980s was the Porsche 956.*

OPPOSITE TOP *The Porsche 911 was still one of the world's outstanding road cars, well over 20 years after its introduction. The 1972 911E and 1973 Carrera RS (provided by Barry Sumner and John Locke respectively) illustrate the contrasting images these engineering masterpieces can create through cosmetics.*

OPPOSITE BELOW *1985 Gruppe B Porsche carries the traditional 911 shape (created by 'Butzi' Porsche in the early 1960s) a stage further.*

from Italy to Argentina following a deal with Peron.

In the meantime, in June 1947, work began on the first car to be called a Porsche. From 1937, Porsche had been working upon the idea of a VW-based sports car, and a team had been prepared (for a Berlin–Rome race, cancelled when war was declared in September 1939). In August 1947, now well into his seventies, the founder was set free and he travelled immediately to the former sawmill at Gmünd where his workshops were still located in the southern Austrian hills.

The first Porsche had the VW engine and transmission units, turned through 180 degrees, giving good weight distribution but space for only two seats. It ran, for the first time, early in 1948. From the second car onwards, the layout reverted to the regular VW arrangement, with the engine behind the gearbox and transaxle to provide interior accommodation for some luggage, or even for two small rear seats. The first Porsches had the type name 356, which was simply a

successful single model in the world. On his return to Stuttgart he had a stroke, and died on 30 January 1951. He was one of the greatest engineers the world has seen, and an influence on many great marques besides his own.

The Porsche 356 enjoyed a brilliant life, and took many forms for road, rally and race use. From 1951, when it won its class at the first attempt, Porsche returned annually to Le Mans, where it has become the dominant marque of recent times.

There was no basic change in the body style until 1963 when Ferry Porsche's eldest son 'Butzi' (another Ferdinand) made fame with the classic 911 shape, still as popular as ever in the mid-1980s. It remains one of the world's supercars, despite the rear-mounted air-cooled engine, and has by no means been ousted by today's front-engined 'modern' Porsche road cars, the 924, 944, and 928, or by any other high-performance car for that matter.

In motor racing, Porsche has reached all of the important pinnacles, the highest being achieved by the flat-12 four-camshaft-engined 917 which, in 1970, brought Ford's domination of Le Mans to an end. A 1973 version of this amazing car (the 5.4-litre 917-30, with twin turbochargers) had a quoted power output of 1100 bhp, which made it one of the fastest of all circuit racers.

Porsche was still dominating Le Mans and the World Sports Car racing series in the 1980s, and likely to continue to do so barring sudden changes of policy. The company has also kept its unique consultancy role and, in that capacity, provided the turbo power and the reliability that gave Niki Lauda, Alain Prost, and the McLaren Grand Prix team their virtual monopoly of the 1984 Formula One World Championship.

Porsche is justifiably a great marque, for it has created more history in its relatively short life than almost any other car, and continues to do so.

RENAULT France

Louis Renault was born in 1877, the fourth son of a family of six. In the view of the French writer André Maurois, Renault had the look of a poet, and would have been head of General Motors had he been born American. Renault's great work was, sadly, clouded by his untimely death in prison (accused of collaboration with Nazi Germany) in 1944. After that, the firm he had founded with his brothers Fernand and Marcel was nationalized – yet it kept the Renault name, which has achieved respect throughout the world of motoring.

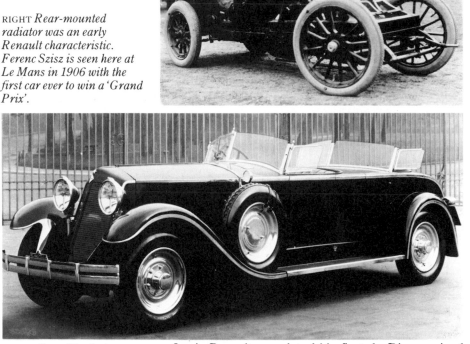

RIGHT *Rear-mounted radiator was an early Renault characteristic. Ferenc Szisz is seen here at Le Mans in 1906 with the first car ever to win a 'Grand Prix'.*

ABOVE *One of the last prestige Renaults before a general tendency to America styling, this superb 1934 Reinastella straight-8 has coachwork by Million Guiet. The radiator is now at the front.*

Louis Renault completed his first de Dion-engined shaft-drive prototype voiturette in late 1898, and in February 1899 the Renault Frères began trading.

Outstanding performances in racing came almost immediately, and Marcel Renault was the toast of France when he won the 1902 Paris–Vienna race from Count Louis Zborowski's Mercedes.

The following year came the Paris–Madrid, the last of the old inter-city races. Tragically, there were many accidents, among them the fatal one to Marcel Renault. Louis Renault, lying second in the race when it was brought to a halt at Bordeaux, vowed not to race again. Although he did not do so personally, his cars were soon in the headlines again, and in 1906 one of his big 13-litre machines won the first-ever French Grand Prix, run on a large circuit east of Le Mans. The driver was Renault tester Ferenc Szisz of Hungary. The two-part race, totalling over 12 hours of driving,

proved the great advantage of detachable wheel rims for quick tyre changing. Even so the Renault, although not the most powerful car in the race, was the fastest on the straights: it touched 160 km/h (100 mph) and was recorded over one kilometre of acceleration through the grandstand area at nearly 148 km/h (92 mph), no doubt helped by the streamlined nose, permitted by the characteristic scuttle-mounted radiator.

The publicity from racing proved invaluable, and Renault sold over 3000 cars in 1907, more than double the previous year. By 1908 the figure was approaching 5000. In that year Fernand Renault died, and the company name was changed to SA des Usines Renault. All the time, the company expanded at its original Billancourt site on the Seine, making a variety of 2-, 4- and 6-cylinder chassis, to which other firms fitted the coachwork. Of these the 'Marne Taxi' was the most celebrated, after being requisitioned for the massive troop movements needed to keep the Germans out of Paris in 1914. Light tanks, commercial vehicles and aero engines were also produced by the Renault empire during the First World War.

During the 1920s Renault car production covered everything from small family cars to the large and luxurious 9.1-litre six-cylinder 40CV, variations of which won the Monte Carlo Rally and took a number of long-distance speed records. In 1929 came the introduction of the 7.1-litre Reinastella, an elegant straight-8 with front-mounted radiator: a pattern to be adopted across the Renault range. Its successor, the 5.4-litre Nervastella, maintained the big Renault's reputation with a second Monte Carlo Rally victory – a decade after the first – in 1935, plus shared victories in the Liège–Rome–Liège marathons of 1934 and 1935, all with Lahaye driving.

Following a 1930s trend towards smaller cars, the rear-engined Renault 4CV, or 760, was inspired by the Volkswagen and developed during the Second World War, and it marked the beginning of a new era of advanced Renault designs. It had a chirpy French appearance, and an agility that brought it success in its class in early postwar rallies and races – perhaps one reason for its reduction from 760 to 750 cc in 1951?

The 1955 Dauphine was another attractive rear-engined family Renault. Then, soon afterwards, tuning wizard Amédée Gordini, renowned for his work on SIMCAs/FIATs, and for his own competition cars, began a long period of association with Renault, adding a sporting tang to a once-staid marque. The last important new rear-engined model was the Renault 8.

In 1961, Renault replaced the 4CV with the Renault 4 and this, like the more amusing but basic 2CV Citroën, was still being produced for local family and goods transport in many nations into the late 1980s.

After the Renault 4 came the Renault 16 of 1965 and a general front-wheel-drive policy has been maintained for new models since then, except in the case of the associated Alpine-Renault: a fine sports car, and one of the most effective rally cars of the early 1970s, but not part of the mainstream Renault range.

RIGHT *One of the most loved of all modern small cars, the chic Renault 5. This 1983 Turbo model is from The Patrick Collection.*

BELOW *The Renault 9 (or Alliance in the United States), announced in late 1981: a thoroughly practical 'three-box' front-wheel-drive saloon, typical of modern design practice, if not as 'homely' as some of its predecessors.*

History repeated itself when, after an absence of 70 years, Renault returned to Grand Prix racing with the first of the new breed of turbocharged Formula One cars. These scored many wins between 1979 and 1983, but by 1985 they were still looking for their first championship: the dream of every manufacturer who takes part in racing.

The biggest single investment of all came in 1980 when Renault launched out in a big way in the United States. In 1954, Hudson and Nash had merged to form the American Motors Corporation; and there had already been cooperation with Renault who had manufactured a joint product, the Rambler, for a few years in the 1960s.

In 1978, Renault and an ailing AMC were talking once again, and this led to the purchase by the Régie Nationale des Usines Renault of 46.4 per cent of the American company's equity. Further integration meant that AMC-Renault was producing not only the indigenous four-wheel-drive Eagle and Jeep ranges, but many of the popular modern Renault models – including the well-named Alliance (the Renault 9, Car of the Year in 1982), for which there was a soft-top option in 1985. By then, all Renaults were thoroughly modern, with a new prestige saloon (the 25) and a completely updated baby (the 5) at opposite ends of the scale; and a space age family wagon, the Espace, devised in conjunction with newly acquired Matra. Renault had, indeed, moved with the times. Only the surprise 1985 departure of top man Bernard Hanon in favour of Georges Besse led to slight concern for the state-owned giant's well-being.

HIGHLIGHTS

1898: Renault Frères established at Billancourt (Paris).

1902: Marcel Renault wins Paris–Vienna race.

1906: Ferenc Szisz (Renault) wins first Grand Prix.

1925: First Renault victory in Monte Carlo Rally.

1929: Beginning of general switch of radiator position from bulkhead to front of chassis.

1944: Death of Louis Renault, followed by nationalization of company.

1947: Introduction of Renault 4CV.

1955: First appearance of Jean Redélé's Renault-based Alpine sports car.

1961: Renault 4 starts trend to front-wheel drive.

1978: First serious talks with American Motors.

1982: Renault 9 voted 'Car of the Year'.

RILEY Great Britain

BELOW *One of the most beautiful early postwar cars was the Riley. What a pity this concept was not developed by BMC. This 1½-litre RM saloon in The Patrick Collection dates from 1954.*

The Riley Cycle Company of Coventry experimented with car manufacture as early as 1898, but made its name with proprietary-engined tricycles that became more akin to motor cars as their design progressed. Four-wheeled cars soon followed; but the introduction of a detachable wheel, which was sold to other makers, proved the most important commercial activity of the era before the First World War. As Riley (Coventry) Ltd, the company made reasonable progress until 1927, when it launched the first of its real gems: Percy Riley's Nine, announced in 1926. It had a 1.1-litre engine with two gear-driven camshafts placed high in the crankcase to reduce pushrod length. The overhead valves were set at 90 degrees to one another, and the combustion chambers were hemispherical. All subse-

quent new Rileys up to and including the first of the BMC Pathfinders had engines based on this unit. The Nine and its successors were exceptional performers, and the tuners had many a field day. Among them were Parry Thomas in the last days before his death (*see* Leyland); Reid Railton; and above all Freddie Dixon, the former motorcycle racer whose spectacular assault on the rather more genteel car racing world took him through a hedge and into a vegetable garden while leading the 1932 Ulster Tourist Trophy in his lightened Nine! He was to make up for this by winning the 1935 and 1936 TTs in later Rileys.

A six-cylinder supercharged version of the Riley engine provided the power of the 1934 ERA, and the Riley company itself produced a fine range of sports and touring models throughout this period (many of these had the Wilson preselect gearchange system). But the range was far too wide. By 1937 it was becoming impossible to make such carefully built cars at acceptable prices, and that was also the year a Riley subsidiary, Autovia Cars, introduced a luxury model with a V8 engine based on two fours (this was not actually Riley's first attempt at this configuration). The Autovia's price was too high for it to find ready sales. In 1938, financial circumstances led to a takeover by the Nuffield group, which had already managed to give a touch of the Morris to Wolseley and even M.G., and was about to do the same to Riley. Indeed, the last prewar saloons had a bland, even blank, look about them, although they did keep the shapely Riley radiator cowl.

The 1946 cars, among the first postwar models to be announced, gave Riley a new lease of life. The proportions of the new low-slung saloons were a delight to the eye, and the fabric-covered roof (unlike recent revivals of this gimmick) was totally in keeping with the overall theme. Almost simultaneously Donald Healey, who had had Riley connections earlier, began offering the 2.4-litre Riley engine, which was still capable of giving a very good performance, in a car of his own (*see* Healey).

The postwar Riley drophead coupé and roadster models were not as satisfying as the saloons, but it was an excellent series just the same; and it was the last of its kind.

At first, the slab-sided 1953 Pathfinder had the good old Riley engine, but in 1957 it was forced into using the BMC C-series engine from the Wolseley 6/90, which already had the same body.

An intended, but not really necessary, Morris Minor replacement structure was fitted with a two-carburettor version of the BMC B-series engine in 1957 and called the Riley 1.5. It was a potent little saloon of some charm, and a Rapier-baiter on the race circuits, but it was not a *real* Riley. Neither the Farina-styled 4/68 and 4/72, nor the front-wheel-drive Elf (Mini) and Kestrel (BMC 1100), did anything at all for the Riley name and in 1969, shortly after the formation of British Leyland, the marque was brought to an end – perhaps mercifully.

ROLLS-ROYCE Great Britain

As with several other makes – notably the Packard – the Rolls-Royce motor car came into being after a perfection-seeking engineer had bought himself an early vehicle, only to find himself dissatisfied with his purchase. The engineer's answer to that problem was to construct a car to his own standards. The outcome of Frederick Henry Royce's efforts was to bring him the accolade: maker of the Best Car in the World.

When he was ten Henry Royce, whose father had died young and poor, was a newspaper seller for W.H. Smith. Then an aunt paid for him to start on an apprenticeship at the Great Northern Railway Works, Peterborough; but the money ran out after three years and at the age of 17 Royce was job hunting. He worked long hours for a Leeds toolmaker, then found a job with the Electric Light and Power Company, first in London, later in Liverpool; and all the while, he was expanding his technical knowledge, so that by the age of 21 he was an accomplished electrical engineer.

In 1884, Royce and a friend, Ernest Claremont, scraped together sufficient capital to rent a room in Cooke Street, Manchester, and to start making electrical components. Over the years, their company became known for the quality of its work: electric motors, dynamos, switchgear and, latterly, electrically operated cranes. There was expansion at Cooke Street and in Manchester's Trafford Park industrial estate, and by the turn of the century Claremont and Royce were wealthy men, able to take an interest in the newfangled activity of motoring. France was the only country producing cars in quantity at that time, and the partners chose de Dion-Bouton quadricycles – well enough engineered, but a form of transport that

RIGHT *1913 Rolls-Royce 40/50 by Mulliner. Although there was only one car named Silver Ghost, the term became generally used for the 40/50. Provided by the Merle Norman Classic Beauty Collection.*

BELOW *1936 Phantom III with Saoutchik coachwork from France. This former Barbara Hutton property was provided for photography by the Briggs Cunningham Automotive Museum.*

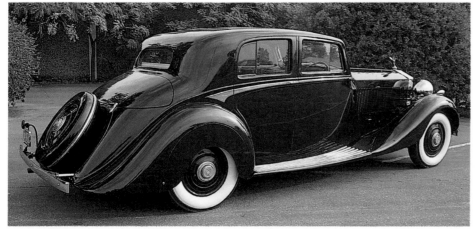

exposed the user to the mercy of all the elements.

Royce was not a healthy man, and was advised by his doctor to get a 'real' car. So he bought a second-hand Decauville. Although short-lived (1898 to 1910), the Decauville light cars from Corbeil were quite advanced and well respected in their day. One of the first German car factories – at Eisenach, later to become the home of BMW – built Decauvilles under licence (as Wartburgs). So did Orio & Marchand of Italy.

There was probably relatively little wrong with Royce's Decauville which was sent by rail to Manchester in 1902 but nevertheless, it embarrassed its new owner by refusing to start when he went to collect it. On taking the car apart, and applying his own perfectionism, Royce's thoughts turned to making something similar but better. Claremont and another

The Rolls-Royce Silver Shadow II (foreground) was launched in 1977 – 12 years after the original 'Shadow' – as was the long-wheelbase version known as the Silver Wraith II (also in this picture); both were provided for photography by Kenneth Smith. Their successors for the 1980s were called the Silver Spirit and the Silver Spur respectively.

director, Henry Edmunds, went along with the idea of using Royce's design skills, and the company's many and varied manufacturing facilities; for the foundry and machine shops were, at the time, under-utilized.

Begun in 1903 and completed the following year, the three original Royce cars were based on the twin-cylinder Decauville. Royce, Claremont and Edmunds had one each. Edmunds was already a keen motorist and a member of the same club as the Hon. Charles Rolls, a noted pioneer who had bought his first car, a Peugeot, in 1896, had already raced abroad, and had just (in 1902) set up in business as a London motor trader. His business manager from 1903 was Claude Johnson, former secretary of the club (the Automobile Club of Great Britain and Ireland, later to become the RAC).

Edmunds persuaded Rolls to meet Royce; they did so in March 1904, when they lunched in the Midland Hotel, Manchester, before inspecting one of the cars. Rolls agreed to be the sole selling agent, and the contract with Royce became formal in December of that year. The name Rolls-Royce was chosen simply because they thought it sounded well that way. Rolls claimed no precedence; he liked Royce, and considered him the most brilliant engineer he had met.

By the end of 1904, the first range of two-, three-, four- and six-cylinder Rolls-Royces were ready to show their distinctive radiator cowls in public, and in 1905 there was an experimental V8 model. Claude Johnson was made the managing director of a new company which was formed officially in 1906, as Rolls-Royce Ltd, and kept separate from the old Royce firm. Claremont was the first chairman.

Having come second to an Arrol-Johnston in the 1905 Tourist Trophy race, a Rolls-Royce (driven by

Rolls himself) turned the tables in 1906 to win outright. Although there were to be many other public demonstrations of Rolls-Royce performance and durability, the company would not take part in such events after the First World War. The chief home rival, Napier, was fading by then anyway.

It was the 40/50 hp model, launched in the autumn of 1906, that set Rolls-Royce on course for immortality. This was a 7-litre six-cylinder luxury car, not in any way revolutionary, but of exquisite workmanship and of ultra-smooth operation. Johnson had the Barker coachwork of one of the first cars painted and plated in silver for publicity purposes, naming it the 'Silver Ghost'. The name stuck, and came to be applied to the 40/50 generally.

By 1910, Rolls had taken a back seat, as he was more interested in flying. Sadly, he was killed in an aircraft crash that year. Johnson's commercial skill was shown time after time. For ten years from 1921 Rolls-Royce made 40/50s, and their successors the Phantoms, in the United States to reduce the effect of import taxes on the already costly cars. The Wall Street crash of 1929 led to the decision to close down after nearly 3000 American Rolls-Royces had been made. By then, the company was being run by Arthur Sidgreaves, following the early death of the hard-working and brilliant Johnson. Sir Henry Royce, deservedly knighted, spent his later years on the French Riviera or in the peace of Sussex countryside, where he worked on car and aero engine design right up to his death in 1933.

So it was that none of the founding fathers of Rolls-Royce lived to see the V12-engined Phantom III, the development of the Derby Bentley, or the move to Crewe. Nor were they to know the age of the jet engine which – like the Rolls-Royce piston engine –

would not only win accolades in the sky, but take several world land speed records, too, including the one achieved by Richard Noble's *Thrust II* in 1983.

The Rolls-Royce marque has suffered many setbacks, especially, it seems, in recent times. Lesser cars could not have weathered all the economic and social crises, but the Rolls-Royce has survived, maintaining the standards set at the very beginning; Sir Henry Royce and his colleagues would have been proud.

Rolls-Royces have never been the most modern cars in the world but, in so many other ways, they are the very best.

ROVER Great Britain

The Rover car's ancestry lies deep in Coventry's industrial antiquity which means, in effect, watch-making and sewing machine manufacture.

The Coventry Sewing Machine Company was set up in 1861 and thus gave birth to the city's bicycle industry. One of the most active participants was John Starley, father of the modern safety bicycle, who used the 'Rover' trade name for some of his machines as early as 1884, but not for his experimental electrically driven three-wheeler of 1888: arguably the only 'car' to come out of Starley's Meteor Works in the West Orchard district of Coventry, for in 1898 the company expanded to premises in Queen Victoria Road.

Starley died young, in 1901, by which time his Rover Cycle Co Ltd, so named in 1896, was the leading bicycle business in town, and on the verge of producing machines with engines. (Rover motorcycles were in fact made, along with bicycles, from 1902 to 1924.)

The first 8 hp single-cylinder Rover car of 1904 was designed by an ex-Daimler man, Edmund Lewis, who left for Armstrong Siddeley within two years. It had a backbone chassis, but later models were of more orthodox construction. A memorable, but relatively isolated, race victory was gained by Ernest Courtis with a 16/20 model in the 1907 Isle of Man TT.

BELOW *Besides the handsome saloons, Rover produced a number of drophead coupés and tourers. This one dates from 1947.*

The company's development was not helped by frequent changes in engineering design policy, and in the late 1920s there were serious financial problems as well as technical ones. Early engineers-in-passing included Owen Clegg (later of Darracq) and Peter Poppe of the engine-making family. A new general manager was needed, and in 1929 the ideal person for the job was chosen – probably only just in time. This was Spencer Wilks who, with John Black, had been running the Hillman company but (like Black) had lost interest when Rootes took over. The opening for Wilks at Rover was, therefore, to the benefit of both parties; moreover Wilks's younger brother Maurice, another fine engineer, came along as well. Between them they ensured for Rover a special niche among British quality cars.

For Rover, the 1930s began with a hiccup: a brave move to produce a really cheap car. The rear-engined Scarab, scheduled to sell for under £90, was withdrawn from the 1931 show catalogues at the last minute. The ever-cautious management, perhaps rightly on this occasion, decided that this baby car was just too basic.

In 1931, Spencer Wilks was appointed managing director, with his brother in charge of engineering. In 1933 the brothers competed in the RAC Rally which finished at Hastings. Maurice came third in his class while Spencer, in a Rover coupé clothed neatly by Carbodies of Coventry, won the coachwork competition for 10 to 16 hp cars. This satisfying result led to the model becoming known as the Hastings; and that shape became an integral part of what could be termed the new 'bargain' Rovers of the 1930s. The P1 and the P2 followed: the significance of the 'P' is not clear. But whatever the symbolism, the P-series brought Rover some solid profits – and, typically, provided doctors and other professional people with eminently suitable transport. Between 1932–3 and 1938–9, Rover production more than doubled, from 5000 to 11,000 cars a year.

The 'shadow factory' scheme of the Second World War led to Rover expansion, especially in Birmingham, and from 1945 the Solihull factory was the main one.

The Wilks family engineering skills were maintained after the war through their nephew Spencer King and through Peter Wilks. Rover developed the gas turbine engine for road use further than anyone, only to have to shelve it on economic grounds – as other manufacturers have done. By contrast, the 1948 Jeep-inspired Land-Rover lived on into the 1980s as much more than a farmers' workhorse; and the Range Rover, dating from 1970, brought complete sophistication to four-wheel drive in an equally timeless manner.

In 1949 the pretty P3 gave way to the peculiar-looking P4; the P4's central headlamp was, however, soon dropped for convention's sake. Rover was, after all, conventional – for the most part.

The 3-litre, or P5, was introduced in 1958; but it was the 1963 P6, the famous 2000, that brought Rover truly up to date. It was a compact and highly individual saloon, with good looks and good road behaviour.

Alvis was acquired in 1965 and this provided the production facility for a mid-engined Rover coupé, the P6BS; but any chance it might have had was scotched by subsequent BL politics. Rover had a discarded General Motors V8 engine which was also offered in the P5 and P6, giving the company the chance to maintain the high-performance image it had acquired through a serious international rally programme.

Leyland Motors, already in charge of Standard-Triumph, absorbed Rover in 1967, and British Leyland was formed the following year. BL was soon in trouble, resulting in the Ryder Report of 1975 and virtual ownership by the Government. This coincided with the completion of a new factory on the Solihull site and the first rumours of the SD1. This was the bulky, David Bache-styled four-door Rover hatchback, introduced with the 3.5-litre V8 engine in 1976 and subsequently offered with smaller petrol and diesel options.

In 1982, what remained of BL Cars was renamed Austin-Rover. By 1985 the Triumph marque, with which Rover had been linked for so long, was gone; its last model, the Acclaim, was succeeded by the diminished Rover 200 series – a Honda Ballade by any other name! For a traditional Rover, it was necessary in the late 1980s to look at the Land-Rover and Range Rover of Solihull. By then the saloons were being built at Cowley in any case.

Erik Carlsson started winning big rallies for Saab in the late 1950s; it was, however, his British RAC Rally hat trick of 1960 to 1962 that brought not only the sport of forest-stage rallying, but the Saab to a wider public.

A three-cylinder two-stroke engine was used from the mid-1950s, but then a full decade passed before the V4 Ford four-stroke engine gave the Saab 96 a new lease of life: with more rally victories, including the 1968 and 1971 RAC events, thanks to Simo Lampinen and Stig Blomqvist respectively.

Blomqvist worked wonders as a rally campaigner with the Saab 99, but it was not a true rally machine like its forebears: more of a sophisticated road car for the sporting business person. The first of the new generation Saabs, introduced in 1969, it featured a Triumph-designed overhead-camshaft engine. In that year, too, the long-established Swedish company Scania-Vabis was acquired. The old 96 soldiered on, to the delight of its many fans, throughout the 1970s.

The Saab 99 became a real innovation when first turbocharged in 1978, and the 900 of the mid-1980s maintained the company's reputation for performance and individuality; the latter quality applied in particular to the body shape, which seemed to follow no orthodox aesthetic rules yet did not offend the eye.

A totally modern, multi-national look came to Saab in 1984 with the introduction of the 9000, a smooth four-door saloon, built in cooperation with Lancia, with wind-cheating bodywork to accompany the famous

SAAB Sweden

The original two-stroke Saab prototype of 1947 followed the stillborn 1946 Philipson as Sweden's postwar answer to the DKW. (The DKW had been the best-selling car in the Scandinavian countries, but it had fallen victim to the war and the formation of two new Germanys.)

SAAB stands for Svenska Aeroplan Aktiebolaget (Swedish Aeroplane Co), and from the outset the diminutive four-seater, Sweden's only modern production car apart from the Volvo, was given the flowing lines that are second nature to aircraft builders.

Unusual, but certainly not unpleasant, looks gave the early Saabs a special appeal. Their front-wheel drive and free-wheel features were endearing, too.

ABOVE *A new departure in the mid-1980s was the introduction of convertible coachwork for the sophisticated Saab 900 Turbo.*

Swedish attribute of longevity. It was the smartest Saab yet evolved and put the Linköping company firmly into the luxury bracket. The engine was a fuel-injected twin overhead-camshaft 2-litre and there was even a pollen filter in the ventilation system – suggesting that we should be looking ahead to see what else we may need to keep out of our capsules in the future.

SINGER Great Britain

FAR RIGHT *From 1935 the Bantam kept Singer afloat until wartime, after which the company remained independent only while the seller's market lasted.*

BELOW *Singers were popular sports cars for every kind of competition. Here Joseph Patrick, head of Patrick Motors of Birmingham, competes in a 1934 club event with a works 1.5-litre.*

Like many Coventry marques, Singer made bicycles, and then motorcycles and tricycles, before producing its first car, a Lea and Francis design, in 1905. The most significant of George Singer's early cars was, however, the 1.1-litre Ten of 1912, which was extremely light and economical and could be bought for £185: probably the best buy on the British market until the £175 Morris Cowley appeared a year later. Lionel Martin tuned a Singer Ten and did well with it in hill climbs, including the one at Aston Clinton, near Tring, Hertfordshire. (This led him to choose the name Aston Martin when he began building cars.) The Rootes brothers' climb to fame and fortune started with their selling Singer cars; and later, of course, they would become the owners of the company.

Singer stopped making its motorcycles after the First World War. So did another local firm, Coventry-

Premier (although its German branch moved to what had become Czechoslovakia, and kept the Premier marque going until 1933). In 1920 Singer acquired Coventry-Premier, by then making a three-wheeler. This was turned into a four-wheel machine, a simple but effective vehicle well-suited to the days when few people had the experience of maintaining a motor car. The Coventry-Premier marque soon vanished, surplus to requirements, as Singer found itself with a range that was too complex.

In 1927 came the company's first overhead-camshaft four-cylinder model, the Junior, and from 1934 all Singers – fours and sixes – had this engine configuration. In that year, Singer acquired an old BSA factory in Coventry Road, Birmingham, in order to expand.

The 1935 Singer Bantam saloon was similar in its appearance, size and performance to the Morris 8, which was itself a copy of the Ford Popular. Any hope the Bantam might have had of competing seriously with Morris or Ford was hindered by two events in 1935: one was the price reduction of the Y-type Ford to £100; the other, the failure of the steering ball joints of three Singer sports car entries in the Ulster TT race. No one was hurt in the ensuing crashes, but they did the Singer reputation no good at all. In fact, the Singer Le Mans of that period was a good and often successful car in rallies and trials, driven by such experts as the Barnes brothers (Donald and Stanley), Godfrey Imhof, Joe Patrick and Bob Spikins.

Singer survived the Second World War, but did not expand because of it. The five-storey Birmingham factory did not prove suitable for large-scale manufacture and helped to drain the company's funds.

The postwar Singer SM1500 (later revised as the Hunter) was a far from cheap family car, and its dumpy body was not at all attractive. Much prettier was the traditional-looking roadster. In 1956, however, the Rootes brothers acquired Singer Motors Ltd, soon transferring production to their own factories and converting the Singer factory block into a spares centre. Subsequent models were very much Rootes products. No cars were called Singer after 1970, so at least the marque did not become a Chrysler when even the Rootes era passed into history.

STANDARD Great Britain

Today, the 'standard' model in a car range may be taken as the basic one, which few customers buy – preferring the De Luxe, the GLE, the Super, the GTi, or whatever skilfully marketed version is the most appealing.

It is, therefore, necessary to recall that cars were once simply cars, and that standards were banners to wave, or high ideals. 'Standard of the World' was the phrase adopted for the Cadillac after one of its early demonstrations of manufacturing quality (see Cadillac).

Britain's Standard car, built in Coventry, was so named with a similar thought in mind, and the subsequent adoption of the Union Jack as its emblem helped to emphasize the implied integrity of the product.

Reginald Maudslay came from a famous engineering family, another member of which had already begun making 'Maudslay' vehicles: which is possibly why he chose a different name. The first product of his Standard Motor Co Ltd was a single-cylinder 1-litre machine, the work of Alexander Craig, who was responsible for several other early Coventry designs.

The Standard range broadened quickly, and included some of Britain's earliest six-cylinder engines.

ABOVE *Created by Alan Jensen (before he and his brother Richard joined Patrick Motors), the 1930 Avon Standard Special was the first sports car to bear the Standard name. The New Avon coachbuilding company of Warwick retained a close association with Standard throughout the 1930s.*

In 1916, the first moves were made to create the factory site which is today the Austin-Rover headquarters at Canley, on the western edge of the city. However, the 1920s did not bring the consolidation Maudslay's company needed, and E. J. Corbett of Barclays Bank became a board member when finance caused problems. It was at Corbett's instigation that John Paul Black was invited to join the company in 1928, and become Maudslay's deputy although in effect this former Tank Corps officer was Standard's kingpin from the moment he arrived. Since 1919, when he was 24, Black had been with Hillman, latterly running the company jointly with his brother-in-law Spencer Wilks (each had married one of William

Hillman's six daughters). When the Rootes brothers began to take charge of Hillman, Black and Wilks were ready to apply their undoubted talents elsewhere. Wilks, as recorded earlier, became Rover's probable saviour; Black, likewise, brought Standard through the Depression and on to considerable success.

The Standard range of the late 1920s represented good value, but was as mundane as most contemporary everyday cars. It needed the independent coach-building trade to offer a measure of individuality and personal style to people for whom car ownership was by now a practical possibility. The New Avon company of Warwick had a long association with the firm, and Avon Standard Specials (created by the Jensen brothers before they joined Joseph Patrick in Birmingham) were the first really sporting Standards. Maudslay's son ran New Avon for a while, but it was the work of William Lyons, newly arrived in Coventry from Blackpool, and his Swallow Sidecar and Coachbuilding Company that intrigued Black the most. A Swallow-bodied Standard was first shown at Olympia in London in 1929.

Captain Black (he liked to use his old army rank) admired Lyons and could see that he was going to get on. He therefore agreed to provide Swallow with Standard engines and specially lowered chassis. From 1931 he even agreed that Lyons's new cars, resulting from this cooperation, should be called S/S – without any actual reference to the name Standard. As the SS marque progressed, so Black realized that Lyons was steadfast in his determination to stay independent. The cooperation continued but, when 'SS' cars became 'Jaguars', Lyons had reached a stage where he was no longer reliant upon the Standard company. Meanwhile, in 1934, Maudslay had died.

Throughout the 1930s, therefore, Black was faced with having to sharpen the Standard's image from within. The famous fastback range of Flying Standards, from a neat little Eight to a Twenty, were his answer. For a while, a V8 was offered but it was not a success, even in a sports car developed independently by Raymond Mays (creator of the ERA racing car). It would not be until 1944 that Black acquired a company of the type he was seeking (see Triumph). He also took a lease on a former Government 'shadow' factory at Banner Lane in 1945; for he had increased annual production sevenfold, to over 50,000, in his first decade with Standard, and was determined to do better still.

The 1947 Standard Vanguard confirmed Black's urge to succeed in export markets. It was big for a 2-litre car, but it made good use of the interior space and looked modern in an American way. After the Vanguard no other new Standards were announced for six years. During that period the Banner Lane factory was developed not for car manufacture but for the construction of tractors! (Black knew that Harry Ferguson was looking for a new factory and a new engine, and was quixotic enough at one stage to consider switching to tractor production altogether.

In fact, Ferguson and Massey-Harris merged in 1953 and took over the Banner Lane factory six years later.)

From 1953 a new Standard Eight was produced at Canley, soon to be followed by a more powerful Ten, which performed well for a saloon with an engine of less than 1 litre, winning outright (and the team prize) in a snowbound 1955 RAC Rally. But the small postwar Standards were dull and were not developed for the 1960s. The group, now known as Standard-Triumph, was putting more and more emphasis on the second name of its title, and the bigger Standards – the new-style Vanguard and the Ensign – were dropped in 1963. Sadly, the Standard name had gone, but the Triumph marque would live on for another twenty years under Leyland rule.

STUDEBAKER USA/Canada

All five Studebaker brothers were involved in carriage building at their smithy at South Bend, Indiana, from the middle of the 19th century, so in one sense Studebaker, which expired in the 1960s, could be regarded as America's oldest road-vehicle maker.

The Studebaker was a solid seller in the early days of the car. The first cars, in 1902, were electrically powered but internal combustion orthodoxy followed.

Studebaker produced more than 45,000 cars in 1915, placing the marque sixth among the American manufacturers, but this level was not maintained consistently. From 1927 to 1933 Studebaker owned Pierce-Arrow only to run into financial trouble itself in 1934 (*see* Pierce-Arrow); but it recovered. After the Second World War, Studebaker took the lead in style: first with the Virgil Exner/Raymond Loewy 'panoramic' effect of 1947, achieved with a wrap-around rear window; then with the more convincing Bob Bourke/Loewy cars of 1953. Meanwhile, production

at South Bend had reached an all-time high point of over 320,000 vehicles in the 1950 model year – but by then, this was good enough only for eighth place in North American standings! From 1952, Studebaker production fell away alarmingly, but this decline does not seem to have been noticed by Packard, who had rarely exceeded 100,000 in a year. Packard needed its merger with Studebaker in 1954 to survive; neither of the famous companies was able to deal with the colossal Ford versus GM war then being waged.

Studebaker can be considered great not merely because of its age, but because of the beauty of those 1953 models, the most handsome of all early postwar American cars. Regrettably, they kept their elegant good looks only for a few years before falling victim to styling excess; or maybe it was panic, for Studebaker dragged Packard down quickly after their merger. The very last Packards of 1958 were shaped like Studebakers.

Packard was gone when, in 1962, the Loewy-styled glass-fibre-bodied Avanti coupé was produced as Studebaker's final fling; but it was not enough.

Studebaker kept going in its Canadian plant (at Hamilton, Ontario) with Brooks Stevens 'facelifts' until 1966: two years after the Indiana plant had been abandoned. Part of the South Bend factory, however, was used by two enthusiasts who obtained the go-ahead and the tooling to build Avantis with Chevrolet V8 engines in small numbers there, and they still had a faithful following in the 1980s.

STUTZ USA

There were two distinct phases in the production life of the Stutz. During the first, from 1911 to 1918, Harry C. Stutz was in charge. His company (with its great rival, Mercer) may be considered America's first sports car maker. Like the Mercer and other early cult cars, the Stutz Bearcat featured a 'monocle' windscreen and rakish looks, but was technically orthodox.

Harry Stutz left the company to start another, and from 1919 his cars bore the name H.C.S. The early models were similar in character to the Stutz, being big and expensive, but the last H.C.S. products were taxis, and the firm closed down in 1925 (the year that Mercer also failed).

Meanwhile, the Stutz Motor Car Co of Indianapolis was grappling with the problems of a 'playboy' image, as attitudes to the automobile changed and its sales dropped away.

The firm's second great phase began in 1925 when its owner, tycoon Charles Schwab (who also owned Bethlehem Steel and was an important sponsor of the Atlantic City Speedway) brought in several top men from neighbouring Marmon. This was an older marque with a similar clientele – but a company that had also been technically advanced from its outset. Schwab's greatest 'scoop' came in obtaining the services of Frederick E. Moskcovics, another great racing advo-

ABOVE RIGHT The 1929 Stutz Model M's Vertical Eight engine was subsequently rechristened the SV-16 to distinguish it from the new (1931) DV-32, which featured double overhead camshafts and 32 valves.

cate, to lead a team of fine engineers. Among them was Paul Bastien whose background, like that of Moskcovics, had included European automobile design.

The product of the reorganized company was the overhead camshaft-engined new Stutz Vertical Eight, which soon re-established the marque's reputation in the fashionable driveways and on the racetracks of America. Stutz cars put up several creditable performances at Le Mans, finishing a strong second to Bentley in 1928.

The last Stutz cars were the glorious but doomed products of the Depression. The performance of the DV32 was prodigious, in roadholding as well as power. Launched in 1931, it had an eight-cylinder nine-bearing engine, bored out to 5.3 litres, with four valves per cylinder (hence the car's designation) operated by two overhead camshafts. Probably more than any other single sporting car, the Stutz DV32 represented the finest possible blend of American and European perfectionist design practice.

Perfectionism can lead to insolvency, for this is not a perfect world. No cars were made after 1934; a switch to lightweight commercial vehicles was attempted, but the losses mounted up and in 1938 a Federal judge oversaw the sale of assets to the Diamond T truck company.

The name Stutz appeared again from 1970, for a new series of exotic American-built high-price specials.

SUNBEAM Great Britain

Louis Coatalen, a Breton who had worked for de Dion-Bouton before making England his home, joined the Sunbeam Motor Car Company by way of Crowden, Humber, and Hillman where he had been chief engineer.

Sunbeam cars had been made from 1899 by John Marston Ltd of Wolverhampton, general engineers and bicycle makers, but it was Coatalen's arrival ten years later that transformed the marque. There was a marked increase in racing activity, first with the 1911 Coatalen-designed 3-litre four-cylinder Coupe de l'Auto model, but most effectively with the 1923 Grand Prix car, designed largely by Vincenzo Bertarione who joined Sunbeam from FIAT with the Italian company's own six-cylinder 2-litre racer fresh in his mind. Henry Segrave won the 1923 French Grand Prix in one of these cars to give Britain its biggest racing success to date. He went on to take the world land speed record twice with Sunbeams, using a supercharged 4-litre V12 (based on two GP engine blocks) for the first of these successes in 1926. This was not the first V12, for Coatalen's wartime aero engines had also been used for motor racing. Early in the 1920s (when Sunbeam, Talbot and Darracq had joined forces commercially), there was a less successful straight-8. The ultimate Sunbeam record breaker was the 1000 hp (twin-engined) machine with which Segrave took the world record to over 320 km/h (200 mph) in 1927.

The Sunbeam road cars of that period were of outstanding specification, including a double-overhead camshaft six with dry-sump lubrication and, at the top of the range, a 5.4-litre straight-8, priced in the Rolls-Royce class.

The STD organization did not weather the Depression very well, and disintegrated in 1935. William Lyons of SS Cars Ltd made what he thought was a successful bid for Sunbeam but the Rootes brothers managed to

RIGHT A fine example of an underrated classic, the 1924 six-cylinder overhead-valve 4.5-litre Sunbeam 24/70 tourer.

RIGHT 1961 Sunbeam Alpine II, an attractive two-seater based upon the Rapier. More exciting was the V8 Ford-powered variation known as the Tiger.

acquire both the Sunbeam and the Talbot marques.

Sunbeam production at Wolverhampton was phased out in 1937, and the 'Sunbeam-Talbot' marketed by Rootes from 1938, although attractive, was essentially an up-market Hillman with sporting overtones.

With the Alpine two-seater convertible of 1953, the marque name Sunbeam was restored. In 1955 a Sunbeam 90 saloon won the Monte Carlo Rally, and a new line of two-door saloons began with the launch of the Rapier in 1956. It maintained the Rootes reputation for outstanding performance in competitions with a win in the 1958 RAC Rally, and class victories in numerous other races and rallies.

A new Sunbeam Alpine sports car appeared in 1959 and then in 1964 a very special version was introduced as the Tiger. This had a 4.2-litre American Ford V8 engine, and car assembly was carried out by Jensen. In 1967, the power plant of this civilized, Cobra-inspired sports-tourer went up to 4.7 litres: but then, soon afterwards, politics took a hand. Chrysler, by now the master of Rootes, did not like using the engines of its rival, Ford; and, it was said, did not have a V8 power unit that could be shoehorned into the Tiger's tight under-bonnet space. Then with the coming of the US Federal emission and safety laws, and with natural obsolescence, the Alpine and Tiger were soon out of production. However, the Alpine name was revived in a basic version of the last, fastback, Rapier which (with the Hillman Imp-based Stiletto) brought the Sunbeam marque name to an end for the second time. New models from Humber Road and Ryton, Coventry, became Chryslers in 1976.

In 1978, however, a small saloon called the Chrysler Sunbeam was announced. Then came the Peugeot takeover, so the car became the Talbot Sunbeam: at which point it is probably best to move on to the British Talbot.

TALBOT Great Britain

The Earl of Shrewsbury and Talbot was the main sponsor of the British firm of Clément-Talbot Ltd, founded in 1903 to import Clément cars from France. Soon assembly was taking place at a factory in Barlby Road, West London, and from 1906 the Talbot was very British – and not a Clément or a Clément-Bayard.

The greatest Talbot exploit before the First World War occurred at Brooklands in 1913, when Percy Lambert became the first person to cover more than 160 km (100 miles) in an hour. Immediately after the war, however, Talbot became engulfed in a new group called STD Motors. This included the Darracq and

Sunbeam firms, which kept up their sporting activities, whereas Talbot concentrated on the manufacture of bread-and-butter light cars of high quality. The outstanding model of the early 1920s was the 10/23, which had been developed from a badge-engineered Darracq by the Swiss engineer Georges Roesch.

In 1925 Louis Coatalen, the leading light at STD, appointed Roesch chief executive at Clément-Talbot. Roesch helped the company through the next very difficult years with his 14/45, a 1.9-litre light six model aimed at the sophisticated customer who wanted smoothness and performance comparable to those of a Rolls-Royce 20, but in a car of less size and cost.

The 14/45 (or Type 65) was the first of an illustrious series of Roesch Talbots: the 2.3-litre 75 and 90, followed by the 3-litre 95 and 105, and ultimately the 3.4-litre 110. These were superb road cars, equally adaptable for racing or rallying. Fox & Nicholl prepared teams of Talbots for several big events. Third place at Le Mans was taken in three successive years (1930, 1931 and 1932), but it was in the 1931, 1932 and 1934 Alpine Trials that the model shone. In those three years seven Talbot 105s were entered and all of them finished without penalty in those gruelling events.

Georges Roesch approved of the Fox & Nicholl activity up to the end of 1932, after which these Surrey garage owners and tuning specialists concentrated their attention on Lagonda, to win Le Mans with that marque in 1935. Roesch was more concerned with providing superbly engineered, understated cars of great distinction, at reasonable prices. A 4.5-litre straight-8 Talbot was on the way when the axe fell. The fact that Talbot of London may well have been profitable at the time was not allowed to affect the STD group, which failed in 1935. The Rootes brothers picked up the famous names of Sunbeam and Talbot, and put them into their existing (Hillman and Humber) melting pot.

The last Roesch Talbots were listed until 1938, by which time there were two new Hillman-cum-Humber derivatives wearing the Talbot badge, and London manufacture was to cease.

Roesch had left, mortified, and purists voiced their objections, strongly, to the loss of 'their' car. This may have been one reason for introducing the Sunbeam Talbot, from which the 'Talbot' was dropped in 1954. Meanwhile, the former Darracq plant in France had been making Talbots and Talbot-Lagos (*see* Darracq).

By the late 1970s Rootes' successor Chrysler was in real trouble at home and ready to back out of Europe. Peugeot-Citroën took over and unearthed the name Talbot for British Chryslers and French SIMCAs.

Peugeot itself was a reputable name, however, and by the mid-1980s the future of the Talbot marque – British or French – seemed open to question. The 1980 RAC Rally and the 1981 World Rally Championship, however, were won by small orthodox cars bearing the name Talbot Sunbeam-Lotus which, in a way, was a backhanded tribute to the achievements of those great London-built Talbots of another age.

TATRA Czechoslovakia

Alongside Ferdinand Porsche (himself a Bohemian by birth), Hans Ledwinka and Edmund Rumpler – both born near the centre of the Austro-Hungarian empire – rank among the greatest of visionaries in the pioneering days of the motor car, men who were able to anticipate by many years features that have since become commonplace.

Ledwinka was 18 when he left college in Vienna in 1896 to join the Nesselsdorfer Wagenbau-Fabriks-Gesellschaft, which had been founded as the Schustala cart and carriage making firm in 1853 and, since 1882, had been one of Europe's most important railway rolling stock producers.

In 1897, the 24-year-old Edmund Rumpler, newly qualified in engineering (also in Vienna), was a leader of the team that put together the first Nesselsdorf car, inspired by the contemporary flat-twin Benz. Ledwinka was one of the assistants.

Rumpler left Nesselsdorf in 1898 to pursue a distinguished if unconventional engineering career; his best-known exercise was the 'teardrop' car, which he displayed at the 1921 Berlin motor show. Ledwinka left the company, too, but only briefly, and from 1905 his career was bound up with the products of the tiny village of Nesselsdorf (with the notable exception of a four-year period when he was wooed by Steyr, to switch production from arms to motor vehicles). This time he returned, in 1921, to a Nesselsdorf now renamed Kopřivnice: for Czechoslovakia had beome a republic, and German was no longer the first language. Progress was accelerated not only by Ledwinka's return, but by the backing of the Ringhoffer industrial group of Prague. From now on, the products carried the name Tatra.

Late in 1922 Ledwinka put into effect a combination of features which made Czechoslovakia the producer of the world's first modern economy car. Its two-cylinder engine was an air-cooled flat-twin of just over a litre's capacity. It had no frame as such, but a hefty central tube, or backbone, containing the propeller shaft, which drove through independent swinging rear half-axles (as patented by Rumpler much earlier). This brilliantly conceived light car was called the Tatra 11. In 1925 it became famous when a sports version won its class in the Targa Florio race, and in the following year the production model was given four-wheel brakes to become the Tatra 12. The next important advance was a series of larger air-cooled models built on the same principle, but with flat-4 engines. The last of these front-engined cars, the Tatra 57B, was discontinued in 1948 or 1949.

The early Nesselsdorf range had consisted largely of luxury models – the 1910 S-40/50, with six-cylinder 5-litre overhead-camshaft Ledwinka engine, was outstanding (and the inspiration for the first Steyr). In the 1930s, even after the popularization of motoring, the company continued to produce limited numbers of water-cooled front-engined 'state cars', including a magnificent V12 6-litre, the Tatra 80. From 1933 to 1938, the marque was exported to a number of overseas countries, including Britain.

However, it is the air-cooled rear-engined Tatra for which Hans Ledwinka is best remembered. His first

RIGHT *Announced in late 1922, the Tatra 11 led to a whole series of practical and original family cars with backbone chassis, swing-axle suspension and air-cooled engines. The first update, in 1925, was the four-wheel-braked twin-cylinder Tatra 12 (far right). Most popular of its successors was the flat-four Tatra 57 seen (near right) in mid-1930s tourer form.*

1931 prototype was a small two-seat coupé which, in retrospect, can be seen to have anticipated the 'Beetle' (*see* Volkswagen). A saloon, the V570, with a 0.9-litre two-cylinder engine beneath its streamlined tail, was made in 1933. It, too, remained a prototype: perhaps because of the continued popularity of the front-engined cars, or maybe Tatra could not build it in economic quantities?

The final translation of the fastback, rear-engined saloon to production reality came dramatically in 1934 in the form of the Tatra 77. This full-sized four-door car was powered by a new 90-degree V8 3-litre (later 3.4-litre) engine, and the very earliest examples had a central driving position! From then on, all new Tatra cars followed the principle of uncompromising aerodynamic shape and air-cooled V8 or four-cylinder engine mounted at the rear (largely to reduce noise for the occupants).

From 1938, German control over Czechoslovakia led to a reduction in choice for customers and, very soon, a concentration upon military vehicle manufacture. After the Second World War, the nationalized Tatra corporation (Tatra Narodny Podnik) continued to develop Ledwinka's design principles. Ledwinka himself was imprisoned – presumably as a capitalist – but was able to retire to Munich, West Germany, after some six years of internment. He did not, however, benefit from the partially successful action taken against Volkswagen by the Austrian arm of the Ringhoffer empire concerning his Tatra patents. At

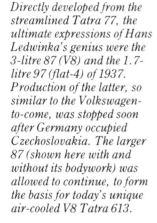

Directly developed from the streamlined Tatra 77, the ultimate expressions of Hans Ledwinka's genius were the 3-litre 87 (V8) and the 1.7-litre 97 (flat-4) of 1937. Production of the latter, so similar to the Volkswagen-to-come, was stopped soon after Germany occupied Czechoslovakia. The larger 87 (shown here with and without its bodywork) was allowed to continue, to form the basis for today's unique air-cooled V8 Tatra 613.

HIGHLIGHTS

1822: Birth of Ignác Šustala (Ignaz Schustala), founder.

1853: Šustala opens coachbuilding workshop at Nesselsdorf in Austrian crown land of Mähren (Moravia).

1867: Formation of dual monarchy of Austro-Hungary.

1872: Birth of Edmund Rumpler.

1878: Birth of Hans Ledwinka.

1897: First Nesselsdorf car, the Präsident, designed by engineers Sage and Rumpler, with Ledwinka and others assisting.

1898: First NW truck, based on original car; Rumpler leaves Nesselsdorf.

1899: Baron Theodor von Liebieg, textile magnate, wins Vienna race in Nesselsdorf car.

1905: Ledwinka returns to Nesselsdorf after three years with a Viennese steam engineering company, Knoller-Friedmann.

1918: Moravia becomes part of new Czechoslovak republic; Nesselsdorf renamed Kopřivnice (both names allude to nettles).

1922: Launch of Tatra 11.

1931: First rear-engined prototype baby Tatra built.

1934: Aerodynamic air-cooled V8-powered Tatra 77 introduced.

1938: Munich Pact leads to division of republic; Bohemia and Moravia ceded to Germany.

1948: Czechoslovakia re-emerges as part of Soviet bloc; Tatra 600 (or Tatraplan) introduced.

1956: V8 engine returns, in new Tatra 603.

1967: Death of Hans Ledwinka.

1975: Series production of Tatra 613 begins; updated version still in production ten years later.

Kopřivnice itself there is no reticence about acknowledging the man whose picture on the wall of the works museum is captioned 'Jan Ledvinka'.

For a while, it looked as if car production would stop. Certainly, for many years Kopřivnice has been devoted to heavy-duty truck manufacture. In 1969, however, came the prototype of a large, modern saloon, with a four-camshaft 3.5-litre air-cooled V8 engine, mounted over the final drive, rather than behind it. For the first time, the now dated fastback style was abandoned for a crisp, well-proportioned body by Vignale of Italy. Full production, in a separate factory at Příbor, began in 1975 and the Tatra 613 was still being made in the mid-1980s, which gives it the longest heritage of any Central European car.

TOYOTA Japan

TOYOTA

If Japanese technical progress remained relatively unaffected by the First World War, it was to be shattered by the disastrous earthquake of 1923. The country had had a late start in any case, for Japan was in no hurry to replace the rickshaw. When all forms of transport were disrupted in 1923, the Americans were quick to bring their technology. By 1928 the Big Three – Chrysler, Ford and General Motors – were well-established and, until local restrictions were imposed, they led the industry. The Second World War and its aftermath forced Japan to start all over again. It was

ABOVE *The world's best-selling modern car range, Toyota's Corolla. This GT version dates from 1985, the year in which production of the 12 millionth Corolla was anticipated.*

not until the 1950s that her motor cars would even begin to make an impression on the rest of the world.

Toyota is the classic example. The Toyoda family began making weaving equipment in 1926, and then from 1933 personnel were recruited, mainly from GM Japan, to start a vehicle division. In 1935 came the launch of an ungainly saloon car, copied from the Chrysler/DeSoto Airflow and fitted with a Chevrolet-type 3.4-litre six-cylinder overhead-valve engine.

The first cars and trucks to emerge from the Nagoya factory carried the Chinese characters for the name Toyoda. In July 1936, a competition was held to establish a trade mark. This resulted in a new name, 'Toyota', which could be formed more simply than Toyoda: with eight brush strokes instead of ten.

The first Toyotas were made in very small numbers, as was the Toyopet SA, a smaller saloon built in the late 1940s, when the Occupation authorities maintained strict limits on Japanese production, and morale was still low. In 1950 the sales outlook was bleak, and there was a three-month strike; but Toyota pursued its new policy of making totally home-produced cars and the 1955 1.5-litre 4-cylinder Crown marked the company's turning point. Exports to the United States began with the arrival of two Crowns at Los Angeles in August 1957, accompanied by Miss Japan. A headquarters was set up at the Statler (later Hilton) Hotel. It was the beginning of the great reversal of roles: the first promotion of Japanese cars in the land that had taught the world mass production. Five years later, Toyota had passed the million mark in vehicle production, and in 1963 its export drive to Europe began.

The year 1966 was important, for it marked the arrival of the first of the best-selling Toyota Corolla saloons. Hino and Daihatsu were among Toyota's acquisitions in the late 1960s. (Daihatsu was the first company to sell Japanese cars to Britain, in 1966.)

By the 1970s, Toyota was holding on to its lead among the manufacturers involved in Japan's magnificent demonstration of how to make and sell fully equipped, reliable and attractive cars in the markets of the world. Its annual production was approaching two million vehicles. This positioned it third (ahead of Nissan-Datsun), and only General Motors and Ford were in front of Toyota in overall rankings!

Toyota entered the 1980s with over 30 million vehicles behind it, and a bewildering variety of new models. Although they do not quite have the sporting image of Honda, Mazda, Mitsubishi, or even Nissan, Toyota production models have proved themselves in competitions on many occasions, sometimes winning against powerful odds. Hannu Mikkola's 1975 triumph in the Thousand Lakes Rally showed the Corolla's possibilities; and Björn Waldegård's mighty deeds with the Celica Turbo in the 1983 Ivory Coast and 1984 East African Safari rallies proved that four-wheel drive by itself was not a foolproof passport to victory in the world's toughest marathons. Dependability still counted, above all.

The best-selling car in the world by the 1980s, the Toyota Corolla, switched to transverse engine and front-wheel drive in the wake of the European trend. The most exciting new Toyota for the late 1980s also had its power unit mounted crossways, but behind the driver. This was the MR2, or 'Midship Runabout 2-seater', a neat high-performance machine to challenge the Pontiac Fiero in the medium-priced super-coupé class. For some reason, its badge was a bird. Fifty years earlier, the first Toyoda bonnet badge featured symbolic wings. Whatever the thought behind the emblem, Toyota has flown quicker than other car producers in the world – and further than most.

TRACTA France

Front-wheel drive has been in existence almost as long as the car itself. The Gräf brothers of Vienna should probably be counted as first in the field, in 1899. Since the 1970s, it has become the standard configuration used by the world's high-volume car producers. It gives the modern car compactness, a flat floor, and a natural controllability. Until the 1920s, however, front-wheel drive was not available in any 'off-the-peg' touring car. After all, handling was a sophistication as yet irrelevant to everyday motoring, and there was a special problem: how to overcome harshness and wear in the steering mechanism, caused by irregularity of driven-shaft velocity when lock was applied. The principle of a double joint, to give the effect of constant velocity, was propounded by Robert Hooke, an English scientist, towards the end of the 17th century. Pierre Fenaille and Jean Grégoire were the creators of the patented Tracta Homokinetic joint – their literal translation for a joint 'of constant velocity' – in the '20s.

Fenaille was the financier and often an ideas man. Grégoire was a technician, a salesman, and an enthusiast, who ran a garage in Versailles.

Several hundred front-wheel-drive Tractas, with proprietary engines by SCAP, Continental and, ultimately, Hotchkiss, were sold to the public between 1927 and 1932. They had underslung chassis, which allowed them to have long, low lines. The gearbox was placed ahead of the engine, and the independent front suspension was on the simple sliding-pillar principle.

Despite their good looks, virtually all Tracta cars were sold at a loss; however, sale of the Tracta joint patent rights and further design consultancy work made up for this. Grégoire was responsible for the all-independently sprung Amilcar Compound, which Hotchkiss built in the late 1930s. At his Asnières works he made the advanced Aluminium Français-Grégoire lightweight prototype secretly, during the Occupation, and it nearly went into production after the Second World War in America (Kaiser), Australia (Hartnett), and Britain (Kendall). (See also Panhard.)

Between 1945 and 1962 Grégoire created a number of interesting but abortive cars bearing his own name; but his most historic work is reflected in the Tracta, for which his friend Fenaille had been the inspiration: not least, financially.

From 1932, when the Triumph company commissioned Patrick Motors of Birmingham to make a sports body for the Southern Cross chassis, a performance image had begun to emerge. Through rally successes, Donald Healey helped create and promote the excellent Gloria and Dolomite models with their distinctive Walter Belgrove styling, but the Alfa Romeo-inspired Straight Eight supercar was scrapped at the project stage. That was just the tip of the dangerous iceberg. Triumph was becoming too specialized in an area – the 1.5- to 2-litre quality market – that already contained too many poor-but-honest makers for any comfort. Moreover, Triumph had more factory space than it could use effectively after the motorcycles were moved out. In June 1939 the Triumph Motor Company went into receivership.

During the Second World War the Sheffield engineering firm of Thomas Ward held the title to the

Triumph car business, but put it on the market in 1944; and Sir John Black (the former Captain Black – *see* Standard) took it on.

It was not just that he wanted a good, reputable sporting marque to enhance postwar trade for his relatively lacklustre Standard company. Thwarted in all his attempts to team up with the equally strong-willed William Lyons of SS Cars Ltd (soon to become Jaguar Cars Ltd), Black went on record as saying he had bought Triumph to put Lyons out of business.

Black's Triumph cars were very individual and personal. The roadster shape with rumble seat (or dickey) was designed in Coventry by Frank Callaby; the boldly attractive Town and Country (or Renown) razor-edge saloon was largely the work of Louis Antweiler and his colleagues at the Mulliner, Birmingham

TRIUMPH Great Britain

Siegfried Bettmann and Mauritz Schulte, the German founder-partners of the Coventry firm of Triumph, manufactured bicycles and motorcycles. The company turned to cars as late as 1923, probably persuaded to do so by Claude Holbrook, who later was to succeed Bettmann as chief executive. The company's use of hydraulic brakes brought it early fame as did its small saloon car, the Super Seven.

ABOVE *The handsome 1934 Triumph Gloria Vitesse had a twin-carburettor Coventry Climax-designed 2-litre six-cylinder engine with overhead inlet and side exhaust valves. Provided by The Patrick Collection.*

LEFT *The Triumph TR series of sports cars were fine roadgoing and competition machines. Works driver and Swiss dealer Jean-Jacques Thuner is seen taking part in the 1964 Monte Carlo Rally with a TR4.*

BELOW *Final manifestation of the Triumph sports car was the wedge-shaped TR7.*

body plant. Both were in complete contrast to the Standard Vanguard, whose engine they shared from 1948. (The later Mayflower was much less successful, aesthetically, than its bigger brother, the Renown.)

The 2.1-litre Vanguard engine was sold for use in the Morgan Plus Four and Doretti sports cars – the latter was made by the Walsall company that by now owned the Swallow Sidecar business. It was as a passenger in a Swallow Doretti that Sir John Black suffered injuries that were to provide an opportunity for his removal from his position as head of Standard-Triumph in January 1954 at the age of 58. The real reason was that he had been behaving in a most arbitrary manner, culminating in his sacking his most senior engineer, Edward Grinham. This led to a board rebellion. Alick Dick was Black's successor.

There were several false starts at making a true Triumph sports car but the 1953 TR2, largely the creation of Harry Webster, was the one that made the grade. It preceded 20 years of brilliant, traditional-style TR models, leading up to the fuel-injected 2.5-litre TR6, which would be replaced in 1975 by the wedge-shaped TR7. All TRs produced worthy competition results, as did their smaller sisters, the Spitfire and GT6. The most sophisticated of all the sporting Triumphs was the 3-litre V8 Stag of 1970.

From 1959 the small Standard saloons were superseded by the Herald/Vitesse series with Michelotti styling and independent rear suspension by swinging half-axles. From 1961, Leyland Motors controlled Standard-Triumph which, almost immediately, became simply Triumph. No British cars were called Standards after 1963, although the Herald was to be assembled as a 'Standard' in India right up to the 1980s.

The finest series of saloons to come from Triumph in the 1960s was the 2000, a rival of the Rover P6.

The scaled-down version, the front-wheel-drive 1300, did not sell very well but its successors with rear-wheel drive came in attractive packages; the most exotic was the Dolomite Sprint, with its high-performance 2-litre overhead-camshaft engine.

From 1967, Rover was part of the Leyland group, which meant that one of Triumph's main competitors was suddenly an ally – but was it? The formation of British Leyland in 1968 raised even bigger question marks, and the launch of Rover's SD1 in 1976 spelled an end to Triumph's bigger model range. The sports cars petered out in the early 1980s. After the worst ravages of BL were over, Triumph finished up the loser, as all its models became outdated: or, in the case of the TR7/8, unloved in the United States where its main market should have been. The end was nigh.

Under Sir Michael Edwardes, the unsuccessful conglomerate, BL, was brought to heel. The Triumph name was used for a Honda-based model, the Acclaim. It was replaced in 1984 by the Rover 200.

TVR Great Britain

The TVR has achieved greatness not only through the product but also through its very survival. For over 30 years it has battled for existence in the sea air of Blackpool, Lancashire (where the seeds of the Jaguar idea first flourished).

Many kit cars have been, and still are, offered to the customer who wants something different. The TVR is outstanding for the way in which it has become one of the world's exclusive sports cars, despite financial problems, and at least four changes of management.

The 1954 TVR was good looking from the start: a fastback two-door fixed-head coupé in glass fibre, built around a light multi-tube frame and powered by a modified version of the 1.2-litre engine usually found in those famous 'West Country' Austins, the Devon, the Dorset and the Somerset.

In 1956, the very neat coupé shape known as the Grantura was evolved, and powered initially by the Coventry Climax FWA 1.1-litre engine, with cheaper Ford units optional. A few open-top versions were sent to the United States and developed for SCCA sports car racing as Jomar Mk 2s. TVR Engineering Ltd was formed at this stage, run by Bernard Williams and *Trevor* Wilkinson, the founder after whose abbreviated first name it was called.

A second link with the United States resulted in the fitting of 4.7-litre Ford V8 engines for a while, and the well-known British driver Gerry Marshall gained a number of fine victories in his early racing days with this model, sold as a Griffith-TVR, later as a Griffith.

Another beautiful coupé was the 1956 TVR Trident, again a V8-powered machine; but it had to be sold off immediately to enable TVR to stay in business. (The Trident remained a separate marque, built in Suffolk, until 1978.) The old TVR Grantura lived on, with a longer bonnet now to accommodate the six-cylinder Triumph engine, although other units were still available. Its later designations were Vixen and (in 1977 hatchback form) Taimar.

Glass-fibre bodies and tubular all-independently sprung chassis, and a selection of engines were the tried formula of the Tasmin range, introduced by the small company's aggressive young management team of 1980. The open or closed Tasmin was sharply styled and well finished, and appealed strongly in special markets such as the Middle East, where the regular engine was the Rover V8. By the mid-1980s, the TVR was a great British sports car that had, truly, made the grade the hard way.

BELOW *For years, TVR relied on the compact Grantura shape for its most popular models. Then came this eye-catching Tasmin for the 1980s, offered with several proprietary engine options.*

VAUXHALL Great Britain

From the outset Vauxhall car styling incorporated a ridge around the bonnet and this was developed into the famous flutes that were to be a feature of every new model for more than 50 years, but ultimately vanishing as full-width bodywork became universal. The first cars were made in 1903 in the Vauxhall Iron Works, London – hence the marque name.

Early success brought the need to move to a location where further expansion was possible, and from 1905 Vauxhall's headquarters were situated in the rolling Bedfordshire countryside, close to Luton.

From then on, the company was directed by Percy Kidner, whose policy was to make larger cars and to compete in motor racing and trials – in which he and

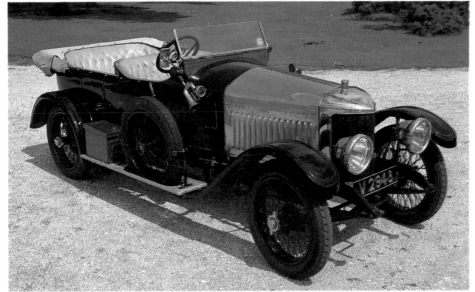

ABOVE *The Prince Henry Vauxhall was one of the finest of the early high-quality sports-tourers: but the Vauxhall image would have to change radically for the marque to stay in business.*

TOP RIGHT *A complete contrast to the old Vauxhalls, the 'Car of the Year 1985' was GM's European Astra/Kadett. This small, aerodynamic four-seater is seen (in the foreground) in its high-performance form for the British market: the Vauxhall Astra GTE.*

Vauxhall's general manager-to-be, A. J. Hancock, were particularly successful.

Laurence H. Pomeroy was the young engineer largely responsible for the high-revving 3-litre 20 hp model, built specially for the 1908 Royal Automobile Club and Royal Scottish Automobile Club 2000-mile trial in which Kidner put up best performance. This fine car was the forerunner of a whole series of high-performance touring models, the most famous being the 4-litre 'Prince Henry' of 1911. It was named after the Prinz Heinrich (of Prussia) trials, in which Kidner and Hancock achieved excellent results from trouble-free performances. At this point, and with this machine, Vauxhall could be said to have taken over from Napier and Wolseley as the makers of Britain's premier sporting cars. The next super-sports model to appear was the 30/98 prototype, built for sprint driver Joseph Higginson who broke the Shelsley Walsh record with it in 1913. In 1914, there was even a fully fledged Pomeroy-designed lightweight Grand Prix racing car but it was not a great success.

Despite selling big sixes to the Russian nobility, breaking the Melbourne-to-Sydney record, coming out

with the magnificent definitive 30/98 OE sports model (4.2 litres, four cylinders, overhead valves, giving 112 bhp at 3400 rpm), and generally adding to its reputation around the world, Vauxhall was in deep trouble in the 1920s. Pomeroy had left in 1919 for America (later he would join Daimler of Coventry); yet the urge to go racing remained.

It took General Motors' cadaverous, clever boss Alfred P. Sloan Jr, and his chief export executive James D. Mooney, to find a future for the Vauxhall car: but on their terms. In his autobiography, Sloan referred to the progress of the motor industry in the 1920s as 'explosive' – a very accurate description, for GM nearly bought out Citroën and Austin. The planned deal with Austin fell through in 1925 and, as Sloan wrote, the acquisition of the smaller Vauxhall company late that year was 'a much less controversial matter for General Motors . . . It was in no sense a substitute for Austin; indeed, I looked on it only as a kind of experiment in overseas manufacturing.' (GM took over Vauxhall before Opel of Germany.)

The Vauxhall changed in character under GM rule, but so did most cars in that restless period of industrial turbulence and realignment. It now ceased to be an expensive luxury car, although the early, tentative, American-style Vauxhalls of 1928 were considerably larger than the average British family saloon.

In 1931 the Bedford range of trucks and buses was introduced and there was an increasing tendency towards smaller, family-sized cars: with the compensation of the early use in Britain of GM developments such as synchromesh gearchange, independent front suspension and unit construction. Annual output had usually been well under 2000 cars a year in the 1920s. GM took Vauxhall to 9000 in 1930 and 60,000 in 1938.

GM's styling skills seemed to pass Britain by in the 1940s and 1950s, however, after which Vauxhall had to overcome a crisis of confidence. Tighter organization and closer links with Opel led to a near-miraculous change of image. In the 1960s a sense of style began to be restored, and the old qualities of sporting performance and longevity were again evident.

By the mid-1980s Vauxhall had three outstanding front-wheel-drive models among the ten top sellers in Britain. The popularity of the Cavalier (GM's 'J' car) was particularly impressive – second only to the smaller Ford Escort by 1985, and ahead of all other individual Austin-M.G. or Ford models. The small Nova (which Opel called the Corsa) was making its mark while the new Astra (Opel Kadett) was voted 1985's Car of the Year. Even if it was in a different world from the 30/98, the Vauxhall had returned to greatness.

VOLKSWAGEN Germany/Brazil/Mexico, etc

Over 50 models of car have achieved the goal of a million sales around the world, but only one has passed the 20 million mark: the ubiquitous and much-loved, air-cooled flat-four rear-engined Volkswagen *Käfer*, or 'Beetle', still being made in the 1980s in Brazil, Mexico, and Nigeria.

The world's most successful car grew out of Adolf Hitler's dream of mass mobility for the people of his Third Reich. Ferdinand Porsche was the engineer appointed to carry through this project for a 'people's car', but there were a number of other significant pioneers whose ideas were also incorporated in the first Volkswagen.

In Kopřivnice (then known by its German name of Nesselsdorf) Edmund Rumpler had worked with the slightly younger Hans Ledwinka when the Moravian wagon works first turned its hand to car making. Rumpler had gone his own way, introducing his streamlined, independently sprung, rear-engined *Tropfen-Auto*, or 'teardrop car', to a bewildered public at the 1921 Berlin show. Hans Nibel, technical chief with Benz, induced his company to take on Rumpler's

BELOW *Still being made in several countries, the Beetle has long passed the 20 million mark: a unique production record for one model. This 1978 convertible is in The Patrick Collection, Britain's newly established motor museum containing great cars of every age and every price category.*

design and develop it. The most famous development was the 1923 Benz Grand Prix car which, of course, became available to Mercedes (where Porsche was working) when those companies merged. At the same period Ledwinka created the first Czechoslovak 'people's car', the Tatra 11, which had a backbone chassis and a variation of the Rumpler swing-axle independent rear suspension. In 1931, Ledwinka produced a lightweight air-cooled rear-engined coupé and, in 1933, this was updated as a beetle-shaped fastback baby saloon.

Budapest-born Josef Ganz, editor of Germany's *Motor Kritik* magazine, was more than 20 years younger than Ledwinka, Rumpler or Porsche. In addition he was a German citizen and a Jew, otherwise his ideas of 1928 for a *Deutschen Volkswagen* (German people's car) might have borne fruit; as it was, he would have a rather brief moment of glory with the Swiss Rapid light car before emigrating to Australia in 1950, receiving an honorarium from VW soon afterwards; but Ledwinka was not so lucky (*see* Tatra).

Ferdinand Porsche was just three years older than Ledwinka and they knew one another well, for they spent much of their youth in and around Vienna, and their technical aspirations were similar. Porsche had already influenced and been influenced by several companies when in 1930 he set up his own engineering consultancy in Stuttgart in Germany, as a result of a bank crisis in Austria. He made small rear-engined fastback saloons for Zündapp in 1932 and NSU in 1933, when he also conceived a rear-engined Grand Prix car for Germany's new Auto Union. That was also the year that Hitler became chancellor. In 1934, Porsche was commissioned by the German government to produce three prototypes, and in this he was assisted by neighbouring Mercedes-Benz. This company was already turning out a small (but short-lived) rear-engined car. The three cars were produced in 1936, followed in 1937 by 30 more Daimler-Benz built pre-production models. Only in 1938 did Hitler lay the foundation stone for the factory where the car called the *KdF-Wagen* was to be made. The letters 'KdF' stood for the recreational movement *Kraft durch Freude* or 'Strength through Joy'. In turn, the town that housed the factory workers was called Stadt des KdF-Wagens, and was situated east of Hanover. At this time, Porsche produced three special coupés for a race (aborted due to the outbreak of the Second World War), and these were to be the inspiration for his son's new sports car (*see* Porsche).

In 1945 the British, now one of the occupying powers, did not really recognize the potential of the Volkswagen. In any case, under their supervision, the works were allowed to return to German control again in 1949 (the town was renamed Wolfsburg), and from then on the Volkswagen began its headlong rush to fame.

By comparison with its success, the subsequent difficulty of replacing the VW in sophisticated markets pales into insignificance. Several quite unsatisfactory

ABOVE *In complete contrast to the Beetle, the typical modern Volkswagen has water-cooling and front-wheel drive. With the small sports car virtually extinct by the 1980s, the more practical hatchback had effectively taken over its role, and the VW Golf GTi set the parameters. This example dates from 1981.*

variations on the 'Beetle' theme were tried before an Audi-NSU prototype brought VW finally into the front-wheel-drive water-cooled category with the 1971 K70: a new departure indeed, although it meant the end for the NSU marque.

Most successful of the subsequent VWs have been the front-wheel-drive Passat, Polo, and Golf. The last-named was (in GTi form) the small sports saloon of the early 1980s by which all others were judged.

Cooperation with China and Japan has led to the manufacture of the bigger VW – the Santana – in those countries, maintaining the marque's modern reputation as a car for the people of all the world – not just the *Volk* for whom it originally was designed.

VOLVO Sweden

VOLVO

ABOVE RIGHT *Tom Trana, European Rally Champion of 1964, taking part in the previous year's Monte Carlo Rally in a works Volvo PV544. This development of the PV444 set new standards of performance for family saloons, much to the surprise of its rivals – for the name Volvo was not familiar in overseas markets until the late 1950s.*

Although there were earlier small-scale producers, the Volvo Car Corporation of Gothenburg (Göteborg), Sweden, is Scandinavia's oldest active car maker.

Ten 'GL' prototypes were made in Stockholm in 1925–6, the initials being those of their designer, an engineer named Gustaf Larson. He and a colleague, Assar Gabrielsson, worked for the SKF ball bearing company (Svenska Kullagerfabriken) whom they persuaded to help them start a motor factory.

The first cars and commercial vehicles to be called Volvo (an unused SKF trade name) were built in a surplus ball-bearing works near Gothenburg in 1927. Early Volvos were little known internationally. They owed much to American design and production techniques. 'Styling' was attempted, but not very successfully, in the PV36 of 1935, which was an unfortunate amalgam of American ideas thought to be *avant garde* at the time. Its successor, the PV51, was a more orthodox model and, with a fine range of commercial vehicles, it established a strong home market for Volvo in the late 1930s ('PV' stood for *personvagn*: the Swedish for passenger car).

In 1939 there were plans for a two-stroke eight-cylinder small rear-engined car; but this was shelved, for Volvo was a cautious company and the four-cylinder PV44 (first presented in Stockholm in 1944 – hence the nomenclature) became the design that took the marque around the world. Although it looked American the car was designed mainly by Erik Jern, if inspired by a 1939 German Hanomag fastback that never reached full production, but had promised speed with economy.

The Volvo PV444 (1947–58), PV544 (1958–65) and estate car derivatives (up to 1969) were tough and compact, and handled well enough to gain major race and rally honours. This began to catch the public eye with Gunnar Andersson's surprise winning of the 1958 European Rally Championship. Thereafter Andersson guided the Volvo competition effort, which produced outright victories in the very toughest rallies, by star drivers such as Tom Trana, Carl-Magnus Skogh and Joginder Singh.

From 1956, the Amazon (or 120) series of Jan Wilsgaard-styled saloons and estate cars brought Volvo more friends and more international victories. There was a short-lived glass-fibre sports car, the P1900, and a GT model, the P1800, which was developed into a distinguished 'sportshatch' in the early 1970s – but that was to be a blind alley for Volvo.

Since 1967, the 140/240 and 160/260 series and their derivatives have given the Volvo an enviable reputation as an energetic workhorse of high quality. Despite its foursquare looks, the turbocharged 240 became, suddenly, a force to be reckoned with in European Group A (touring car) racing from the time it began winning in 1984.

From the mid-1970s, and acquisition of the Dutch DAF concern, Volvo developed a new, scaled-down family saloon series, the 340/360. There was cooperation with Peugeot and Renault on petrol engines, and with Volkswagen on diesels. The 740/760 range of Volvo saloons, launched in the early 1980s, had controversial styling but could not be faulted on space utilization.

Aktiebolaget Volvo is perhaps best known for its replacement, back in the 1970s, of conventional assembly line methods of production at Kalmar by small teams working flexibly, fully involved in all aspects and stages of the process. It is now the biggest industrial group in Scandinavia, producing over 250,000 passenger cars a year in addition to its other interests.

WOLSELEY Great Britain

Frederick York Wolseley was a machinery maker for the sheep-shearing stations of Australia and needed an engineer to improve the reliability of his equipment. The man he found to do it was Herbert Austin, who had left England to gain experience.

Austin returned to Britain in 1893, when he was 27 years old, and became general manager of the Wolseley company which had, in the meantime, moved to Birmingham, its period in Australia having been relatively brief. As a sheep-shearing machine company it was not a success. Wolseley himself resigned in 1894 and died in 1899. Austin (who, from 1896, had made several experimental cars) came to an arrangement with Vickers Sons & Maxim Ltd to form a subsidiary company to make cars with the Wolseley name.

Besides production models there were some long, low racing cars that qualified for the Gordon Bennett and other big races, although no wins were recorded. Austin insisted on horizontal engines for all Wolseleys and left the company in 1905 when the other board members questioned his policy (*see* Austin section for the rest of his story).

John Siddeley influenced the company both during and after Austin's tenure, but he moved to Coventry (*see* Armstrong Siddeley).

Wolseley motor cars at this stage were large and well-made; but there was no planned model programme. There was no doubt about the firm's engineering capability, for it was still first and foremost a machine tool company and took on any profitable-looking project. A variety of solid war contracts helped the company stay solvent, and manufacture of Hispano-Suiza aero engines led to some important

postwar overhead camshaft-engined Wolseley cars.

In the mid-1920s there was a fight for possession of Wolseley, which was then in the hands of the receivers. Sir William Morris (Lord Nuffield) outbid Austin and GM, and created a new company, Wolseley Motors 1927 Ltd.

This move led to a complete change of character for the Wolseley whose first new model of 1930 was, in effect, a Morris Minor with two extra cylinders. (From 1927, Wolseley engineers had been making a small four-cylinder overhead-camshaft engine for the little Morris.) The six-cylinder Wolsley Hornet chassis was fitted with sports bodywork by many coachbuilders, including such famous names as Eustace Watkins, Patrick, and Swallow. This was also the engine that provided the basis for all the great overhead-camshaft M.G.s of the 1930s. During that decade the Wolseleys were established as the prestige cars of the Nuffield Group, and turned away from the sporting side altogether. Miles Thomas, later Lord Nuffield's deputy, was in charge, and gave the Wolseley enough character and distinction to enable it to survive for many years – usually recognizable at night, if not in the daytime, by the post-1933 gimmick of an illuminated radiator badge.

The last new Birmingham Wolseleys were a batch of 'Nuffield' taxicabs, and from 1949 all car production went to Cowley, Oxford. There, a return was made to overhead camshafts for the very smart Wolseley 4/50 and 6/80, which had a hint of the elegance of the 1941 Packard One Eighty LeBaron about them. They lasted from 1948 to 1953, after which the Wolseley radiator was applied rather indiscriminately to a variety of models from BMC, or its successor BL, until 1975 when, suddenly, the last model became a Princess, which later became the Austin Ambassador.

The 1936 1.8-litre six-cylinder 14/56 was priced very competitively at £265, yet the imposing grille with illuminating Wolseley badge helped the marque remain one up on Morris in the Nuffield pecking order.

INDEX

Figures in *italics* refer to captions to illustrations; figures in **bold** type indicate main references.

ACKNOWLEDGEMENTS
The publishers wish to thank the following for their kind permission to reproduce the photographs in this book:
Alfa Romeo 20 above; Auburn-Cord-Duesenberg Museum 15 below, 58; Austin-Rover 32 below; Autopress 125; Neill Bruce 11 below, 13 above inset, 22 above, 64, 76 below, 89, 101 below, 119 above, 126 above, 147 above, 148; Cadillac 50 below; Citroën 9 inset, 55 above; FIAT 79 below; Focalpoint 107 below; Ford 15 above; Geoff Goddard 18 below, 26 below, 57 below, 60, 63, 71, 73, 82 below, 101 above, 105 below, 107 above, 108, 111, 118, 142 above, 152 above, 155 left; Chris Harvey 99 above, 124 below; Jaguar 153 below; LAT 26 above, 29 above, 109 below, 127 below, 131 above, 149 above; Chris Linton 13 inset below, 116 below; Andrew Morland 67, 68, 97, 103 above, 114 above, 121 above, 134 above, 147 below; Don Morley 134 below; National Motor Museum 24 below, 32 above, 33 above, 44, 49 above, 57 above, 59, 66, 83, 86 above, 91 below, 96 above, 131 below, 145 below, 157 above; Oldsmobile 126 below left; The Patrick Collection 143 below; Peugeot 130, Pontiac 132 below; Porsche 135 below; Cyril Posthumus 36 above; Quadrant Picture Library (*Thoroughbred & Classic Cars*) 8-9, (*Autocar*) 18 above, 43 above, 88, 90, 129, 143 centre; Renault 136, 137 below; Peter Roberts 8 inset, 11 above, 24 above, 30, 36 below, 48, 72 below, 81, 106 below, 122, 141, 142 below, 152 below, 157 below; Rolls-Royce Motors Ltd 35 below; Saab-Scania 143 top; Rainer Schlegelmilch 7 and inset left, 38, 40, 41, 113; C. G. Smedley 119 below; Toyota 151; TVR 154; VAG (UK) Ltd 29 below; Vauxhall 51 inset, 155 right; Volkswagen 70; Andrew Whyte 23, 28 below, 39 below, 42, 84, 123, 144, 149 below, 150; Nicky Wright 4-5, 16, (Auburn-Cord-Duesenberg Museum) 28 above, 33 below, 49 below, 50 above, 61 above, 72 above, 74, 75, 76 above, 80, 82 above, 87, 99 below, 100.
Special Photography: Ian Dawson 1, 2-3, (4-5 Patrick Collection edition only), 10, 12-13, 19, 20 below, 21, 22 below, 25, 27, 31, 34, 35 above, 37, 39 above, 43 below, 45, 46, 47 above, 51-54, 55 below, 56, 61 below, 62, 69, 77, 78, 79 above, 85, 91 above, 92-95, 98, 102, 103 below, 104, 105 above, 106 above, 109 above, 110, 112, 114 below, 116 above, 117, 121 below, 122 inset, 124 above, 127 above, 132 above, 133, 135 above, 137 above, 138-140, 146, 153 above, 156.
The publishers would like to thank The Baton Press Limited for providing several of the car badges.